Tutankhamun hunting birds, in a detail from his Golden Shrine

Canopic stopper of Tutankhamun

# TUTANKHAMUN
## AND THE GOLDEN AGE OF THE PHARAOHS

## ZAHI HAWASS

### PHOTOGRAPHS BY KENNETH GARRETT

NATIONAL GEOGRAPHIC

WASHINGTON, D.C.

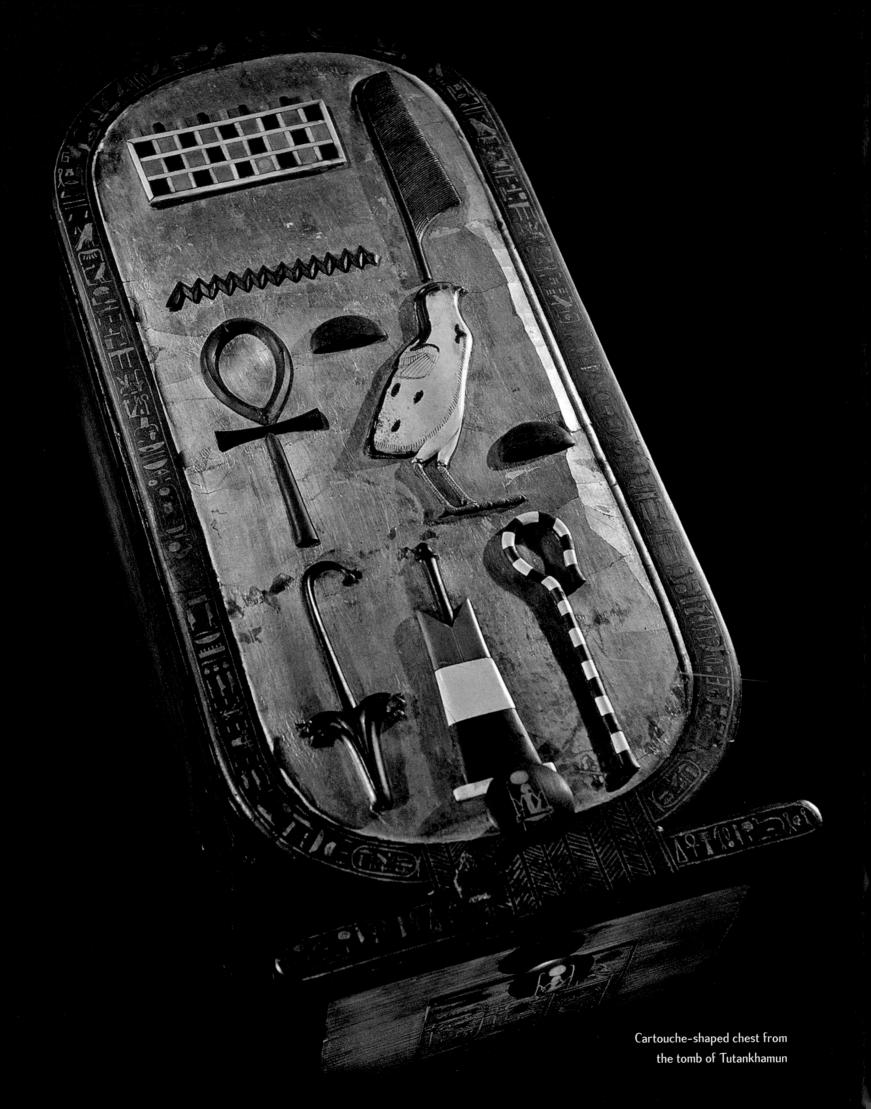

Cartouche-shaped chest from
the tomb of Tutankhamun

# CONTENTS

# FOREWORD

The civilization of the pharaohs has long stood as a beacon to the world, a symbol of what is possible when people work together toward common goals. The kings of Egypt ruled for thousands of years over a land of harmony and prosperity, building pyramids that still stand tall, tunneling elaborate underground tombs, and erecting great temples to the gods. Egyptian artisans and craftsmen were the most skilled in the world, producing masterpieces of sculpture and exquisite jewels for all to admire, and for other cultures to imitate. Although the pharaohs waged war when they had to, the ancient Egyptians valued tranquility and reconciliation, and signed the first peace treaty in history. Using diplomacy instead of force, they married the sisters and daughters of their former enemies, and brought young princes from vassal states to be raised with their own sons.

As modern Egyptians, we follow in the path laid down by our ancestors, and strive for harmony and peace among nations. We have suffered greatly from war, and believe that the time for bloodshed is over. We must speak to one another in the language of civilization, and the beautiful monuments and artifacts that are the legacy of the pharaohs provide us with a unique means of communication. Egypt offers these beautiful objects from the tomb of Tutankhamun, along with equally exquisite pieces from the era that preceded him, in a spirit of peace and goodwill. Study of the past can illuminate the future, and by talking to one another and working together, we can strive to build a new era of greatness.

H. E. Suzanne Mubarak
First Lady of Egypt

Culture is the bridge on which peoples meet to resolve political differences and instabilities, for culture is a reflection of the integrity of human conscience and enlightenment. This in turn is an expression of our present and of our long history, which together have shaped the main features of international relations.

The exhibition of Tutankhamun comes to the United States of America with a noble message that gains its credibility and validity from centuries of ancient Egyptian history and wisdom. This noble message is a message of peace, the peace that the world seeks. It is also an enlightened message that encourages dialogue among civilizations with the aim of helping all nations reach a common future. This future should depend on culture as a major instrument for comprehensive peace.

Farouk Hosni
Minister of Culture

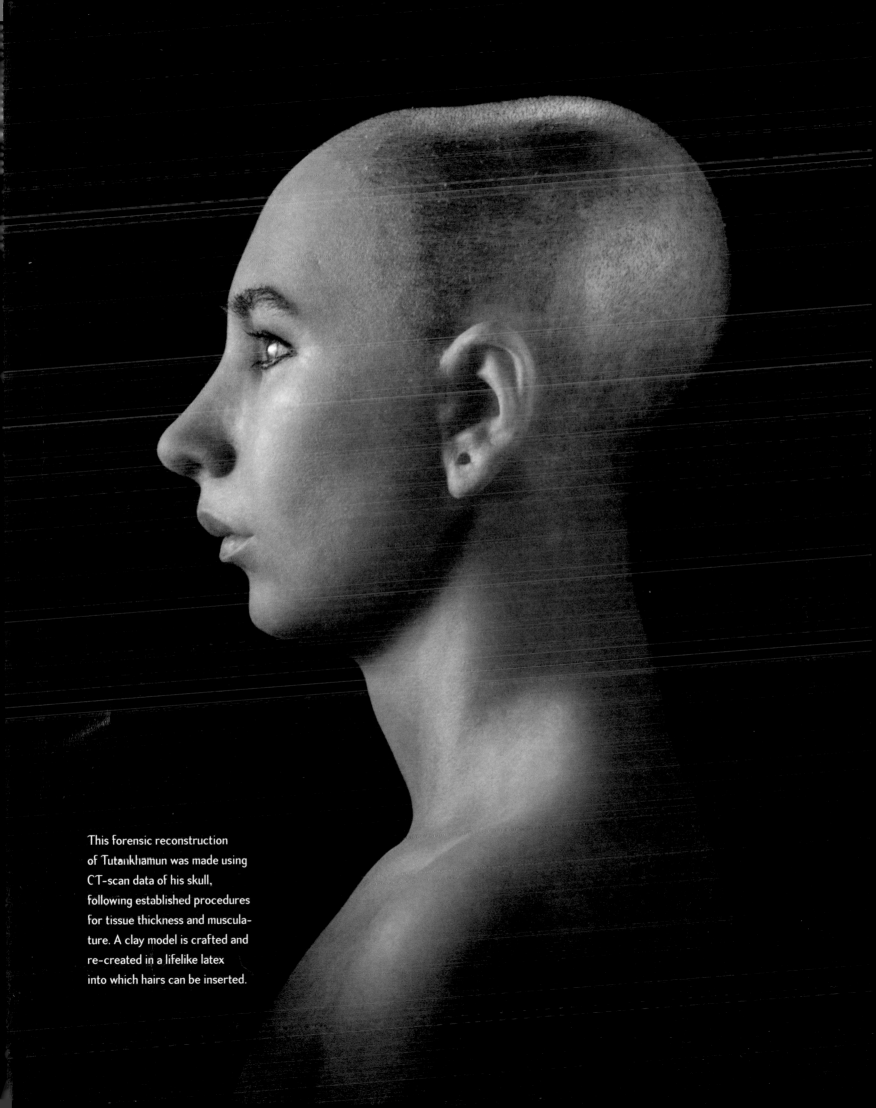

This forensic reconstruction
of Tutankhamun was made using
CT-scan data of his skull,
following established procedures
for tissue thickness and muscula-
ture. A clay model is crafted and
re-created in a lifelike latex
into which hairs can be inserted.

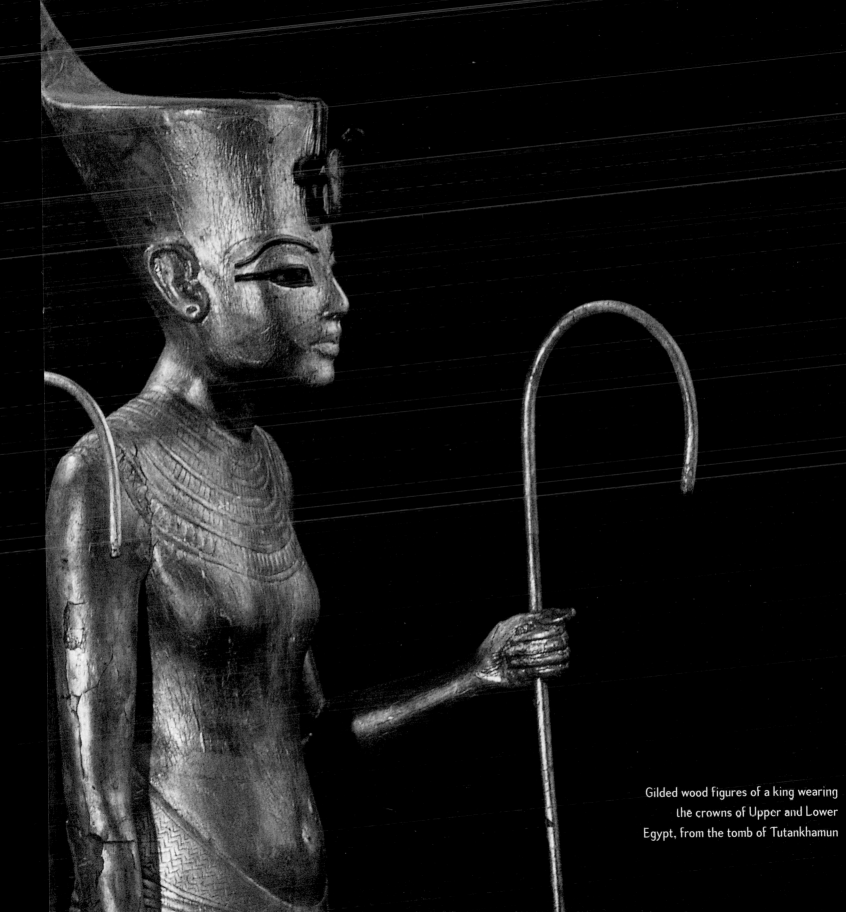

Gilded wood figures of a king wearing
the crowns of Upper and Lower
Egypt, from the tomb of Tutankhamun

# INTRODUCTION

*Since the discovery of his tomb in 1922, Tutankhamun has fascinated the world. His name alone conjures up images of glittering gold and gleaming jewels, of riches beyond the imagination, and of a life cut tragically short. His treasures have attracted millions of visitors, both to their permanent home in Cairo and to traveling exhibitions that have circled the globe.*

Only about eight or nine years old when he came to the throne in about 1332 B.C., Tutankhamun was heir to an immense realm that stretched north almost to the Euphrates River and south to the Fourth Cataract of the Nile. His principal allies—and his main rivals for regional supremacy— were the Hittites in modern-day Turkey and Syria and the Babylonians and Assyrians who lived in what is now Iraq. The Mycenaean Greeks dominated the Aegean.

By the time Tutankhamun was born, Egypt had been a superpower for almost two centuries, and had been in periodic conflict with its neighbors for most of this time. The kings who came before him had fought to build an empire, conquering the lands to the south and forcing the city-states to the north into vassaldom. The booty these monarchs brought back from their campaigns poured into the royal coffers and the treasure houses of the principal state god, Amun. Amenhotep II, Tutankhamun's putative great-great grandfather, was the last warrior king of his line. He began his reign with war and ended it with the promise of a peace that came to fruition

The goddess Selket guards the canopic shrine of Tutankhamun.

under his son, Tuthmosis IV, who married the daughters of Egypt's old enemies instead of confronting them on the battlefield. The next monarch, Amenhotep III, inherited a stable kingdom and access to unmatched wealth.

But this moment of calm was not to last. Two decades before Tutankhamun ascended the throne, a new player stepped onto the stage of Egyptian history. Eldest surviving son of Amenhotep III and his great queen Tiye, the "heretic" pharaoh Akhenaten and his wife Nefertiti changed the state religion of Egypt, closing the temples of the great state gods and dedicating their extensive holdings to the sun-disk Aten. Some see this controversial king as a saint, others as a monster. Many scholars believe that Tutankhamun was his son.

Soon after he became king, Tutankhamun rejected the teachings of Akhenaten, bringing back the traditional religion and restoring the wealth and power of Amun. When he died after fewer than ten years on the throne, he was laid to rest in a small tomb in the Valley of the Kings, a remote canyon on the west bank of the Nile in Thebes. Tutankhamun passed away without an heir, as did his elderly successor, Aye. Perhaps because of his association with the hated Akhenaten, the next kings wiped his name from the annals of history. Little did they know that by erasing his existence from official records, they would be ensuring that his name would live forever: While all of the later royal tombs were robbed and their treasures scattered to the winds, Tutankhamun's remained untouched, hidden beneath the sands.

On November 4, 1922, English archaeologist Howard Carter found the long-forgotten burial, a discovery that fired the imagination of the public. For the next decade, the world watched in amazement as thousands of objects of gold, alabaster, semiprecious stone, precious wood, and glass—each piece more astonishing than the last—poured from the tomb's packed chambers and traveled to their permanent home at the Cairo Museum.

In 1961, some of Tutankhamun's treasures left Egypt for the first time. Other traveling exhibitions followed: Between 1961 and 1981, thousands of people stood in line for hours to catch a glimpse of these riches as they were displayed around the world. In the late 1970s, a special exhibition of 50 of the best objects from the tomb launched a frenzy of Tutmania.

The West has always been fascinated by the world of the pharaohs. The ancient Greeks and Romans were the first Egyptophiles, adopting the cults of certain Egyptian gods and developing the first Egyptian-style sculpture. After the Arab invasion of Egypt, the pharaonic past was hidden from most Western eyes for centuries, until Renaissance scholars rediscovered the wonders of the ancient world. In the 15th and 16th centuries, cities such as Rome erected obelisks and practitioners of the fine and decorative arts began to incorporate Egyptian elements into their work. Napoleon's expedition to Egypt in 1798 prompted still more curiosity, and Egyptomania, expressed in art, architecture, and even opera, continued to grow.

The discovery of Tutankhamun pushed ancient Egypt to the forefront of public awareness. Advertisers of products from cigarettes to soap borrowed Egyptian images and themes, top-end clothing designers turned to pharaonic art for ideas, and carmakers even produced a beetle-like automobile called the Scarab. The Art Deco movement was heavily indebted to ancient Egypt for its forms and details. Hollywood jumped on the bandwagon, producing many films, such as *The Mummy*, exploiting the pharaonic era. Tutankhamun and ancient Egypt continue to inspire books, movies, clothes, adver-

tising campaigns, art, and architecture, and the public's thirst for both scientific knowledge and mystical "truths" from the land of the pharaohs seems insatiable.

Two decades ago the cobra on the headdress of the goddess Selket that once guarded Tutankhamun's canopic chest was damaged while traveling in Germany. Expert conservators were able to restore the goddess to her original glory, and she is now back in Cairo. As a result of this accident as well as an increasing awareness of the unavoidable wear and tear of travel on objects, the Egyptian Parliament requested that the treasures of the king not leave the country again. This ban held for over 20 years, denying an entire generation (at least those not fortunate enough to come to Egypt themselves) the opportunity to see artifacts from Tutankhamun's tomb.

In 2002 representatives of the Antikenmuseum, Basel, approached Egypt's Supreme Council of Antiquities and proposed a new traveling exhibition featuring the treasures of Tutankhamun. Due in large part to the excellent relationship that Switzerland and Egypt enjoy, the Parliament agreed to allow a carefully chosen selection of pieces to travel, so that the world could once again experience the wonders of the boy king firsthand. After Basel, the exhibition went to Bonn, Germany, and then to the United States, where it will be on display at the Los Angeles County Museum of Art, the Museum of Art in Fort Lauderdale, the Field Museum of Chicago, and the Franklin Institute in Philadelphia. After it closes in America, the exhibition will go to London before returning to Egypt.

Tutankhamun's treasures are not traveling alone; with them come objects spanning a century of Egyptian history. Most are from the burial ground of the pharaohs—the Valley of the Kings. There are pieces from the tombs of Amenhotep II and his son, Tuthmosis IV; from the burial of Amenhotep III's parents-in-law, Yuya and Tjuya, and from the mysterious Tomb 55, which may have held the body of Akhenaten himself. The exhibition also showcases objects from the temples on the east bank at Thebes (across the river from the royal valley) and from Akhenaten's capital city, Tell el Amarna. These pieces illuminate the world into which the boy king was born and tell the story of the Golden Age of Egypt, when the Egyptian empire was at its height and gold flowed like dust in the land of the pharaohs.

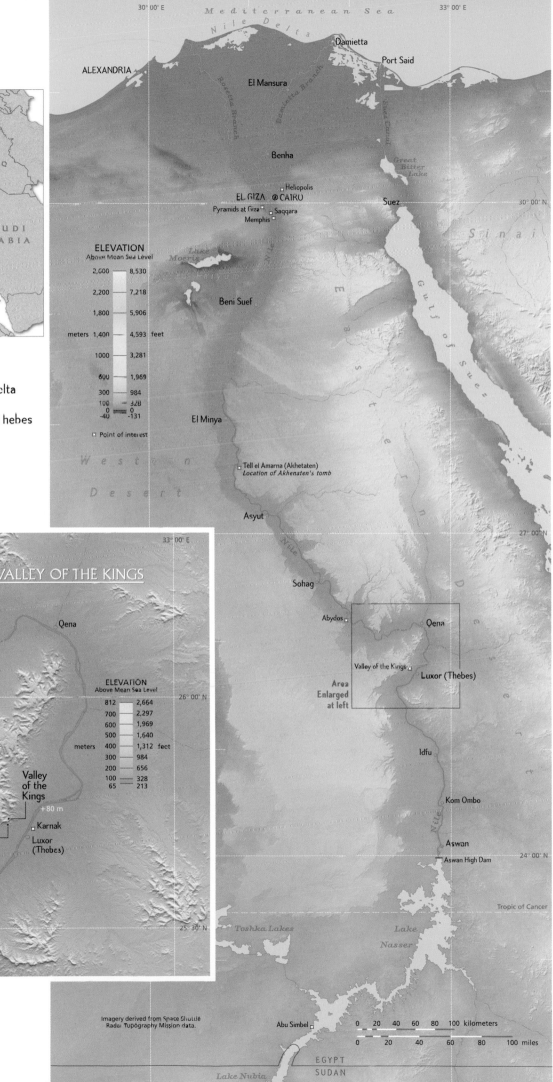

TOP: Egypt today

RIGHT: Nile River valley and delta

BOTTOM INSET: The region of Thebes in the New Kingdom

## ELEVATION
### Above Mean Sea Level

| meters | feet |
|---|---|
| 2,600 | 8,530 |
| 2,200 | 7,218 |
| 1,800 | 5,906 |
| 1,400 | 4,593 |
| 1000 | 3,281 |
| 600 | 1,969 |
| 300 | 984 |
| 100 | 328 |
| 0 | 0 |
| -40 | -131 |

□ Point of interest

Tell el Amarna (Akhetaten)
*Location of Akhenaten's tomb*

## VALLEY OF THE KINGS

### ELEVATION
#### Above Mean Sea Level

| meters | feet |
|---|---|
| 812 | 2,664 |
| 700 | 2,297 |
| 600 | 1,969 |
| 500 | 1,640 |
| 400 | 1,312 |
| 300 | 984 |
| 200 | 656 |
| 100 | 328 |
| 65 | 213 |

Valley of the Kings

Valley of the Queens

Karnak

Luxor (Thebes)

Qena

Imagery derived from Space Shuttle Radar Topography Mission data.

Height 73.5 cm; width 41.5 cm; depth 30.3 cm
Dynasty 18, reign of Tutankhamun
Thebes, Valley of the Kings, tomb of Tutankhamun (KV 62)
Carter 116

Found partially hidden behind one of Tutankhamun's chariots in the Antechamber of his tomb, this figure of gessoed and painted wood is truly without parallel. A life-size model of the head and torso of the young king, it includes his hips as far as the top of the groin and the upper part of his arms. There is no sign that other pieces were once attached. The torso has been painted a pale yellow, perhaps in imitation of a gauzelike shirt. In contrast, the face is a dark reddish brown, the traditional color for male skin since early in Egyptian history. The face is oval, with high cheekbones, full cheeks, and a small rounded chin. Lightly arched brows surmount large, doe-like eyes. The nose is rounded yet fine, the Cupid's-bow lips are full, and the pierced ears are large and slightly protuberant.

The figure's cylindrical crown widens toward its flat top and is painted yellow, perhaps in imitation of gold. At the king's brow is a uraeus, its body painted in red on the front and then winding over the top of the headdress, its head worked separately and adorned with gold leaf and red and blue paint. This crown is similar in shape and proportions to the leather bonnet worn by the great god Amun. However, Amun's crown does not include a uraeus, and in other respects, such as the lack of the divine beard and the clothing, the bust does not resemble images of this god. It also recalls a platform crown worn by Akhenaten in at least one relief from Amarna, the meaning of which is uncertain.

The excavator, Howard Carter, suggested that this object was a mannequin, used to hold the king's robes and jewelry, or perhaps even used for fittings like a modern dressmaker's dummy. In fact, marks on the surface suggest that the figure once wore a jeweled corselet, an actual example of which was found in the tomb. If this is the case, it might have stood in either a temple or a palace and held costumes of state for ceremonial purposes.

However, it also possible that it was a ritual figure of some sort. It is similar in scale and style to a wooden head of the child king as Nefertem, the sun god at dawn, rising from an open lotus blossom. Found in the debris of the entrance corridor, the Nefertem head is generally understood to be an image of the king in a perpetual state of rebirth. It would have insured magically both that Tutankhamun would be resurrected eternally and that, through his identification with the sun god, the sun would rise each morning.

The mannequin may have served a similar purpose, although its interpretation is not as clear. It is unlikely that it represents the aspect of the king that would have received offerings (the *ka*), as all known ka statues have arms with which to receive gifts. It might stand for the king as a blessed spirit. It does not correspond exactly to any known examples of such images, but is at least similar in that it is an armless bust. Whatever its intended purpose, the figure now provides the modern viewer with an exquisite and unforgettable image of the boy king.

THE COLONNADE OF LUXOR TEMPLE CATCHES THE LIGHT
TO THE LEFT OF THE SUN COURT OF AMENHOTEP III.

# Prelude to Tutankhamun

*The pharaonic civilization to which Tutankhamun was heir*
*first appears in the historical record in about 3150 B.C.,*
*near the end of what Egyptologists call the Predynastic Period.*
*During this era, Egypt was already developing a complex*
*hierarchical culture ruled by local chieftains.*

The hierarchy is reflected in the archaeological record by cemeteries with significant differentiation in the size and elaboration of burials. At this critical moment, the Egyptians invented a unique writing system: the hieroglyphic script. This was used at first to write names and label commodities, and soon developed to the point where the Egyptians were able to record historical events.

By about 3050 B.C., all of Egypt had been brought under the control of a single king. From this point forward, modern scholars divide the history of Egypt into periods and dynasties, based on a system laid out by the Greek-Egyptian priest Manetho in the 3rd century B.C. Many of the artistic conventions and fundamental tenets of Egyptian kingship were put in place very early in the first historic era (the Early Dynastic Period). The country was divided symbolically into two lands, Upper Egypt (the Nile Valley) and Lower Egypt (the Delta), each with its own symbols and tutelary deities: The vulture goddess Nekhbet, the white crown, the sedge

This exquisite quartzite statue of Amenhotep III as the god Atum was found in 1989 below the floor of Luxor Temple. Its idealized, childlike features indicate that it was carved after the king's first festival of rejuvenation.

plant, and the lily or lotus stood for Upper Egypt; and the cobra goddess Wadjet, the red crown, bee, and papyrus plant symbolized Lower Egypt. One of the king's primary tasks was to preserve the unity of these two regions.

Out of the Early Dynastic Period grew the Old Kingdom (Dynasties 4 to 8), the first great era of Egyptian civilization. For five centuries (c. 2575 to 2150 B.C.), Egypt, well protected by deserts to the east and west, impassable cataracts to the south, and the Mediterranean to the north, was strong, secure, and wealthy enough to import luxury goods such as coniferous woods unknown in Egypt, ivory, and exotic animals. A highly centralized royal government ruled from the strategically important Memphite region, near the juncture of Upper and Lower Egypt and at the entrance to vital trade routes. It was during this era that the first monumental stone structure—the Step Pyramid of Djoser—was built and the great pyramids at Giza erected, attesting to an advanced state of technical skill and scientific knowledge. The hieroglyphic language developed to the point where it could be used to write narratives and complex religious texts; artisans carved elegant, harmonious reliefs and statues. The most important state deities were Re, the sun god; Osiris, lord of the dead; and Ptah, patron of Memphis.

The Step Pyramid of 3rd-dynasty king Djoser, seen from the floodplain, rises from the sands of the western desert.

By the end of the exceptionally long reign of the last king of the 6th dynasty, significant power had been transferred into the hands of provincial nobles and administrators, and the central government was on the verge of collapse. Some scholars also believe that the internal politics of the late Old Kingdom were affected by drought and perhaps famine. By about 2150 B.C., the country had splintered into regions headed by competing ruling houses centered around Thebes in the south and Herakleopolis Magna in the north. Egyptologists refer to this era of decentralization as the First Intermediate Period.

A little more than one hundred years later, a king from the southern 11th dynasty succeeded in reuniting the country under the Theban banner, founding the Middle Kingdom. The 11th, 12th, and 13th dynasties held power for four centuries (c. 1975–1640 B.C.),

during which time they tried to recapture the glories of the past. The 11th dynasty ruled from Thebes, but the 12th dynasty kings moved their capital back to the north, most likely near the mouth of El Faiyum. Like their Old Kingdom predecessors, these kings were buried under pyramids, but they were not the massive, well-built structures of the past. Constructed instead of mud brick and cased only with stone, their burial apartments were complex mazes of corridors, designed perhaps in part to thwart robbers but also as models of the Underworld. It was in the Middle Kingdom that Amun, principal deity of the Theban region, first became important. The kings of this era erected temples at a cult center now known as Karnak on the east bank of the Nile at Thebes, where they worshipped Amun along with his consort, Mut, and their son, Khonsu. The art and literature of this period reflect a new awareness of the fragility of life, seen, for example, in the careworn and very human portraits of the later kings of the 12th dynasty.

The rulers of the 12th dynasty built a chain of fortresses in Lower Nubia (the northern part of the land directly south of Egypt) to control trade with the south. The Kushites yet farther south in Upper Nubia remained independent and developed their own advanced civilization. Toward the end of the Middle Kingdom, evidence of an influx of foreigners appears in the archaeological record of the Delta. These were primarily merchants, their material culture linked to the nearby civilizations of Syria-Palestine. As the power of the central government began to wane under the kings of the 13th dynasty, either the Asiatics that had settled earlier in the Delta or other closely related invaders from the northeast took over part of Egypt, forcing the Memphite kings to retreat south to Thebes. For the first time in Egyptian history, foreigners controlled Egyptian soil. The Asiatic kings were called the *heka khasut*, "rulers of foreign lands," or the Hyksos (after the Greek version of their title); they ruled from Avaris in the eastern Delta. In the south, the Nubian kingdom of Kerma, based near the Third Cataract, grew in strength and sophistication until it was powerful enough to take back Lower Nubia from the Egyptians and even threaten the southern border of Egypt.

## The Dawn of the New Kingdom

By c. 1580 B.C., a native dynasty, the 17th, had come to power in Thebes, perhaps as vassals to the Hyksos, and had begun a war for independence. The mummified head of this dynasty's penultimate king, Seqenenre Taa II, bears the marks of Asiatic battle-axes, testimony to his death in battle against the Hyksos invaders. Taa II's mother, Tetisheri, was the first in a long line of powerful queens, and his wife, Ahhotep, may have been his full sister. Ahhotep and Seqenenre Taa II are thought to have had two sons, Kamosis and Ahmosis.

After the death of Taa II, Kamosis continued the war against the northerners. An important text from his short reign tells of how his scouts captured a messenger carrying a letter from the Hyksos monarch to the Kerma king, complaining of the aggressiveness of the Egyptians and suggesting an alliance. Kamosis was able to retake at least a part of Lower Nubia, after which he marched to the north and pushed the Hyksos back into their stronghold at Avaris.

But it was left to his much younger brother, Ahmosis, to complete the defeat of the Hyksos. For the first years of this king's rule, his mother, Ahhotep, acted as regent and may even have led some military sorties. When he reached adulthood, Ahmosis continued the war of independence, laying siege to Avaris. After the Hyksos citadel fell, Ahmosis chased the foreigners into southern Palestine and besieged them for six years at the town of Sharuhen before claiming final victory. He also mounted campaigns south into Nubia, doing battle with the army of the Kushite king.

Considered the first ruler of the 18th dynasty and thus the founder of the New Kingdom, Ahmosis set the pattern for the kings who came after him by acting as both war leader and builder. With his sister-wife Ahmosis-Nefertari, he left monuments at sites including Avaris, Abydos (mythical birthplace of the god Osiris), and Karnak, where the 18th-dynasty kings expanded the Middle Kingdom temple to Amun. Although Thebes (or Waset, as it was known in ancient times) became the religious center of the country, the 18th dynasty rulers moved their political seat back to the Memphite region.

From at least the time of Seqenenre Taa II and Ahhotep, kings of the 17th and 18th dynasties usually married a princess of the royal house, thus concentrating the family's power and wealth within a closed circle. Royal women were crucial to the rituals that magically maintained the proper order of the cosmos. Perhaps due to the king's symbolic identification as both the son of Amun and an incarnation of the god himself, certain royal women of the 18th dynasty played the important role of God's Wife of Amun. The holders of this title, of whom Ahmosis-Nefertari was the first, seem to have wielded significant power independent of the king.

The Hyksos invasion had taught the Egyptians that they were no longer safe within their own borders; in order to protect their land (as well as increase their wealth), they needed to expand. Egyptian pharaohs of the 18th dynasty followed a two-part military strategy. First, each king marched south in order to secure his back and collect prisoners of war to serve in his armies.

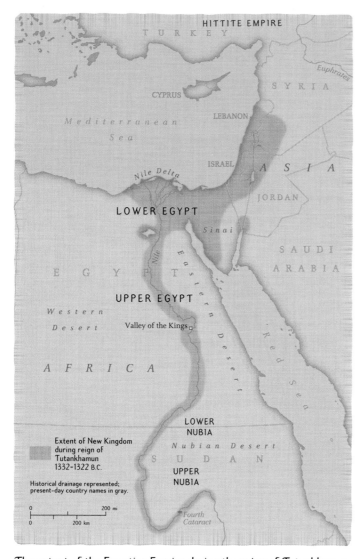

The extent of the Egyptian Empire during the reign of Tutankhamun

and mines to provide material for his many building projects. These included a chapel at Karnak, bark stations—places where the sacred boats of the gods could rest during their festival journeys—on the west bank of Thebes, and monuments at Abydos as well as in the region of the First Cataract of the Nile, the southern border of Egypt proper.

## The Tuthmosids and the Rise of Empire

Amenhotep I does not seem to have left behind any sons. The next king, thought by some to have been from a family connected with the priesthood of Amun, was Tuthmosis I. The name of this king's principal consort, Ahmosis, suggests that she may have been linked with the previous ruling line; in any event the transition of power from the Ahmosids who founded the dynasty to the Tuthmosids who would dominate Egypt for the next two hundred years seems to have been smooth.

Tuthmosis I ruled for about 11 years, campaigning vigorously for much of his reign. It is likely that he was responsible for the final defeat of the Kingdom of Kerma and the extension of the southern border of Egypt to somewhere between the Second and Third Cataracts. This region became an Egyptian territory under the charge of an Egyptian viceroy.

After securing the south, Tuthmosis I moved against the city-states of the northeast, mounting an expedition to northern Syria to battle Egypt's principal rivals in this area, the Mitanni, on their own ground. He reached the Euphrates River, the boundary of the Mitanni homeland, and erected a victory stela (an inscribed slab of stone) on its shores. The Mitanni remained a powerful presence in Syria, challenging Egyptian control of the region for several more generations.

Tuthmosis I's most significant building projects were additions to the temple of Amun at Karnak, where he built pylons (monumental entranceways) as well as a number of other monuments. At Abydos, he donated objects and statues to the cults of his predecessors. Other sites such as Giza, where the kings of the 4th dynasty had built their pyramids and carved the Great Sphinx, also received his attention. Tuthmosis I

In this way Lower Nubia, and eventually Upper Nubia as well, became provinces of Egypt. After Nubia was "pacified," the pharaoh could turn his attention north and east and mount campaigns into Syria-Palestine. This empire building had the added benefits of guaranteeing trade routes and bringing in booty from foreign lands. New weaponry such as the duck-billed axe, the scimitar, and the chariot—all originally introduced by the Hyksos—helped to make the Egyptian armies formidable foes.

Amenhotep I, son of Ahmosis and Ahmosis-Nefertari, ruled for about 20 years and continued to build the empire for which his father had planted the seeds. His successful Nubian wars replenished the kingdom's coffers and he opened a number of quarries is thought to have been the first king to carve his tomb into the rocky slopes of the Valley of the Kings.

Queen Ahmosis and Tuthmosis I had a daughter named Hatshepsut, but no surviving sons. The next king, Tuthmosis II, Tuthmosis I's son by a secondary wife, secured his right to the throne by marrying his half-sister Hatshepsut. Ruling for only about three years, he carried out at least one campaign into Nubia and did some building at Karnak. Tuthmosis II and Hatshepsut had one daughter (and perhaps a second), but no known sons.

Tuthmosis II was followed on the throne by the son of a minor wife. This heir, Tuthmosis III, was still a child, so his stepmother Hatshepsut—who bore the important title of God's Wife of Amun—became his regent. Biographical texts inscribed in the tombs of several high officials of the period make it clear that this powerful queen held the reins of government tightly from the beginning of her stepson's rule.

Sometime between her second and seventh year as regent, Hatshepsut took on the full title and powers of a reigning pharaoh. Women were essential to the royal dogma—kings could not rule without their queens beside them—but in theory only men could take on the role of pharaoh. Although several queens had ruled Egypt before, none of them appear to have assumed full kingly status. In order to reinforce her legitimacy, Hatshepsut claimed to have been placed on the throne by an oracle of Amun, and she commissioned a series of scenes for her mortuary temple illustrating her birth from a union between her mother and this god. In most of her reliefs and sculptures she had herself portrayed as male, in full pharaonic regalia.

Hatshepsut ruled for more than 20 years. The rightful king, Tuthmosis III, remained her co-regent, but stayed in her shadow. Hatshepsut poured the resources of the country into ambitious building projects all the way from Nubia to the old Hyksos capital of Avaris, but the majority of her attention was focused on Thebes. On its east bank, she significantly embellished the temple at Karnak and built a chapel for Amun two miles to the south on the site that would become Luxor Temple. On its west bank, she erected her mortuary temple at Deir el Bahri and began another Amun temple to the south at Medinet Habu.

In two reliefs from the 20th year of their joint reign, Hatshepsut and Tuthmosis III are depicted side by side, shown as equals. Soon afterward, by about 1481 B.C., Hatshepsut disappears from the official historical record and Tuthmosis III emerges as the sole ruler of the Two Lands. There is no evidence for the fate of this energetic, unique female pharaoh; it is most likely that she simply passed away.

Late in his 54-year reign, Tuthmosis III ordered his stepmother's name chiseled from her monuments and attempted to erase her very existence from history. This may have been to pave the way for his son, Amenhotep II, to serve as co-regent and sit beside him on the throne of the Two Lands. There is no evidence that this *damnatio memoriae* was spurred by any personal animosity, and indeed, the fact that it was not carried out until more than 20 years after Hatshepsut's disappearance suggests that the relationship between the two monarchs had been civil.

Tuthmosis III is remembered as a great military leader, both a man of courage and a brilliant strategist. As soon as he became sole ruler, he launched an attack against a coalition of Syro-Palestinian princes gathered at the city of Megiddo. Choosing to approach the fortress by the most dangerous path, he took the enemy by surprise and defeated them decisively. By the end of his reign, the Egyptian empire had reached its farthest extent, from the Fourth Cataract of the Nile in the south to the Euphrates River in the north. Booty from Tuthmosis III's frequent campaigns flowed into the royal coffers and into the treasure houses of the god Amun, providing the king with enormous resources to fund his ambitious building programs. He is known to have constructed more than 50 temples, including monuments in Syria-Palestine and Nubia. His most important contributions to Egypt's sacred landscape were at Karnak in the precinct of Amun, who had by this time been fused with the ancient sun god Re to become Amun-Re, king of the gods.

A scholar as well as a warrior, Tuthmosis III brought artists along on his military expeditions to record the exotic flora and fauna the soldiers encountered in their travels (including birds that might be chickens). Lists of these were engraved on the walls of Karnak Temple, along with extensive annals describing

the victories of the king and the wealth that these conquests enabled him to offer to Amun.

## The Height of Empire

Like his father, Amenhotep II was a warrior, proud of his prowess in the arts of the battlefield. He boasts, for example, of being able to shoot arrows through thick copper targets while driving his own chariot. Over the course of a 25- to 35-year reign, he consolidated the empire and ushered in a golden age of stability and prosperity. Among his achievements was the building of a diplomatic relationship with the Mitanni, who had appealed to him for peace.

Amenhotep II carried out building projects all over Egypt, but most of these are now fragmentary, having been dismantled, built over, or reused by the kings who came after him. Among his surviving works is a temple at Giza dedicated to the Great Sphinx as the sun god Horemakhet (Horus in the Horizon). Like all kings of his line, Amenhotep II also built at Thebes.

This king had many children, at least nine or ten of them male, by his wives and concubines, and the succession was probably disputed, perhaps violently. Tuthmosis IV, son of a lesser queen named Tiaa, became the next ruler. According to a stela that he left between the paws of the Great Sphinx at Giza, he had come to the Memphite desert on a hunting trip while still a prince, and had fallen asleep in the ancient statue's shadow. As he slept, the Sphinx spoke to him and asked him to clear the sand from around its body. In return for this service, the Sphinx promised him the kingship, and both king and statue kept their word. Having inherited a country fundamentally at peace, Tuthmosis IV had little campaigning to do. During his eight-year reign, he sealed the Egyptian alliance with the powerful Mitanni through marriage with a daughter of their king, Artatama I.

A queen named Mutemwiya, whom some scholars have suggested be identified as Tuthmosis IV's Mitanni

The mortuary temple of Hatshepsut is set into an imposing bay of cliffs at Deir el Bahri, its terraces and ramps echoing the natural landscape. In the upper left corner of the temple, beside a dismantled monument of Tuthmosis III, is a chapel to Hathor.

princess, gave birth to the next king, Amenhotep III. At the age of about 12, this youthful king inherited the vast Egyptian empire. The state and temple treasuries were filled with gold, and Egypt's vassals bowed down before the mighty ruler of the Two Lands.

By the second year of his reign, Amenhotep III had taken a girl named Tiye as his queen. Her father, Yuya, was a master of the horse, commander of chariotry, and overseer of the cattle of Min (the god of fertility); her mother, Tjuya, was a priestess of Amun, Hathor (one of the great goddesses of the pantheon), and Min. The connection of both husband and wife with the fertility god Min suggests that they came from Akhmim, site of a great temple complex to this god. Some scholars believe that Yuya and Tjuya were of foreign birth, although there is no particular evidence for this. Yuya and Tjuya are known to have had at least one child in addition to Tiye; this was Aanen, high priest of the sun god, Re, and second priest of Amun under Amenhotep III. Another important official named Aye, who ruled Egypt for a short time near the end of the dynasty, may also have been their son.

Tiye held a position of unusual prominence during her husband's reign. In a significant change of policy, she immediately became Great Royal Wife and outranked even Amenhotep III's mother. Tiye is shown at the same scale as her husband in a number of statues and is depicted in ways heretofore reserved for the king, such as in the form of a sphinx trampling enemies. Since Tiye's parents were not royal, scholars once assumed that the marriage was a love match. However, it is possible that Yuya and Tjuya held significant power in the central administration under Tuthmosis IV, and may even have served as regents during the minority of Amenhotep III. In the early part of his reign, this king issued a series of large commemorative scarabs; two types mention not only Tiye, but also her parents. One of these series, dated to the 11th year of the king's reign, celebrates the opening of a new lake that had been dug especially for the queen, perhaps near her home town of Akhmim; the king states that he was rowed on this lake in his royal barge, the *Dazzling Aten*. Yuya and Tjuya were granted the rare privilege of burial in the Valley of the Kings, where their partially plundered but still rich tomb was discovered in 1905.

Between the massive paws of the Great Sphinx at
Giza stands the Dream Stela of Tuthmosis IV.

Amenhotep III and Tiye had at least six children: two sons, Tuthmosis and Amenhotep, and four daughters—Sitamun, Henuttaneb, Isis, and Nebetah. Other than Tiye, the king's harem included princesses from southern Syria, Mitanni, Babylon, and a province of southeast Asia Minor called Arzawa; he also seems to have married several of his own daughters. The eldest son of Amenhotep III and Tiye, Tuthmosis, was designated crown prince at an early age. However, he died before his father, and his younger brother, Amenhotep, took his place.

## The Amarna Period

Although many scholars believe that Amenhotep IV (later known as Akhenaten) ascended the throne of Egypt only at the death of his father, others think the younger king was raised to the status of co-regent before this time. There is convincing evidence on both sides of the issue, but nothing that is widely considered conclusive. The situation is complicated further by the fact that those who favor a co-regency vote for a joint reign of anywhere from two to twelve years. Lack of agreement on this fundamental point makes outlining the history of this fascinating period extremely complex.

Amenhotep III died in about the 38th year of his reign, and his son either took the throne for the first time or continued as sole ruler. From the beginning of his reign Amenhotep IV is linked with his Great Royal Wife, Nefertiti—The Beautiful One Comes—who played an important role in his court. Some believe that Nefertiti was a member of Tiye's family (perhaps the daughter of Aye), but there is no conclusive evidence for or against this. Amenhotep IV and Nefertiti had six daughters together, but apparently no sons. Another of his wives, Kiya, was given the special title, "greatly beloved wife of the king"; she may have been Tutankhamun's mother.

Amenhotep IV began his reign with a campaign into Nubia; in Syria-Palestine, he continued his predecessors' policy of mixing diplomacy with shows of military strength. In his early years of rule, the king undertook an ambitious building program at Karnak, but the temples he erected were not for Amun, but were rather dedicated to a deity manifested as the disk of the sun, the Aten. The artistic style seen in these temples and in other monuments from this period is remarkable, unique in the history of Egyptian art. In contrast to the idealized, youthful images of the king seen in traditional Egyptian art, Amenhotep IV had himself represented in an exaggerated fashion, with a long, narrow face, prominent chin, high cheekbones, a long neck, narrow shoulders, pronounced breasts, wide hips, a sagging belly, and spindly arms and legs.

Debate has raged for decades on the reason the king and, by extension, members of the royal family and the elite chose to be shown in this fashion. Important new artistic developments had already begun to appear during the eras of his grandfather and father. Scholars have even argued that the innovations of the later reign of Amenhotep III were concurrent with the artistic revolution of Amenhotep IV, and that the Aten was in actuality the elder king, deified after his 30th year of rule. Whether or not this is the case, the new king went far beyond his predecessors, creating a drastically different artistic vocabulary.

Some believe that this new style was a reflection of the king's actual appearance. If this was the case, he may have suffered from a genetic disorder, recently suggested to be Marfan's syndrome. People with this disease often have long, narrow faces with pendant jaws, extremely long, thin limbs, pear-shaped bodies, and shortened life spans. Other scholars think that the king's features and body shape reflect his religious beliefs, and represent a desire to reflect the androgynous nature of his principal god, the sun disk, to whom the "Great Hymn to the Aten" (composed by the king himself) attributes the roles of both mother and father and the responsibility for the fertility of the universe. It is also possible that both theories are valid: that the king did suffer from Marfan's syndrome, and also chose to exaggerate his features for religious and symbolic

This colossal statue of sandstone originally adorned one of Akhenaten's temples to the Aten at Karnak. Carved in the early years of Akhenaten's reign, it shows the radical style of this era. On his chest and wrists, the king wears the cartouches of the Aten, a deity manifested as the disk of the sun.

reasons. As the reign progressed, this style of art gradually became less exaggerated and more naturalistic, although certain traces of the first style, such as a slightly sagging belly, continue far into the next period.

At some point between the fifth and seventh years of his rule, Amenhotep IV, "Amun is Satisfied," changed his name to Akhenaten, "The Transfigured Spirit of the Aten." At about the same time, Nefertiti was given a second name, Neferneferuaten "the most beautiful one of the Aten." From the outset of her husband's reign, Nefertiti, like the queens just before her, enclosed her name in a cartouche—an oval ring bearing the king's name. With the addition of a second cartouche, her status was raised even closer to that of a pharaoh. Akhenaten transformed his supreme deity, the Aten, into the sole creator god from whom everything issued. As part of his spiritual revolution, Akhenaten abandoned Thebes as Egypt's religious center and built a new city dedicated to the cult of the Aten.

The royal family moved to Akhetaten, the "horizon of the Aten"—better known by its modern name of Tell el Amarna, or Amarna—sometime after the fifth year of Akhenaten's reign. This move, although it had clear symbolic significance, may also reflect a struggle with the priesthood of Amun, which had enjoyed enormous power and wealth until this time. Queen Tiye also came to Amarna; if her husband was still alive, he might have lived in or visited the new city as well. One stela, found in a private home at Amarna, depicts the older royal couple seated side by side, and there is other evidence, although generally considered circumstantial, that Amenhotep III was in Amarna at some point in his life. The Black Plague may have come to the Mediterranean basin around this time, so it is possible that the move was partially prompted by a desire to flee disease-infested centers of population. (However, if this was the case, it was unsuccessful, as traces of the Black Plague have recently been found at Amarna.)

Discovered in 1912 in the workshop of the chief sculptor Tuthmosis at Amarna, this painted limestone head of Queen Nefertiti is now in Berlin. Probably never meant as a finished piece for display, it most likely served as a sculptors' model for composite statues carved from more expensive stone.

When Akhenaten laid out his city, he commanded that a series of boundary stelae be carved in the cliffs surrounding the site. Among other things, these state that if he were to die outside of Akhetaten, his body should be brought back and buried in the tomb that was being prepared for him there, in the Great Wadi (canyon) that cut through the eastern cliffs. The pharaoh carried out building projects in Nubia, and erected temples to the Aten in Memphis, Heliopolis, and possibly other locations. Although the religious capital of the country was moved from Thebes to Amarna, Memphis may well have continued as a key center of administration. Certainly high officials of Akhenaten's court, such as Aperel, one of his viziers, and Meryre, a high priest of the Aten, were buried here.

Foreign relations during the reigns of Amenhotep III, Akhenaten, and their immediate successors are illuminated by a group of clay tablets found in 1887 by a peasant woman digging in the ancient ruins at Amarna for fertilizer. Written in cuneiform script and a form of the Akkadian language, these are known as the Amarna letters, and consist primarily of missives from independent Near Eastern rulers and Egyptian vassals with whom the kings had diplomatic relations. The picture that emerges from these letters is of a world in flux. There were six other great kingdoms in the Near East: Kassite Babylonia, based in southern Iraq; Assyria in the upper Tigris River area; the Mitanni of northern Syria and northern Iraq; the Hatti (Hittites) of central Turkey; Arzawa in southwestern Turkey; and Cyprus (known as Alashiya).

The two superpowers—the Mitanni and Egypt—had developed an excellent relationship. Amenhotep III was married to both a daughter and a sister of the king, Tushratta. But the Hittites were gaining power, threatening Mitanni supremacy in the north. The Hittite king began to court Egyptian favor, proposing an alliance between the two lands. Sometime early in Akhenaten's reign, the Hittites attacked the Mitanni empire and took over its north Syrian lands as far south as the Lebanon mountains. Akhenaten did nothing to help his Mitanni allies, and soon afterward appears to have signed a new treaty with the Hittites. Some scholars believe that Akhenaten stayed out of

# VALLEY OF THE KINGS
## East Valley

KV 1
KV 2
KV 46
KV 3
Generator House
KV 4
Ghafir's Hut
KV 5
KV 45    KV 44
KV 7
KV 6
KV 28
KV 27
KV 8
KV 55
KV 21
Rest Area
KV 62
Tutankhamun
Rest Area
KV 9
KV 17
KV 16
KV 60    KV 20
KV 56
KV 10
KV 18
KV 19
KV 54
KV 11
KV 58
KV 57
KV 12
Approximate location of KV 48, KV 50-52
Approximate location of KV 53
KV 49
KV 43
KV 35
KV 36
KV 61
KV 29
KV 13
KV 47
KV 40
KV 26
KV 14
KV 59
KV 38
KV 30
KV 31
KV 32
KV 37
KV 15
KV F
KV 42    KV 33
KV 34

THEBAN HILLS

| 0 | 10 20 30 40 50 | 100 meters |
| 0 | 100 | 200 | 300 | 400 feet |

Contour interval 5 meters

KV 62  Tomb featured in exhibit
KV 7   Other tomb
        Aboveground pathway

Source: Theban Mapping Project

### PRINCIPAL LEADERS OF THE 18TH DYNASTY

| Ahmosis | 1539-1514 | |
| Amenhotep I | 1514-1493 | KV 39? |
| Tuthmosis I | 1493-1483 | KV 20, KV 38 |
| Tuthmosis II | 1483-1479 | |
| Queen Hatshepsut | 1479-1458 | KV 20 |
| Tuthmosis III | 1479-1426 | KV 34 |
| Amenhotep II | 1426-1400 | KV 35 |
| Tuthmosis IV | 1400-1390 | KV 43 |
| Amenhotep III | 1390-1353 | KV 22 |
| Akhenaten | 1353-1336 | |
| Tutankhamun | 1332-1322 | KV 62 |
| Aye | 1323-1319 | KV 23 |
| Horemheb | 1319-1392 | KV 57 |

TUTANKHAMUN
ca 1332-1322 B.C.

| 3000 | 2500 | 2000 | 1500 | 1000 | 500 | A.D. |

18th dynasty

| Late Predynastic circa 3100 B.C. | Early Dynastic ca 2950-2575 B.C. | Old Kingdom ca 2575-2150 B.C. | 1st Intermediate Period ca 2125-1975 B.C. | Middle Kingdom ca 1975-1640 B.C. | 2nd Intermediate Period ca 1630-1520 B.C. | New Kingdom ca 1539-1075 B.C. | 3rd Intermediate Period ca 1075-715 B.C. | Late Period ca 715-332 B.C. | Greco-Roman Period 332 B.C.-A.D. 395 | Roman conquest 30 B.C. |

these affairs because he was concentrating instead on his religious changes: It has even been suggested that Akhenaten could not send troops north because he needed them in Egypt to enforce his revolution. It is also possible that he was playing a waiting game, sensing that Egypt's best long-term interests lay with the Hittites rather than the Mitanni. However, it was not long before the Hittites took advantage of local rebellions in Egyptian territory to annex part of Egypt's northern empire. This provoked a war that lasted, on and off, for 100 years.

The 12th year of Akhenaten's reign was marked by a celebration in which tribute was brought to the king by his foreign vassals. According to subscribers to the co-regency theory, this ceremony could have marked the junior king's promotion to senior king. However, those who believe in a short co-regency or the consecutive rules of Amenhotep III and his son argue instead that this was simply a normal ceremony of tribute that might have occurred at regular intervals, or was associated with a Sed festival—a royal jubilee at which the king celebrated his rejuvenation and reaffirmed his competence to rule.

Soon after this ceremony, Nefertiti dropped out of sight, and a new king appeared, ruling with Akhenaten as co-regent. This king was named Ankhkheprure Neferneferuaten. Scholars once assumed that Nefertiti (also named Neferneferuaten) either died or fell from favor, but many now believe that she may have changed her name, and is to be identified as new coregent. In some inscriptions, a feminizing 't' is added to the name Ankh(et)kheprure, adding even more credence to this theory. Meritaten, the eldest daughter of the royal pair, replaced her mother as Great Royal Wife, a position that might have been primarily ceremonial. The appearance of a daughter, Meritaten the Younger, however, might mean that the elder Meritaten was her father's consort in more than name. Kiya disappears at this point, and her name is

effaced and replaced by the name of Meritaten on many monuments.

Tiye died in about the 14th year of her son's reign. Fragments of a sarcophagus found in Akhenaten's tomb at Amarna suggest that she was originally buried there and later moved to a small tomb in the Valley of the Kings (KV 55), where objects bearing her name, including pieces of a large gilded wooden shrine, were found. Her body, however, was not found in that tomb either, so she must have been moved again sometime in antiquity. A mummy found reburied in the tomb of Amenhotep II has been tentatively identified as this queen on the basis of a hair sample (which may match a lock of hair labeled as Tiye's from the tomb of Tutankhamun) and the similarity of the shape of its skull to Tutankhamun's.

Akhenaten died after 17 years of rule. His rock-cut tomb in the Great Wadi at Amarna was never completed, but fragments of a red granite sarcophagus were discovered in the burial chamber there. A male body found in KV 55, within a royal sarcophagus originally made for a queen but adapted for a king, is thought by some to be that of Akhenaten himself. The cartouches on this coffin had been deliberately chiseled out: Although the body was allowed a proper burial, its identity was taken from it.

Exactly what happened toward the end of Akhenaten's reign and after his death is still a matter of debate. After Ankhkheprure Neferneferuaten, the names of another king, Ankhkheprure Smenkhkare, also known as Djeserkheprure Smenkhkare, appear briefly in the historical record. This king appears at least once with Meritaten as his consort. Smenkhkare was once assumed to be the son of Akhenaten and the brother of Tutankhamun, although there is no direct evidence for this. In fact, even the existence of this king is debated, as some would like to see him as yet another incarnation of Ankhkheprure Neferneferuaten/Nefertiti. Others believe that he did exist and that the body in KV 55 is his. Whether male or female, Nefertiti, a son or brother of Akhenaten's, or even, as has also been suggested, Akhenaten's eldest daughter Meritaten, the king who ruled with and/or after Akhenaten died only about two or three years after ascending the throne, leaving Egypt in the untried hands of a young boy named Tutankhaten.

The Valley of the Kings is a group of wadis (canyons), with two main arms and a number of smaller tributaries. Most of the royal tombs are in the eastern arm, hidden high in the cliffs or dug, like Tutankhamun's tomb, into the valley floor.

This life-size statue depicts Tuthmosis IV with his mother Tiaa. Discovered in 1903 in the Temple of Amun at Karnak, it had been deliberately buried only a few centimeters below the ancient surface, placed almost vertically near the east wall of one of the inner rooms of the temple. Mother and son sit side by side on a high-backed throne, each with one arm around the other and the other arm resting flat upon the thigh. Tuthmosis IV holds an ankh, symbol of life, in his right hand. He wears a round shoulder-length wig topped by a uraeus (a hooding cobra that represents both Wadjet, tutelary deity of the Delta, and the sun god, Re) and a knee-length kilt of a type known as the *shendyt,* generally reserved for royalty. His throne name, Menkheprure, given to him at his coronation, is carved on the kilt's waistband, which is decorated with a lozenge pattern. A bull's tail that dangled from the back of his belt can be seen between his legs. His bare feet rest upon the Nine Bows, symbols of the enemies of Egypt. By his left leg is an inscription that reads: "The good god, Menkheprure, beloved of Amun-Re, Lord of the Thrones of the Two Lands, given life."

2  Statue of Tuthmosis IV and His Mother
Gray granite
Height 111.5 cm; width 68.2 cm; depth 80.7 cm
Dynasty 18, reign of Tuthmosis IV
Karnak, Temple of Amun
CG 42080

Tiaa wears a long tripartite wig, over which can be seen the vulture headdress worn by queens and goddesses from at least the Old Kingdom onward, with the damaged head of the bird protruding at her brow. This vulture was the emblem of Nekhbet, protective goddess of Upper Egypt, and is often seen in conjunction with the cobra of Wadjet. This bird was also closely associated with Mut, consort of Amun. The queen's garment is a tight, ankle-length dress of archaic style; she wears a broad collar around her neck and a bracelet on her visible wrist. The inscription by her right leg reads, "The King's Great Wife, whom he loves, King's Mother, Tiaa, true of voice."

The features of the royal faces are finely worked, and similar to one another. The king's nose is damaged, but the queen's has a narrow bridge and wide nostrils. Both have almond-shaped eyes that slant downward at the inner corner, well-marked eyebrows, and high cheekbones. Their lower lips are slightly fuller and longer than their upper lips, and they seem to be smiling slightly. The statue has been dated stylistically to early in the reign of Tuthmosis IV.

Although this king had a number of wives, it was his mother to whom he gave the greatest rank and importance during his reign. It is interesting that Tiaa held the title of King's Great Wife during her son's reign rather than her husband's. Most scholars believe that she was a minor queen of Amenhotep II and only gained significant status when her son came to the throne.

3  Guardian Statue of Amenhotep II
Wood coated with resin
Height 80 cm; width 22 cm
Dynasty 18, reign of Amenhotep II
Thebes, Valley of the Kings, tomb of Amenhotep II (KV 35)
CG 24598

In the late 1800s, Victor Loret, then head of the Egyptian Antiquities Service, discovered 16 tombs in the Valley of the Kings, all robbed in antiquity. The most spectacular was that of Amenhotep II, which he found in 1898. Although the royal burial had been violated in ancient times and anything of value taken, many archaeologically important objects belonging to the original burial still lay within its chambers. Dominating the burial chamber was a quartzite sarcophagus containing the body of the warrior pharaoh himself. The tomb had been used in antiquity as a cache for a number of royal bodies: One mummy lay within the burial chamber, resting on top of a wooden boat, and twelve others had been left in two of the tomb's side chambers. At least nine of these additional mummies were the bodies of New Kingdom monarchs, including Amenhotep III.

About two-thirds life-size, this statue from the tomb represents Amenhotep II wearing a *nemes* headcloth (usually striped but here plain), a trapezoidal royal beard, and a kilt with a starched front panel. The separately worked uraeus that once adorned the king's forehead is missing, but its emplacement is still visible. The left leg is forward in the typical striding pose for males, seen as early as the Old Kingdom. In the left hand, bent forward at the elbow, the king holds a long staff, only the top of which is now preserved. The king's right arm and both feet are missing, as is the original base on which the statue once stood. When discovered, significantly more of the staff, which had a hand rest in the shape of a papyrus umbel (the top of the plant), the upper part

of the right arm, and parts of both feet were present. Comparison with a similar statue from the tomb of Tutankhamun suggests that the king held a mace in his right hand, which would have hung down by his side.

The wood of this statue was coated with resin or thick paint, giving it the black color of well-watered soil associated with fertility. It is interesting to note that although parts of the Tutankhamun figure were gilded, there is no sign that this statue bore similar decoration. However, the missing uraeus was quite likely of metal, and the fact that the eyes have been gouged out suggests that they were of semiprecious materials.

Since his tomb had been disturbed and robbed before being used as a cache, Amenhotep II's statue was found out of context. In the tomb of Tutankhamun, the statue similar to this (although life-size rather than half human height) was one of a pair found flanking the plastered doorway to the burial chamber, as if to guard it. The second statue of Tutankhamun wore a *khat* headdress, a bag-shaped cloth that fell to just above the shoulders.

Tutankhamun's two figures are often referred to as "guardian statues," and this name may elucidate part of their function. Tutankhamun's statues, and by analogy this piece, also may have played a role in certain funerary rituals, especially the Opening of the Mouth—a rite which served to prepare images of the deceased for eternal life and allow them to receive offerings. Comparable figures were also found in the tombs of Amenhotep II's father, Tuthmosis III, and son, Tuthmosis IV, suggesting that such figures were an essential item of royal funerary equipment.

4  Face from a Royal Composite Statue
Obsidian
Height 19.5 cm; width 14.2 cm; depth 14.2 cm
Dynasty 18, reign of Amenhotep III
Karnak, Precinct of Amun, Court of the Cachette
CG 42101

In the early years of the 20th century, several of the massive columns that held up the great hypostyle hall of Amun at Karnak collapsed. The reconstruction effort was carried out under the supervision of a French Egyptologist named Georges Legrain. Instructed by Gaston Maspero, then head of the Antiquities Service, to explore the area as he rebuilt the columns, Legrain and his workers made a remarkable discovery: Beneath the floor was a cache of artifacts, including 751 statues and statue fragments and more than 17,000 bronzes. These were votive pieces that had been given ritual burial, perhaps in the Roman Period, during one of the many cleanings and refurbishings of the temple. The high water table made the excavations difficult, and work stopped after several years, with many pieces still buried under the mud.

Among the sculptures were a number from the late 18th dynasty, including this face from a composite statue (a statue made up of pieces carved from different materials), a type very popular in the Amarna period. The eyes and eyebrows were originally inlaid and a headdress would have been attached on top. The hole in the center of the brow was made to receive a uraeus, indicating that the face is royal. The back is flat and roughened for attachment to another piece, most likely a wooden core. A foot, an ear, and part of a fist from this statue were found in the same area and part of a neck from a similar statue was also discovered nearby.

The carving of this piece is exquisite. The face, with its round-tipped, wide-bridged nose, narrow, slightly tilted eyes, full lips rimmed by a lip line, rounded cheeks, and square chin, is a masterpiece of the sculptor's art. Its subtle modeling is superb and the surface has been beautifully finished.

Dates given by scholars to this head range from the reign of Tuthmosis III to the 19th dynasty, and it has been interpreted as both male and female. Recent analysis suggests that it was carved in the reign of Amenhotep III and represents the king himself. This is based on study of the features, which correspond to those on images of Amenhotep III from the latter part of his reign, and on careful examination of the ear found nearby, now in the Museum of Fine Arts, Boston, which also bears the characteristics of this king.

The black of the stone was chosen for ritual reasons, as this is the color of water-soaked earth associated with fertility and rebirth. Obsidian was expensive, imported from either Anatolia (Turkey) or Ethiopia. When complete, the statue would have been life-size; a fragment of gold on the fist indicates that it was gilded. It once stood at Karnak, and may have been a focus of the deified king's cult.

This head, also from a composite statue, was discovered at Amarna in the workshop of the sculptor Tuthmosis. This house was a remarkable find, providing a window into the art and technology of the period. With this and other unfinished pieces were sculptor's models, slabs of limestone on which the master artisan had carved the faces of Akhenaten, Nefertiti, and other Amarna figures to provide guidance for the lesser sculptors. These display a new naturalism, removed from the grotesque exaggeration of the king's early reign.

The light brown quartzite of this head was chosen to mimic female skin color as closely as possible. It most likely represents one of the six daughters of Akhenaten and Nefertiti, as these girls are shown elsewhere with this distinctively broadened and elongated skull. This may be a symbolic exaggeration of a real head shape, or else an accurate representation of a skull distorted from youth by tightly wrapped bandages—a practice seen in certain African cultures but unattested from ancient Egypt. Another possibility is that it is a simple convention used to indicate that the portrait is of a child.

The princess has a serene beauty. Her eyes are almond-shaped and slightly tilted under arched brows. Her pupils, cosmetic lines, and eyebrows have been added with paint. Her nose is thin-bridged and straight, slightly rounded at the tip, and her thick lips, bracketed by deep corner dimples, have been tinted red. Her face is triangular, with thin cheeks and a prominent chin. Her ears are large and double-pierced, and lines of the large muscles have been modeled on her long, thin neck.

This is one of a number of sculptures, in various states of completion, of these princesses. It is tempting to identify it as an image of Meritaten, eldest daughter of the king and queen; it could equally well be Meketaten, the second daughter (who died in childbirth), or Ankhsenpaaten, third daughter and queen of Tutankhaten.

5  Sculpted Head of a Princess from Amarna
Height 24.8 cm; width 12.3 cm; depth 16.5 cm
Dynasty 18; reign of Akhenaten
Tell el Amarna; workshop of Tuthmosis
JE 44870

6 Canopic Jar of Queen Kiya

Calcite

Height (including stopper) 52.9 cm; diameter 23.3 cm

Dynasty 18; reign of Akhenaten

Thebes, Valley of the Kings (KV 55)

JE 39637

In 1907, a remarkable new tomb was found in the Valley of the Kings. Dubbed the "Tomb of Queen Tiye" by its excavator, this rock-cut sepulchre (KV 55 according to the official reckoning) held a miscellaneous assemblage of objects bearing the names of various Amarna kings and queens: Tiye, Amenhotep III, Akhenaten, and Tutankhamun. A gilded wooden sarcophagus lay in the center of the main chamber, its form and iconography indicating that it had originally been made for a royal woman, then adapted to hold the body of a king. Inside was the mummy of a man between the ages of 25 and 35; some scholars believe this to be Smenkhkare, shadowy coregent/successor of the heretic pharaoh, while others think it is the body of Akhenaten himself. Whoever it was, his memory had been deliberately destroyed: The face of the coffin had been ripped away and the cartouches had been chiseled out.

Scholars who have studied this tomb believe that Queen Tiye was moved here from her original burial, along with a gilded wooden shrine and other funerary equipment. She was later moved again, perhaps to the tomb of Amenhotep II, where a mummy known as the "Elder Lady" has been tentatively identified as hers. Tomb 55 was then used for the body of an Amarna king. Tutankhamun probably played some part in these reburials, accounting for his name in the tomb.

Illustrated here is one of four vessels for the storage of mummified viscera that were found in a roughly cut side niche of the tomb. When discovered, these elegantly shaped jars, in the traditional form for such containers, still held traces of the owner's internal organs. The stoppers are carved in the likeness of a female head, wearing a short, layered hairstyle known as the Nubian wig (an adaptation of a military style worn by mercenaries from the south) and a broad collar, a type of necklace often worn by the deceased. The beautifully modeled face, with its fine features, full lips, and firm, prominent chin, has been made lifelike by the inlay of the almond-shaped eyes and the arched brows. Above the forehead, a hole indicates where a metal or rock-crystal uraeus was once attached.

The inscriptions that were carved onto the bodies of these jars have been erased, but scholars have been able to reconstruct the cartouches and titles of Akhenaten and the Aten, and the name and title of Kiya, the king's "greatly beloved" wife. Although clearly secondary to Nefertiti, Kiya appears in a number of reliefs from Amarna, and many believe she was Tutankhamun's mother. Although the excavator identified the heads as images of Queen Tiye, scholars now agree that they represent Kiya.

Height 29.5 cm; width 10.8 cm; depth 10.4 cm

Dynasty 18, reign of Amenhotep III

Karnak, Temple of Amun, Court of the Cachette

CG 42083

Discovered in the Karnak cachette, this is one of a series of steatite figures of Amenhotep III dating to the latter part of his reign. It was once glazed with green, of which only traces remain. The king stands, wearing the nemes headdress topped by the double crown (emblem of a united Egypt), the trapezoidal royal beard, a kilt with starched front panel topped by a sporran, a broad collar, and armlets. His right arm hangs by his side while the left crosses his body at waist level. This pose suggests that he originally held a standard of some sort; this, with the hand that once grasped it, is gone. Based on other statues from his reign, the standard may have been a round staff topped by the head of a ram, the animal totem of the god Amun.

The large, almond-shaped eyes and childlike features of the face—rounded cheeks, short nose, and full lips—date this piece to the period after the king's first Sed Festival. At this celebration, which took place in the 30th year of his reign, the aging king was symbolically rejuvenated, and the youthful features with which he is shown afterward reflect this renewal. An extraordinarily large number of statues of the king were carved after this time, representing him in the guise of various gods and connecting him especially with the sun god. The headgear he wears here associates him with Atum, one form of the creator god. The armbands and the striped sporran decorated with uraei (hooding cobras) that he wears over his kilt are solar symbols, formerly seen only in depictions of deceased kings. Here, the symbols indicate his divinized status.

The back pillar, shaped like an obelisk, reinforces the piece's solar imagery. Linked with the sacred *benben* stone kept in the temple of the sun god Re at Heliopolis, the obelisk, with its spire reaching to the sky and its pyramidal top echoing the sun's rays, was a potent solar symbol at least as early as the 5th dynasty. The tip of the pillar, on which a cartouche was carved, is missing. Below, under the sign for sky, is the king's titulary: "The good god, lord of the Two Lands, Nebmaatre, son of Re Amenhotep, ruler of Thebes, [beloved of] Amun, lord of the thrones of the Two Lands...." The placement of the king's name on the top of the obelisk, above the sky, was another way of associating him with the sun god.

Small statues such as this one have been identified as votive images. Many examples have been found at Karnak, where they were dedicated to Amun either by the king himself or by his high officials. One scholar has suggested that the use of steatite may associate this and similar figures with the large commemorative scarabs, also of steatite, dating from earlier in Amenhotep III's reign.

8 Head of a Figurine of Queen Tiye
Serpentine
Height 7.2 cm, width 4.8 cm, depth 5.2 cm
Dynasty 18, reign of Amenhotep III
Serabhit el-Khadim, Sinai, Temple of Hathor
JE 38257

This tiny head of Queen Tiye was discovered by William Flinders Petrie in the temple of Hathor at Serabhit el-Khadim, Sinai. This area was the center of Egyptian turquoise mining and had long been sacred to the great goddess. A temple was first built here in the 12th dynasty; Amenhotep III added to it during his reign, at which time a number of votive statuettes such as this one may have been offered to the deity. Some scholars have suggested, based on its facial features, that this head dates to the reign of Tiye's son, Akhenaten. If there was a co-regency, both datings could be correct.

On the occasion of the first Sed Festival of Amenhotep III, his principal wife Tiye was also divinized and associated with several goddesses. Chief among these was Hathor, daughter and wife of the sun god, Re. Amenhotep III built a temple for himself as the sun god at Soleb in Nubia; a smaller temple to Tiye as Hathor was erected nearby at Sedeinga.

Tiye is shown here with the distinctive features seen in many of her images: a heart-shaped face; a small, elegant nose; prominent cheekbones; narrow, tilted eyes under arched brows; a full mouth turned down at the corners; and a pointed chin. Pronounced grooves from the outside of her nostrils to the corners of her lips may indicate age. She wears a heavy braided wig arranged in layers, topped by a low flat crown adorned in the center with her cartouche; both wig and crown show traces of gilding. Winged cobras, their bodies undulating around the sides of the crown, flank and thus guard her name. From the central point, two more cobras, which may once have worn the crowns of Upper and Lower Egypt, hang down to protect her forehead—a detail typical of this period. Her large ears are pierced for round ear studs.

iscovered in 1915 by American archaeologist Clarence Fisher under a 19th dynasty palace at Memphis, this almost-life-size head is from a composite statue. Popular in the Amarna period, the materials for the individual parts of such statues were carefully chosen for both practical and symbolic reasons. This head, in which the eyes and eyebrows were originally inlaid with other materials, is of a yellowish brown quartzite that imitates female skin in both color and texture and also has solar connotations. It would have been set into a separately carved body; a crown or headdress of some sort would have been set on top, where a tenon has been cut to receive it.

Its style places this piece squarely in the Amarna period; the features are those of Queen Nefertiti. The eyes are slightly tilted, with a distinctive narrowing toward the outer edges. The brows are lightly arched. Most of the nose has been broken away, but enough remains to show that the bridge was narrow and the shape elegant. The cheekbones are high but soft and the mouth full, with even upper and lower lips bracketed on the sides by soft curves. The face is a perfect oval, with a firm, square chin and wide brow. Although the ears have been broken away, a double piercing can still be seen on the left lobe. This double piercing is seen occasionally from the reigns of Amenhotep III and his son and was meant to hold a single heavy earring.

A number of portraits of Nefertiti from the middle to latter part of Akhenaten's reign were found in the studio of the chief royal sculptor, Tuthmosis, at Amarna. One of these was the famous painted limestone bust of Nefertiti now in Berlin, which served as a model for this and other composite statues. The head illustrated here might once have been part of a statue set up at Memphis.

9  Face from a Composite Statue of Nefertiti
Brown quartzite
Height 19.0 cm; width 14.5 cm; depth 19.0 cm
Dynasty 18; reign of Akhenaten
Memphis; Mit Rahina, Palace of Merenptah
JE 45547

THE WINDING RIVER, THE LUSH FLOODPLAIN, AND THE HARSH SANDS
OF THE LOW AND HIGH DESERTS FORM THE LANDSCAPE OF EGYPT.

# Daily Life in Tutankhamun's World

*The drama of the 18th dynasty was played out against a*
*fertile landscape defined by the long ribbon of the Nile River,*
*which flows north for thousands of miles from the highlands*
*of Ethiopia (the Blue Nile) and Uganda (the White Nile)*
*to empty into the Mediterranean Sea.*

From the outcroppings of granite that form the First Cataract at Aswan to the apex of the Delta near modern Cairo, the river cuts a narrow bed into the underlying limestone. North of Cairo, it divides into a number of branches—five in ancient times and two today. The Nile was filled with perch, tilapia, and other edible fish, and was also home to such dangerous creatures as the hippopotamus and crocodile.

Each year, heavy rains in the mountains far to the south send torrents of silt-filled water rushing north to Egypt. From ancient geologic time until the last century, when the High Dam was built at Aswan, the river regularly spilled over its banks and spread across the land. When it receded, it left behind a residue of fertile soil. Over the millennia, this deposit formed a floodplain, narrow in some areas and broader in others, depending on the hardness of the underlying stone. In the Delta, the plain broadened into a vast inverted triangle watered by the ancient branches of the river. Most Egyptians lived on this floodplain; crops were grown and animals husbanded here. The water left in the low-lying ground that fringed the convex floodplain

Modern fishermen ply their trade in the predawn mists of the Delta.

in the Nile Valley and filled many areas of the Delta created swamps that were home to fish, migratory birds, and wild animals hunted by the ancients.

Flanking the floodplain is the low desert, once a savannah teeming with wildlife. Along the length of the Nile Valley, the low desert spreads east and west to the rocky foothills and towering cliffs that lead to the high desert. The Western Desert is punctuated by the fertile depression of the El Faiyum and the five major oases of Egypt: Siwa, Bahariya, Farafra, Dakhla, and Kharga; the Eastern Desert leads to the Sinai and the Red Sea. Ancient Egyptians hunted animals such as wild cattle, ibex, and gazelles in the desert, capturing them or slaughtering them for food. The desert was also the realm of the dead. Those who could afford it used stone to build their tombs, creating dwellings intended to last for eternity. Some cemeteries were in the low desert, and comprised pit or shaft tombs cut into the bedrock and topped by free-standing superstructures; other tombs were carved into the cliffs of the high desert.

The river was the principal artery for transportation and communication, and Egyptian navigation became highly sophisticated. By the New Kingdom, many types of vessels plied the waters of the Nile, from the papyrus skiffs in which kings and nobles hunted in the marshes for ritual and sport to the elegant wooden barks in which the king made visits of state. Stone from far-off quarries was transported by water; one relief in the temple of Hatshepsut at Deir el Bahri shows two enormous, monolithic granite obelisks being loaded onto barges at Aswan before being floated downstream to Karnak. Since the Nile flows from south to north, boats were generally rowed north with the current and sailed south with the prevailing winds. In addition to river-going vessels, the Egyptians had the technology to build seaworthy wooden sailing ships at least as early as the Old Kingdom. In the New Kingdom, such ships were used to transport raw materials, finished luxury goods, and even armies to and from Egypt.

Two temporal cycles defined the orderly world of the ancient Egyptians. The principal cycle was the daily rising and setting of the sun. Imagined as the god Re or Amun-Re in his bark, the solar orb rose each morning in the east and traversed the sky to set in the west, the land of the dead. Each night Re traveled through the Netherworld to be reborn again each morning.

The second cycle was the annual flood, whose arrival was heralded by the appearance of the star Sirius in the night sky. According to the Egyptian calendar, this marked New Year's Day, known to the Egyptians as Wep-Renpet, the "Opening of the Year." The four months of Inundation (Shemu) followed, each divided into three weeks of ten days each. The months during which the flood receded, fields were prepared, and seeds planted were known as Emergence (Peret). Four months later came the Harvest (Akhet), followed again by Inundation. Five "epagomenal" days were inserted at the end of the year in order to bring it up to 365 days. However, a solar year is 365 and $\frac{1}{4}$ days long, so over the centuries the actual year fell out of sync with the civil calendar and the official seasons ceased to correspond with the agricultural cycle. Aided by their skill in astronomy and by their careful record-keeping, the Egyptians were able to correct for this discrepancy and kept a second calendar more closely tied to the changing seasons.

The annual flood also provided the basis for the Egyptian myth of creation. The Egyptians conceived of the primeval universe as endless water (called Nun) and night. Out of the waters of Nun rose a single hillock, analogous to the first bits of earth that emerged as the flood receded. On this primeval mound appeared the creator god, who proceeded to bring the ordered world into being, separating the water from the land, the sky from the earth, and the day from the night. The creation was magically reiterated each day by the rising of the sun, evidence that the sun god had survived his nightly journey through the dangers of the Netherworld. These dangers in turn represented the limitless chaos out of which the cosmos had been born and which surrounded and constantly threatened it.

## The Lives of the Ancient Egyptians

Within a landscape watered by the Nile and illuminated by the sun, the Egyptians of the 18th dynasty enjoyed a regular, seemingly orderly way of life. Their social order is often described by scholars as a pyramid with the king at the top, supported by his family, the highest rank of officials, and the high priests of the major state cults. The uppermost levels of society in the 18th dynasty reached their stations by direct association either with the king or with the cult of one of the major state gods (and often both, as the highest ranks of the priesthood were royal appointments).

Below these were the elite of the court, officials, army commanders, and priests of the higher orders—the men who kept the bureaucracy of state, temple, and army functioning. High-status women worked mainly as mistresses of their family houses and estates and as musicians attached to the cults of the gods. There was a middle class of reasonably well-off and often literate bureaucrats and artisans. Forming the base of the pyramid were the masses of illiterate peasants who tilled the fields and provided the manpower to fight wars, quarry stones, and build the villas, palaces, and temples that adorned the land. Prisoners of war and slaves supplemented this workforce. There was significant social mobility; even slaves are known in some cases to have

A beautifully preserved pair of statues shows Meryre and his wife, who were members of the high elite during the Amarna period. These figures were discovered recently in the couple's tomb at Saqqara.

Sennedjem, an artisan who worked in the Valley of the Kings, and his wife worship Hathor of the sycamore tree.

married into the families of their owners. In the New Kingdom, the army was an important means of social advancement, as military service to the king was highly regarded and could be richly rewarded.

As is the case for many aspects of Egyptian history, our knowledge of daily life in the 18th dynasty centers on the world of the elite. Much of our understanding is based on the paintings and reliefs that decorate high-status tombs as well as the objects with which kings and their courtiers chose to be buried. Although most (if not all) of these scenes and objects have religious and mortuary significance, they also provide a wealth of information about everyday activities. This is supplemented by a relatively small amount of archaeological evidence from settlements. The remains at Akhenaten's royal city of Amarna and the palace complex of

Malkata, built by Amenhotep III on the west bank at Thebes, have preserved the floor plans of elaborate palaces and large villas in mud brick, with painted decoration expressing naturalistic themes. Over the last 100 years, archaeologists excavating the village of Deir el Medina, where the artisans who built the royal tombs made their homes, have found evidence, including household accounts, court trials, and works of literature on papyri and ostraca (flakes of pottery or limestone used as "scrap paper") that temper this narrow view of society. Most of these items date from the Ramesside period (19th and 20th dynasties), but they still give us a good sense of life for the royal artisans of the New Kingdom.

This complex of sources reveals that the ancient Egyptians were not terribly different from people of today. There were brilliant engineers, dedicated family men, and wise mothers on the one hand, and juvenile delinquents, traitors, and thieves on the other. Young people wanted to fall in love, get married, care for their children, and have the resources in later life to build and equip a tomb. Some were content with their lot, while others were ambitious or jealous of their neighbors. In comparison with much of the ancient world, women enjoyed relatively high status and were able, for example, to own property and represent themselves in a court of law.

The ancient Egyptians had a rich and varied diet. Its staples were bread and beer, made from wheat and barley. Vegetable gardens yielded lettuce, onions, leeks, garlic, and pulses such as lentils and peas. Many different fruits were available, including Christ's-thorn (a small round fruit that tastes like apple), Egyptian plums, fruit from the dom palm, sycamore figs, and dates and grapes, which were both eaten and used for wine. Fish were an important food source for all levels of society; in addition to being eaten fresh, their flesh and eggs were dried and salted for longer-term storage.

Domesticated and captured wild animals were kept in pens, where they were fed, cared for, bred, and then eaten. Cattle were highly valued as an important source of meat, eaten mostly by the elite and those laboring for the king. The Egyptians consumed sheep, goats, and pigs (although the last were considered low-status animals), and drank milk plain or made it into yogurt or cheese. They also enjoyed eggs and meat from all sorts of poultry, most often ducks and geese caught in the marshes and kept for breeding, but also including such exotic birds as cranes and ostriches.

Most ancient Egyptians lived in houses made of mud brick, sometimes with elements such as door-jambs and lintels of stone. They chose high ground, out of the reach of the yearly flood. The majority lived in small villages, but the New Kingdom saw the growth of larger towns, even cities, with many-storied dwellings jammed together along narrow streets. The very poor lived in huts, probably simple one-room structures. Many families occupied houses with several rooms, in which they received visitors, slept, cooked, and stored their surpluses. Often they would cook and even sleep on the roof. The elite built villas, the largest of them small estates in themselves, with bakeries and manu-facturing areas as well as sleeping chambers and recep-tion rooms arranged around courtyards. Many houses contained shrines for the worship of gods and ances-tors; larger houses could also have bathrooms. The king and his family lived in palaces scattered around the country at important cities and towns. Most houses were sparsely furnished, but royalty and the elite sat on chairs with their feet resting on stools and ate from small tables. They slept on low-slung beds, their heads propped on high headrests probably wrapped for com-fort. Clothing and valuables would have been kept in boxes and chests of various sizes.

The elite certainly lived lives of luxury and privi-lege. Their clothing was of fine linen, their jewels of gold and semiprecious stone. For festival and official occasions, they wore wigs of human hair or flax and took care to be properly scented with fragrant oils. Men and women applied make-up to their eyes, lips, and cheeks. The middle class, too, aspired to such luxury goods, both for the earthly realm and for life after death. In addition to jewels, wigs, perfumes, and cloth-ing, the ancient Egyptians commissioned a vast array of funerary goods, including coffins and sarcophagi to pro-tect their bodies and statues of wood and stone to house their spirits.

The Egyptian artisans responsible for creating these luxury artifacts were attached primarily to the royal house or the state temples. Although capable of creat-ing great masterpieces, they were, for the most part, anonymous, working under the guidance of the master craftsmen who answered directly to the king or high priest. Statuary, whether royal or private, was essen-tially functional. For instance, sculptors created portrait statues to house the ka, the life force of the person; con-sequently each king had his own ideal type, composed in order to create an identifiable face and body in which the ka could dwell. However, these were not por-traits in the Western sense; they are best thought of as hieroglyphic renderings of an ideal form. The portrait features of the ruling sovereign were also used in pri-vate statuary, reinforcing the importance of loyalty and service to the king in the divine realm.

## Resources and Technology

Raw materials were plentiful and varied, enabling Egypt's master craftsmen to develop efficient and prac-tical technologies. Their methods were generally simple but effective, and artisans were experts in working metal, stone, wood, ceramic, faience (a glazed silicate), and glass.

The most sought-after metal was gold, which the Egyptians identified as the "flesh of the gods." Found in vast deposits along the quartz-rich plateau of the East-ern Desert from just north of Thebes to the Fourth Cataract in Nubia, it could be extracted easily from the earth through panning and shallow surface mines. Col-lected as dust or melted into bar- and ring-shaped ingots, gold provided the New Kingdom pharaohs and their predecessors with raw goods to trade for other luxury materials as well as to use for their own adorn-ment and the glory of the gods. Lead, galena, and cop-per were also found in the Eastern Desert.

Gold is relatively easy to work: It can be manipu-lated cold, and does not tarnish. It was a perfect metal for intricate jewels and other objects meant to last for eternity. Ideally, mummies were clothed in gold in the form of golden or gilded coffins, creating a divine, immutable skin for the deceased. A number of different techniques were used to create masterpieces such as those found with Tutankhamun. Protected by layers of leather or papyrus, sheets of varying thicknesses were

A temporary settlement for ancient workers located halfway
between the Valley of the Kings and Deir el Medina.

A tireless crew of artisans builds and decorates funerary equipment in the tomb of the 18th-dynasty vizier Rekhmire at Thebes.

hammered out using stone beaters against a stone anvil. Thicker sheets, cut into pieces that were then shaped and soldered together, could be used for objects such as vessels and jewelry. Thinner sheets in the form of foil, or even thinner gold leaf, became gilding, decorating the exteriors of coffins, statues, and the like. Gold sheet could be chased (indented on the front with a wooden or metal tool), worked in repoussé (hammered from the inside, creating a relief pattern on the exterior), or engraved (scraped into patterns with a sharp tool). Additional decoration could be created with granulation or wirework. Gold was sometimes (although less commonly) heated and poured into molds: Some objects were cast using the lost-wax method, in which a model of the object was made of wax, coated with clay, then heated so that the wax melted and flowed out, leaving behind an empty mold.

The Egyptian deserts were rich in many kinds of stone. The limestone and sandstone of the Nile Valley provided building material ready to hand for tombs and temples. Finer-quality limestone for statues and reliefs was found at a number of sites, such as Tura in the Memphite region. Granite came from the Aswan area, and basalt, dolerite, and graywacke from the Faiyum. Gebel el Ahmar at the mouth of the Delta supplied most of the quartzite, with additional sources in the Faiyum, and the Nubian desert provided diorite and gneiss. Egyptian alabaster (calcite), used for everything from statues to vessels, came primarily from Hatnub in Middle Egypt. Workers quarried these stones using picks and axes of even harder stone, such as granite, quartzite, flint, and chert; granite quarrying required dolerite pounders. Semiprecious stones, such as carnelian and jasper, were collected from the desert surface, and turquoise was mined in the Sinai. Lapis lazuli was imported from Afghanistan.

Once the stone had been quarried, it was worked with hafted stone hammers, various flint tools, and copper or bronze chisels and adzes, as well as the tubular drill, spun with a bow, and the straight-edge saw. Quartz sand was frequently used as an abrasive. Waste powders were employed for polishing the surfaces of reliefs and statues and were also used in the manufacture of materials such as faience and glazes.

In the New Kingdom, artisans utilized faience primarily for vessels, amulets, and funerary figurines. They began by shaping a paste of finely ground quartz by hand or pressing it into molds, then abrading it to polish the surface. To finish, they glazed most pieces with a slurry of quartz, lime, alkali, and pigment. New Kingdom faience workers also became experts in working glass, a purer silicate; faience and glass-producing workshops were found side by side at a number of sites, including Amarna and the palace of Malkata. Glass was used for luxury vessels and as a substitute for semiprecious stones in jewel and statue inlays.

Egypt had little usable wood. Acacias, figs, and tamarisks, the principal indigenous trees, have poor-quality wood, with a small cross-section and gnarled trunks and branches. As early as the Early Dynastic Period, Egyptians imported large coniferous trees such as cedar from Lebanon to use in ships, coffins, and statues, and for architectural elements. They also brought ebony from the south as a luxury good. Carpenters worked with saws, adzes, chisels, and bow-drills of copper, using sandstone smoothers for polishing. To join separate elements, they employed a variety of techniques, including the mortise and tenon. Wooden objects were often veneered, covered with a thin layer of gold foil, or inlaid with other materials, such as faience.

## Beauty and Symbolism in Everyday Art

The Egyptians had a well-developed aesthetic sense, and even the objects they produced for everyday use had grace and style as well as meaning. The Egyptian worldview was defined in many ways by a desire to protect both the living and the dead and perpetuate the proper order of the cosmos; many artifacts were designed to promote these agendas. Objects created specifically for use in funerary contexts added an additional layer of meaning, as they were needed to help

the deceased on his or her danger-fraught journey to the afterlife.

For both daily life and funerary use, the forms of the objects themselves and the images and symbols with which they were decorated were carefully chosen for religious significance as well as visual pleasure. For instance, unguent vessels, in which goods such as perfumes and scented oils were kept, could be in the shape of the household god Bes (cat. 92), providing extra protection for the user, or in the form of a naked girl, giving it erotic overtones (cat. 93). A cup or bowl could take the shape of the sacred lotus blossom, symbol of the dawn and thus of the eternal renewal of the universe (cat. 102). Meaningful symbols were commonly integrated into the decoration as well. Bes and the goddess of childbirth, Twaret, often adorned household objects, thus magically guarding their owners. Another common symbol is the eye of a falcon, recognizable by the markings that surround it. This is the *wedjat* eye, the sound eye of the falcon god Horus, wounded during a mythical battle with the evil god Seth for the throne of Egypt, and healed by the goddess Hathor. It thus became a representation of the moon as it wanes (is wounded) and waxes (becomes whole). Also frequently seen as an amulet, this stood for protection, healing, and renewed perfection.

Color was very important in the repertoire of Egyptian symbolism. Black was the color of fertile earth soaked by the flood, and thus was used to evoke resurrection. White was associated with purity. Green, the shade of newly sprung vegetation, had connotations of newness and regeneration. Turquoise, mined in the Sinai, was sacred to the goddess Hathor. The disk of the sun and its rays could be referred to as turquoise, and its rising was said to fill the land with this color. Many funerary items were made of turquoise-colored faience to associate the deceased with the reborn sun. Dark blue, the color of lapis lazuli (which was imported and thus expensive and rare) was linked with the night sky and also the primordial waters from which the universe was created. Red and yellow were both colors of the sun, and stones in these hues, such as quartzite and red granite, had solar significance. The skin of the gods was golden yellow, the color of the magical metal that remained unchanging for eternity.

Steatite with limestone base
Statuette: height 24.4 cm; width 11.6 cm; depth 7.5 cm
Base: height 3.8 cm; width 13.5 cm; depth 10.8 cm
Dynasty 18, reign of Amenhotep III
Zagazig
JE 87911 A & B

This small pair statue depicts an official named Khaemwaset and his wife, Manana. The two stand side by side on a base, the high pillar behind them providing space for a lengthy inscription. Khaemwaset wears a complex, shoulder-length wig, a short-sleeved tunic with a tie at the neck, and a calf-length pleated skirt with an elaborate fringed sash. On his chest and right shoulder are the cartouches of the monarch he served, Amenhotep III. Khaemwaset's hands are by his sides, the right in an attitude of prayer and the left holding a cloth or papyrus roll, most likely an indication of his rank. His face has been completely removed in an intentional act of vandalism.

Manana is clothed in an ankle-length, tight-fitting sheath with rosettes over her nipples and a full, pleated shawl. She wears a broad collar around her neck and bracelets on her wrists. Curls or braids on her long, full wig are indicated by engraved zigzags. A wide band holds her hair back from her face at about ear height, and a braid hangs down her back from a fillet of papyrus blossoms. Her real hairline can be seen on her forehead beneath her wig.

The features of Manana's round face are fine and elegant, with slightly slanted, almond-shaped eyes, a narrow-bridged nose, and rosebud lips, similar in its general outlines to the face seen on late representations of Amenhotep III. This is not surprising, as it was usual for private people to adopt the main portrait features of the current ruler. Her left arm is bent and held across her waist; in this hand, Manana holds a beaded necklace. Called a *menat,* this was used as a rattle during the cultic rites of goddesses; here it is an emblem of Manana's position as a priestess of the cat deity Bastet, patroness of the Zagazig area. Her right hand, clenched into a fist, hangs by her side.

The pillar behind Khaemwaset and Manana takes the form of two round-topped stelae joined in the middle. It is inscribed with an offering prayer naming Renutet, goddess of the harvest, and Sekhmet, consort of Ptah and goddess of war. It also lists the names and titles of the couple. Khaemwaset was a member of the nobility, a high official whose most important titles were "Hereditary Prince, High Official, Chief Archer" and "Overseer of all the Northern Foreign Lands"; thus Khaemwaset was a royal ambassador to foreign courts in the ancient Near East. Manana was Lady of the House and Chantress of Bastet. An offering list, asking that food and other necessary items be given to them in perpetuity, is inscribed on top of the steatite base; an offering prayer, now mostly worn away, was carved into the limestone base.

This statue was found during the digging of foundations for a hospital in Zagazig, within the remains of a mud-brick chapel dating to the reign of Amenhotep III. Egyptologist Labib Habachi asked that the building be delayed so that the area could be investigated properly, but his request was denied. The hospital now seals the area, making further excavation impossible.

## 15 Model of a Lotus Bud

Faience
Length 8.9 cm; diameter 4.5 cm
Dynasty 18, reign of Amenhotep II
Thebes, Valley of the Kings, tomb of Amenhotep II (KV 35)
CG 24557

## 16 Model of a Floral Bud

Faience
Length 10 cm; diameter 3.2 cm
Dynasty 18, reign of Amenhotep II
Thebes, Valley of the Kings, tomb of Amenhotep II (KV 35)
CG 24533

## 11 Model of an Unrolled Papyrus

Faience
Length 12.4 cm; width 9.2 cm
Dynasty 18, reign of Amenhotep II
Thebes, Valley of the Kings, tomb of Amenhotep II (KV 35), Room 2
CG 24473

The lotus blossom, represented here by two slightly different examples (center and left), grew in swamps and was associated with the south. It was also an important symbol in Egyptian cosmology. Great observers of nature, the Egyptians noted that these blossoms closed at night and opened in the morning when touched by the sun's rays. Therefore they associated this flower with the rising sun, giving it human form as Nefertem, an incarnation of Re at dawn. The lotus also carried connotations of love and sexual pleasure that made it a symbol of rebirth and resurrection: As it was reborn each day, so was the sun god and, by association, the deceased king.

This model papyrus scroll is unrolled to reveal the throne name of Tuthmosis IV. Papyrus, a symbol of the north, was a common plant found in the swamps of the Delta and on the fringes of the floodplain. Its stalks were crushed into long flat sheets used as writing surfaces. The purpose of the model papyri found in this and other royal tombs is unknown. Some scholars think that they provided material on which the pharaoh could write in the Afterlife; a more plausible suggestion is that they were connected with the funeral ceremonies and eternal cult, magically reiterating the speaking of the king's name.

Nineteen blue faience throwsticks were found in the tomb of Tuthmosis IV. This example is of typical 18th-dynasty shape, its decoration emphasizing its protective and ritual nature. Double horizontal bands divide the body into ten segments painted with stylized flowers, linked to regeneration. On both sides of the throwstick near the front are wedjat eyes guarding the throne name of Tuthmosis IV, magically averting evil.

As hunting tools, throwsticks were initially augmented, and later replaced, with the more efficient method of clapnetting, and hunting with a throwstick became a sport practiced primarily by kings and nobles. The principal significance of fowling scenes is thus symbolic. The papyrus marshes were mystical boundaries between the earthly realm and the cosmos beyond, where chaos pressed upon the ordered world. These swamps, inhabited by wild birds and fish, also represented the dangerous realm of the Netherworld.

By using an archaic weapon in a ritual hunt, the king was acting magically as the defender of the creator god, maintaining the proper order of the Egyptian cosmos. The Coffin Texts, ancient spells meant to aid the deceased in his journey to the hereafter, also refer to the use of throwsticks to fend off enemies of the sun god.

## 12 Model of a Throwstick

Faience
Length 48 cm; width 3.7 cm; depth 1.9 cm
Dynasty 18, reign of Tuthmosis IV
Thebes, Valley of the Kings, tomb of Tuthmosis IV (KV 43)
CG 46404

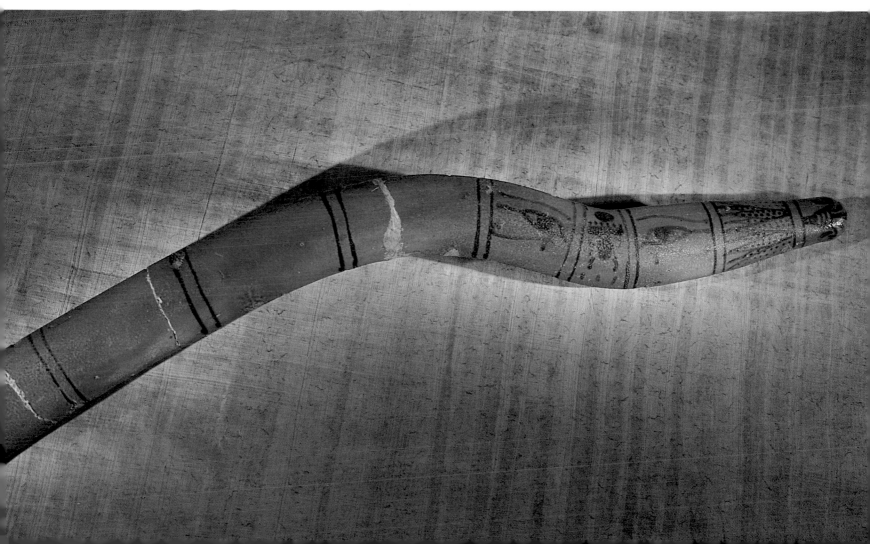

**13 Model of a Pomegranate**
Faience
Height 8 cm; diameter 5.5 cm
CG 24509

**14 Model of a Piece of Fruit**
Faience
Height 7 cm
CG 24517

Dynasty 18, reign of Amenhotep II
Thebes, Valley of the Kings, tomb of Amenhotep II (KV 35)

In 1899 the Victor team discovered a small shaft grave near the sepulchre of Amenhotep II. Mostly intact, the burial contained many funerary furnishings belonging to a king's fan bearer and youth of the royal nursery named Maiherpri, who probably lived during the reign of Tuthmosis IV. About 24 when he died, he appears to have been of mixed Nubian and Egyptian blood. Maiherpri's tomb equipment included arrows, quivers, and wrist guards, suggesting that he was a skilled archer. The tomb also held many vessels, food, jewelry, and a beautiful funerary papyrus.

The ovoid, narrow-necked perfume flask (bottom left, far right) is made of glass, a luxury material seen first in the reign of Tuthmosis III. The blue body is decorated with threads of green, orange, and white dragged into a

**19 Decorated Collar for a Dog**
Leather
Diameter 15 cm; width 7.2 cm; thickness 0.6 cm
JE 33774; CG 24076

**18 Decorated Drinking Bowl**
Faience
Diameter 14 cm; height 5 cm
JE 33825; CG 24058

**17 Polychrome Perfume Bottle**
Glass
Height 15.8 cm; diameter 3.0 cm
JE 33827; CG 24059

Dynasty 18, reign of Amenhotep II to Tuthmosis IV
Thebes, Valley of the Kings, tomb of Maiherpri (KV 36)

pattern. It is stoppered with clay and linen wrapped round with string. A yellowish deposit shows that it once held perfumed fat, used both in life and for the ritual anointing of the mummy and other images of the deceased.

The "Nun" bowl (bottom left, center) is decorated with images linked to the themes of chaos and rebirth. The large fish are tilapia, inhabitants of the watery void of the Nun, and also symbols of fertility and regeneration, a motif enhanced by the lotus buds. The desert gazelle was a symbol of chaos; the suckling calf emphasizes the theme of creation and eternal rebirth. The exterior of the bowl is painted to resemble a lotus blossom. Such bowls were most likely used in life and symbolically after death for drinking water, making offerings to Hathor, and perhaps also for cosmetic purposes.

The dog collar, (bottom left, far left), is one of two examples found in the tomb, and it has been suggested that one of Maiherpri's jobs was to look after the royal hunting dogs. It is made of three layers of leather, the outer of rose, the middle white, and the inner green. The primary decoration, four pairs of facing horses, was made by cutting out the top layer to reveal those underneath. Between each pair of horses are a stylized lotus and a set of gilded bronze bosses. The top and bottom of the collar are adorned with an appliquéd zigzag pattern.

Two of about fifty pieces of model fruits found in the tomb of Amenhotep II, these faience objects represent a pomegranate (top left, left), a fruit from Syria that appears for the first time in Egypt during the reign of Tuthmosis III, and a stemmed fruit (top left, right), perhaps a persea or mandrake. Food was essential for life, and thus a necessary part of the burial equipment as well. Sustenance for the Afterlife could take the form of real fruits, vegetables, spices, and even mummified meat, or could be magical in nature. The iconic image of the deceased seated at a table heaped high with edible offerings is a commonly seen guarantee of eternal nourishment. Lists of the food required for the funerary banquet and Afterlife could be extensive. By the middle of the Old Kingdom, tomb walls were covered with depictions of servants bringing various foodstuffs to the tomb owner. Fruits were generally eaten raw, and are found in mortuary contexts as early as the Predynastic Period. Tutankhamun's burial contained many types of fruits, including dates, the fruit of the dom-palm, dried grapes, jujubes, and persea fruit.

Wood, plastered and painted
20: Height 24 cm; diameter 13.4 cm (red)
CG 51059
21: Height 14.3 cm; diameter 10.3 cm (blue)
CG 51071
22: Height 21.3 cm; diameter 13.8 cm (white)
CG 51077

Dynasty 18, reign of Amenhotep III
Thebes, Valley of the Kings, tomb of Yuya and Tjuya (KV 46)

An American businessman named Theodore Davis held the concession to excavate in the Valley of the Kings for the first decade of the 20th century. With the professional help of a series of Egyptologists, beginning with Howard Carter, Davis and his teams made a number of spectacular discoveries in the royal necropolis. The most remarkable of these was the tomb of Yuya and Tjuya, mother and father of Amenhotep III's great queen Tiye.

On February 6, 1905, Davis's workmen found the top of a staircase cut into the rock. This led to a doorway, still sealed with stone overlaid by mud plaster and bearing the stamp of the necropolis: nine prostrate captives surmounted by the symbol of the jackal god Anubis. Although the presence of the blocking indicated that the larger items of burial equipment might still be inside, an opening in the top right-hand corner told the excavators that the tomb was not completely intact. Davis, with Arthur Wiegall, chief inspector of the Theban area, and Gaston Maspero, head of the Antiquities Department, entered the tomb the next day. Beyond a second doorway—again closed, stamped with necropolis seals, and breached in antiquity—was a dark, stiflingly hot chamber crammed with gilded furniture, including beds, chairs, a small chariot, sarcophagi, coffins, and chests belonging to the burials of Yuya and his wife, Tjuya. The objects had been tossed about, the mummies had been poked and prodded, and boxes lay with their lids ripped off. Ancient robbers had taken everything that could be carried away easily. But what remained was extraordinary.

There were a number of beautiful vessels found in the tomb. In addition to functional examples made from various materials, there were 28 dummy vessels made of wood or clay and painted to look like stones such as calcite, diorite, or red granite. Others were decorated to resemble glass, a novelty item at that time. The three vases here are made of wood, gessoed and painted to look as if they are of another substance. They are completely solid, with the lids either carved from the same piece of wood (20, 22) or attached with a peg (21).

The first piece, shaped like a pot-bellied jug with a long neck, is painted to resemble red granite, with a single handle of the same material. Geometric lotus petals hang in a frieze around the neck and an elaborate rosette has been painted on the top. This was one of a set of three similar vases that were once attached to a base with tenons. Also one of a set of three, the second vessel is bag-shaped, with a short, narrow neck and wide, broad lid. The body has been painted to mimic blue glass decorated in reddish yellow and white; the top bears a geometric pattern formed with triangles. The third vase is similar in shape to the second, but is larger and painted to imitate calcite. A lotus petal frieze in dark blue, red, and green decorates its shoulder, and on its top is a rosette in similar colors.

As imitations of real vessels, dummy vases were designed to provide important substances for the afterlife through representative magic. The three vessels here would, in life, have held various types of unguents—fatty substances mixed with plant essences such as lotus and henna.

This elaborate jewel casket was found on top of a gilded bed in the tomb of Yuya and Tjuya. It had clearly been opened, emptied, and discarded by the thieves who violated the tomb. The box is made of wood, with almost every centimeter of its surface inlaid or gilded. The blue ground that forms the primary field for the decoration of the top and sides is of turquoise faience inset with figures of gilded wood. The vaulted top is divided into two panels that run the length of the box, the two sides mirror images of one another. Each contains the names of Amenhotep III ("Nebmaatre, Amenhotep, ruler of Thebes") inside cartouches topped with the ostrich plumes of Maat and a winged sun disk. Below the cartouches is a figure of Heh, the hieroglyph for one million, seated on the sign for gold. Ankh signs (the hieroglyph for life) have been slung around his arms and hang from his elbows, and in each hand he holds the hieroglyph for "year," notched many times, on top of a *shen* ring (representing the circuit of the sun) and a tadpole, the hieroglyph for one hundred thousand. Above the god's head is the inscription, "May he give life, stability, and dominion," These panels can be read as wishes for the king to be happy, wealthy, and rule for millions of years.

Alternating squares of ebony and white- and pink-dyed ivory adorn the frames of the two panels and the legs of the chest. Its sides are also inlaid with blue faience plaques, below which are horizontal registers of ankh signs alternating with *was* signs (the hieroglyph for dominion), both atop the basket that means "all" on a background of faded pink linen. This common decorative element can be read as a wish for a long life as an effective king. The faience inlays contain texts in gilded wood that give the names and titles of Amenhotep III and his great queen Tiye.

Most likely a gift from the king and queen to the royal parents-in-law, the chest was divided into compartments, probably to hold jewels or cosmetic articles. Two knobs decorated with rosettes closed the box, one on the top and one on the end. A string wound around these knobs would have been daubed with mud and impressed with a seal.

23 Elaborately Decorated Chest
Wood, ivory, ebony, faience
Length 38.5 cm; width 26.8 cm; height 41.0 cm
Dynasty 18, reign of Amenhotep III
Thebes, Valley of the Kings, tomb of Yuya and Tjuya (KV 46)
CG 51118

**25 Unguent Vessel in the Shape of a Servant Bearing a Jar**
Partially painted wood, ivory, colored paste
Statuette: height 13.6 cm; width 5.6 cm; depth 6.9 cm
Base: height 1.8 cm; width 4.6 cm; depth 7.4 cm
Dynasty 18, reign of Amenhotep IV
Sheikh Abd el-Qurn, tomb of Hatiay
CG 44745

peacefully beside Amun, dates the burial to the early part of the reign of Amenhotep IV. The unguent jar was in the coffin of a "Lady of the House" named Siamun.

This beautiful example of a "swimming girl" cosmetic spoon (right) is made of painted and partially gilded wood. The girl has a long, slim body with a slender waist. Her face is oval, with arched eyebrows, narrow eyes that slant upwards at the outer corners, and a small, elegant nose. Her elaborately braided wig falls to just above her shoulders, with a longer group of locks, tied with a band, on one side. Her broad collar has been added in gold leaf, and her wrists sport wide golden bracelets. Two gilded straps, the remnants of a girdle, cross in the center of her back. The bowl that she once held in her long, narrow hands is now gone.

Crafted with care, this object had symbolic as well as practical meaning. The swimming maiden type, first found in the 18th dynasty, has connotations of sexuality, a subject represented covertly in Egyptian art. Duck, gazelle, and fish bowls held by these girls, for example, have erotic meaning, as do bouquets of flowers. A girl who is naked, but adorned with a wig, collar, or girdle, is announcing her readiness for sexual contact. In addition to its innate importance, sexuality was linked to the fundamental theme of rebirth and regeneration, which in turn was essential for eternal life.

Both artifacts here were designed to hold pigments, fat-based perfumes or salves. Above is a charming wooden unguent jar, representing a male servant kneeling to lift a large, heavy vessel. The pot is Syrian in both shape and decoration. Inlaid in ivory and colored paste on the round part of the base and on the top of the lid are calves gamboling among desert plants; geometric motifs adorn the neck. Knobs on the side and the top provide a locking mechanism.

The man's knee-length kilt is rendered skillfully, the fabric draping gracefully around his thighs. His soft upper body is naked, leaving the slightly sagging belly exposed. His face looks rather un-Egyptian, with a broad forehead, almond-shaped eyes with heavy lids, a prominent nose, and a full mouth. This piece was found in an intact tomb at Thebes belonging to Hatiay, a scribe and overseer of the granaries of the mansion of the Aten. Buried with him were three females, including a chantress of Amun named Henutwedjebu. This juxtaposition of titles, with the Aten coexisting

**24 Part of an Unguent Spoon with a Handle in the Shape of a Swimming Female**
Wood, partially gilded and painted
Maximum length 34.2 cm; height 7.2 cm; width 4.7 cm
Dynasty 18, reign of Amenhotep III
Unknown provenance
CG 45118

Tutankhamun's tomb held 35 model boats.

Three large model boats of a similar size and design were found complete in the tomb of Amenhotep II. This one, the best preserved, represents a ceremonial royal barge of the type probably used for state journeys up and down the Nile. A mast, now missing but once set into a hole in the center of the deck, would have held the sail that propelled the barge on its voyages south with the prevailing winds. Ten small seats lining each side of the boat were for the rowers who would have driven the boat north with the current.

Only fragments of the central cabin remain. These are decorated with running spirals, a motif borrowed from the Aegean repertoire, in yellow on a red and blue background, with a border of niches. The edge of a doorway can be seen on one preserved fragment. The cabin probably had a two-level roof with a cornice.

The hull of the vessel, a simple arc extended fore and aft with spars, is painted a bluish green, symbolic of new vegetation and thus fertility. Bow and stern are decorated on both sides with similar but not identical groups of images. These include ram and falcon heads topped with sun disks; falcons protecting the king's name with outstretched wings; human-, ram-, and falcon-headed sphinxes trampling on vanquished enemies; and falcon-headed humans spearing defeated foes. The ram heads represent Amun, the falcon heads Montu, and the winged falcons Horus of Edfu, a powerful sky god. The sphinxes stand for the king as Amun-Re, while the falcon-headed men are identified in the accompanying inscriptions as Montu, god of war, in connection with his four principal cult sites: Thebes, Medamud, Armant, and Tod. The final image on the stern is of Montu, this time as a griffin trampling a Libyan enemy. Set into both bow and stern are small trapezoidal enclosures, each carved with figures of the king as a sphinx wearing the blue war helmet, flanked by cartouches that once bore his name. A prostrate enemy lies under the paws of each royal figure. Other protective symbols in the hull's decoration include wedjat eyes on the bow.

This boat and its companions served several functions within the context of the tomb. As models of the kind of state barge that the king used on the Nile, they would have provided symbolic transportation for the ruler in the afterlife. Since the sphere of the gods and the dead mirrored the earthly realm, these boats would have carried the king and the sun god through the day and night skies. This purpose is enhanced by the barge's decoration, which contains powerful solar imagery and invokes the protection of Montu to aid king and sun god on their journey through the dangerous realm of the night sky. Like many of the objects in the tomb, the ultimate purpose of these boats was most likely to ensure the eternal rebirth of the king.

26  Model boat of Amenhotep II

Painted wood

Height 22 cm; length 213 cm; width 36 cm

Dynasty 18, reign of Amenhotep II

Thebes, Valley of the Kings, tomb of Amenhotep II (KV 35),
    section 5

CG 4945

THE SITE OF TELL EL AMARNA

# Religion Before Tutankhamun

*Religion in ancient Egypt was more than a belief system—*
*it was a way of life, permeating every aspect of existence.*
*The fundamental principal governing this system was maat,*
*an abstract concept often translated as truth or justice but more*
*accurately defined as the way the world was supposed to be.*

Maat was set in place by the creator god at the moment of creation and renewed daily by the dawning of the sun. Within the created universe, every individual had his or her ordained place and function. According to this worldview, the gods and the blessed dead had a direct effect on events in the world of the living, and the living had to provide constant attention to keep the many deities and spirits that hovered just beyond the earthly realm cared for and pacified.

The details of this system and its attendant beings developed slowly over time but remained fundamentally stable for millennia. In the late 18th dynasty, the radical theological innovations of Amenhotep IV/Akhenaten undermined the status quo, and set up repercussions that echoed to the end of the pharaonic era. In order to understand the effect of this religious revolution on the world of Egypt and its consequences for the life and times of Tutankhamun, who lived in its aftermath, it is important first to understand the nature

A painted limestone relief from Deir el Bahri depicts the god Amun-Min, a combination of the great state god Amun and the ancient fertility god Min. His black skin echoes the color of the well-watered soil of the Nile floodplain.

of the traditional religion that defined and shaped the Egyptian world.

## Traditional Religion

The first inhabitants of prehistoric Egypt, like other peoples of that era, were highly attuned to their environment. At some point they began to ask themselves how the world had come into being and who controlled the forces of nature that dominated their lives. They began to imagine hidden beings that inhabited a realm beyond the earth and directed these mysterious powers. They anthropomorphized these beings, gave them names, and assigned them characteristics of the wild animals that shared their land.

The stable environment of Egypt, with its regular agricultural seasons bounded by the annual flooding of the Nile, lay at the foundation of its religious system. The yearly cycle of the Inundation gave rise to the myth of creation, in which a primordial mound rose from limitless darkness and water, providing a platform on which the creator god could stand to work his magic. The sun, with its regular and unchanging cycle, was the most prominent feature of the natural world. It rose each day, bringing light and life to the earth, and disappeared every night, leaving the world in darkness.

This scene from a funerary papyrus shows two figures of the goddess Maat, her head surmounted by her name in the form of an ostrich plume.

It was the visible expression of the daily cycle of creation, symbolically dying as it set on the western horizon and being reborn as it rose in the east, thus reenacting the moment when the universe first came into being.

By the pharaonic era, the Egyptian pantheon was composed of many gods and goddesses. These were represented in art as human, animal, or a combination of the two. Each was linked to one or more towns and identified by specific characteristics. For example, the principal god of Memphis was Ptah, patron of artisans; he was worshiped there with his consort, Sekhmet, goddess of war, and their son, Nefertem. In Abydos, the chief god was Osiris, king of the dead, venerated with his sister-wife Isis and their child Horus.

Other than the creator, who could be identified with a variety of local divinities, the most important member of the Egyptian pantheon was the sun god, Re. This god was originally portrayed as a boatman who rowed across the marshes of creation. By the early historic era, Re had begun to adopt other forms, most often that of a falcon-headed man. His principal cult site was Heliopolis in the Memphite region. His worship there was associated with the sacred benben stone. Represented in art as a pyramid or squat obelisk, this stone was identified with the rays of the sun streaming down to earth and became a key solar symbol. At Idfu, the sun god was imagined in the form of a hawk soaring across the sky, and was linked with the celestial god Horus. As Re-Horakhty (Re-Horus of the Two Horizons), the god was portrayed as a human with a hawk's head topped by the disk of the sun. Surrounding this disk was a snake, identified as the Serpent of Creation and imagined as a symbol of the realm through which the sun god passed each night.

The sun god had two barks, one for day (called *Mandjet*) and the other for night (*Mesketet*). At noon he was Re, a man with a sun disk on his head. With the setting sun he became the Heliopolitan creator god

Atum as an old man. At night, he traveled through the Netherworld to be united with Osiris, god of the dead. At dawn, he was reborn either as the scarab beetle, Khepri, which is also the hieroglyphic sign for "create" or "come into being," or as the child Nefertem, rising from a lotus.

Each major god or group of gods was worshiped in one or more state temples, where their spirits were housed within cult images made of precious materials. These temples were monumental feats of architecture and engineering, requiring massive quantities of stone and the skill of thousands of workers. After the king and his architects chose a site and planned their project, they consecrated the area with a foundation ceremony in which ten separate rituals were performed. The most important of these was the "stretching of the cord," where the king laid out the temple's ground plan. In another part of this ceremony, pottery vessels, building tools, baskets, food offerings, and plaques bearing the name of the king were ritually buried at the corners of the planned structure.

Once work began, tons of limestone or sandstone for the temple core were quarried and transported to the site, along with the finer limestone needed for the relief that would adorn the structure, and the calcite, granite, coniferous wood (imported from Lebanon), and other expensive items for specific purposes. Workers at the site mixed huge amounts of mud and sand for bricks. Tools and equipment were needed, as well as untold quantities of food to keep the artisans and stone haulers healthy and productive. Building techniques developed over thousands of years were generally simple but effective. For example, to make the massive columns needed for pillared halls and courts, rounded slabs were set one atop the other, then finished and decorated in place. After the basic temple was completed, future kings often made their own additions and modifications to the work of their predecessors.

Properly built temples, their walls and obelisks carved with the appropriate scenes and texts, were essential to the continuance of the Egyptian world. They functioned, in fact, as miniature models of the universe. The rituals performed within their sacred spaces served magically to reenact the creation of the world and thus ensure its perpetual survival. It is not surprising that such vast resources were devoted to the construction, decoration, and maintenance of these magnificent structures.

By the New Kingdom, most state temples followed the same basic plan. Each divine precinct was fronted by a pylon, a massive gateway that echoed the hieroglyph for horizon. Before the pylon stood obelisks—narrow, pointed spires sacred to the sun god that soared to the sky. An enclosure wall delimited the rest of the temple precinct and the holy areas within. The outer surfaces of the temple were dedicated to images of the king triumphing over his enemies, symbolically protecting the temple from the forces of chaos.

The architecture of the temple within was designed to mirror the landscape of the cosmos at the moment of creation. Closest to the pylon were colonnaded courtyards and pillared halls representing the primeval swamp of creation, their ceilings held up by columns in the form of marsh plants such as the papyrus and lotus. Beyond the last pillared hall was the innermost shrine, where the divine image was housed, washed, clothed, fed, and otherwise vivified and pacified. Its floor level was higher than that of the outer halls, reinforcing its identification with the primordial mound; in the context of his or her own temple, each deity acted as a creator god. Each day, as light entered the shrine, also conceived of as heaven, the moment of creation was reenacted. Additional rooms in the inner part of the temple could serve as shrines to house the divine boat used to carry the god in festival processions or as dwellings for associated deities.

The walls of state temples were carved with scenes focusing on the relationship between king and god, especially depictions of the rites and rituals that were to be carried out within the sacred spaces. The Egyptians believed in the magical power of word and image: By illustrating their myths, they made them real, and by representing the cult, they ensured that its rituals would be performed magically for eternity, even if priests were no longer available. Other decorative elements emphasized the identification of temple with cosmos. For example, the traditional axis for a temple was east-west; winged sun disks were often carved on the lintels of the doorways that led along this axis, mirroring the daily path of the sun.

Colossal statues and an obelisk of Ramses II mark the
Ramesside pylons of the Luxor Temple to Amun.

Egyptian monarchs were considered semidivine, and their rule was inextricably intertwined with the gods whom they worshiped. The king was both temporal and spiritual leader of Egypt, the link between the earthly and celestial realms. From the earliest periods of Egyptian history, he was considered an embodiment of the sky god Horus on earth, and was responsible for the establishment and maintenance of maat. Ally of the gods and their representative in the world of humankind, he stood against the powers of chaos (primeval darkness and water, represented on earth by wild animals and foreign enemies) that constantly surrounded and threatened the ordered world. As an intermediary between humans and gods, he was—at least in theory—high priest in every temple. Although in actuality the king's role was delegated to priests, in temple art it is always the king who is shown performing the cult rituals and thus caring for the gods and goddesses who dwell therein.

## Religion in the Early 18th Dynasty

In the New Kingdom, the god Amun took center stage. First mentioned in the Pyramid Texts of the Old Kingdom, Amun was originally one of the eight principal gods of Ashmunein, a site in Middle Egypt. With his consort Amunet, Amun, the "hidden one," was chief among these gods, representing the unseen powers of the cosmos. He is most often depicted in human form wearing a knee-length kilt, a long curled beard, and a leather crown topped by two long plumes. His sacred animals were the ram and the goose. With the rise of the Theban 18th dynasty, Amun became the chief god of the state, credited with sponsoring the great military victories of the kings. Syncretized with Re, he became Amun-Re, new king of the gods.

For the kings of the early 18th dynasty, Amun/Amun-Re was first among the creator gods. The creation myth in which he played the central role was linked with the Heliopolitan creation story, and he was identified with Atum, Lord of Heliopolis. Amun was also associated with other important gods, such as Min, an ithyphallic fertility god worshiped at Akhmim, and Khnum, a ram-headed god from Elephantine. Much of the tribute and booty that the monarchs of the 18th

dynasty brought back from their wars abroad went to fill the coffers of Amun as gifts of gratitude. In addition to his principal cult center at Karnak, monuments to this god were built throughout Egypt and Nubia. As the importance of Amun and the wealth of the god's temples increased, so too did the power and influence of his priesthood.

By at least the middle of the 18th dynasty, the right to rule was dependent on Amun. Several kings were proud to proclaim their election to the throne through an oracle of Amun, and both Hatshepsut and Amenhotep III underlined their legitimacy by commissioning scenes that portrayed them as the offspring of the human queen and the god.

The center of Amun's Theban cult was on the east bank at a site now known by its Arabic name of Karnak. To the Egyptians, it was Ipet-sut. Its documented building history goes back to the Middle Kingdom; it is likely that earlier kings had erected monuments here, but these have not survived as standing monuments. The core of this sprawling precinct, which spans about 62 acres, was dedicated to Amun himself, with subsidiary temples and shrines for his Theban consort, Mut, their son, Khonsu, and the god of war, Montu. Every king of the 18th dynasty added his or her mark to this complex in the form of pylons, rooms, shrines, pillared halls, and obelisks. Two axes ran through the temple. The principal axis was east to west, facing the river; a second axis ran from north to south, where an avenue of sphinxes connected the temple of Khonsu with Luxor Temple.

Luxor Temple lay two miles to the south and was called *Ipet-resyt,* "the southern sanctuary." Like Karnak, this temple was dedicated to Amun, Mut, and Khonsu; the earliest remains date to the end of the Middle Kingdom. Ahmosis is said to have built at Luxor, but the first preserved architectural feature from the New Kingdom, a small chapel that is now part of a series of bark shrines to the Theban triad, dates to the reign of Hatshepsut. This was apparently one of six such

Discovered in the Luxor cachette, this beautiful statue of highly polished granodiorite represents the god Amun protecting King Horemheb, Tutankhamun's commander in chief and the successor to Aye in the kingship.

The blocks of sandstone (nicknamed talatat) that made up Akhenaten's temples to the Aten at Karnak were small enough for one man to carry. These enabled the king to build quickly, but also helped his successors tear down the monuments with ease. These blocks were found dismantled inside later monuments at Karnak and reconstructed.

chapels built for the use of Amun and his family during the Opet Festival, a yearly reenactment of the coronation during which the king traveled to Luxor to receive the powers and regalia of kingship from Amun.

Amenhotep III significantly rebuilt and expanded the Luxor Temple, adding, among other things, a court, a pillared hall, a shrine (now replaced by the bark shrine of Alexander the Great), and a "birth room" carved with scenes of the king's divine conception from the coupling of his mother and Amun. However, the current entrance to this monument, including colossal statues, obelisks, pylon, and first court, date to the 19th dynasty king Ramses II.

Luxor's principal axis runs from north to south, but its rear portion, dedicated to a form of Amun known as Amunemopet, is oriented east-west, in line with an Amun Temple on the west bank at Medinet Habu. This west-bank temple was imagined by the ancients to have been built on the Theban mound of creation; it housed its own image of the god in his form of Amun-Kamutef (Amun, Bull of his Mother), an ithyphallic creator god who impregnated his own mother and was closely associated with the king, who was both an individual and an incarnation of his own father.

Also dedicated to the worship of Amun on the west bank—the realm of the setting sun and the land of the dead—were the bark chapels and other shrines used during the Feast of the Valley. Celebrated in the tenth month of the year, this festival (an occasion for families to visit the tombs of their loved ones) was associated with the great goddess Hathor of the West, protector of the realm of the dead. Worshipers carried the divine images of Amun, Mut, and Khonsu across the Nile to the bay of cliffs at Deir el Bahri, where the principal sanctuary of the goddess Hathor was located.

Although king of the gods, Amun/Amun-Re was not the only important divinity in the 18th dynasty. For example, additions were made to the temple of Ptah at Memphis and to the cult places of Atum and Re at Heliopolis. Abydos remained a major center of worship for the great mortuary god Osiris, while the fertility god Min had a cult center at Akhmim. Other significant deities were Horus, Khnum, Montu, Neith, Thoth, and Sobek; many purely local gods and household geniuses, such as Tawaret and Bes, had active cults as well. Another important religious trend was the growth of henotheism, in which Egypt's various gods began to be seen as aspects of a central, universal deity. This development was both usurped and interrupted by the Amarna interlude, but reemerged, forged in the fire of Akhenaten's radical views, after that controversial king's death.

## The Amarna Heresy

The roots of Akhenaten's religious revolution, with its exclusive focus on the cult of the sun god in the form of the solar orb, the Aten, can be traced to the reigns of his immediate predecessors. The reemergence of the northern sun-cult began during the rule of Amenhotep II, who built a temple to the Great Sphinx at Giza as the sun god Horemakhet. Building on the example of his father, Tuthmosis IV gave the cult of the northern sun god great prominence. This king appears in the Sphinx temple at Giza as the deified son of the sun god; his father was then identified with Horemakhet. Other evidence suggests that Tuthmosis IV may have elevated himself to divine status in his lifetime. For example, his later statuary shows him with almond-shaped eyes that lend his face an eerie, unearthly quality that may be associated with this cultic change.

This shift in royal dogma may be due to a number of factors. Some scholars believe that the priesthood of Amun was becoming too strong for the comfort of the royal house; the rise of the sun cult can be seen in part as an attempt to curb its power. Another factor may have been the growth of personal piety seen during the earlier part of the dynasty: By becoming a god himself, Tuthmosis IV could bring cultic focus back to the royal house. The existence of the empire is another potential factor: By becoming one with the sun, always the most important Egyptian god, the king could watch over all of the Egyptian lands from his vantage point in the sky.

The rise in importance of the orb of the sun may also have begun during the reign of Tuthmosis IV. A scarab from this period mentions the Aten, a word that in this context can also be interpreted simply as a noun meaning "sun disk" or "solar orb." This term first appeared in the Pyramid Texts of the Old Kingdom. In texts of the early 18th dynasty, the word was used to mean throne or place of the sun god. It was not until the later part of the dynasty that the Aten was personified as a manifestation of the sun god himself.

The origins of the symbol that became the icon for the Amarna revolution, the solar orb with rays ending in hands reaching down to earth, have been tentatively traced to an image on a stela Tuthmosis IV erected in his father's temple at Giza. Located at the top of the lunette, this shows a winged sun disk with arms embracing the cartouche of the king. Another link to later Amarna material can be seen in Tuthmosis IV's funerary figurines (see cat. 62) which, like those of

Akhenaten (see cat. 38), bear only the king's name rather than the usual magical spell. The artistic style of this period begins to move into a more naturalistic mode, which culminates, in exaggerated form, during Akhenaten's reign.

Tuthmosis IV's son Amenhotep III paid great attention to the god Amun, who remained at the head of the Egyptian pantheon during his reign. Son of a minor queen and married to a commoner, Amenhotep III's right to the throne may have been called into question. He bolstered his legitimacy by building great monuments to the king of the gods and emphasizing his own divine birth as offspring of this deity. However, during his 38-year reign, the solar cult that had begun to flourish under Tuthmosis IV also grew in importance. Some scholars believe that his sons, Tuthmosis (who predeceased him) and Amenhotep, were trained by the priests at Heliopolis, traditional center of the cult of the sun god Re.

A significant change occurred in this king's 30th year on the throne, when he celebrated his first Sed Festival. At this point, Amenhotep III became the living incarnation of various gods, including the god of Memphis, Ptah; the sun god, Re; and the creator god, Atum. He was also identified with the orb of the sun, the Aten: One of his epithets was "The Dazzling Aten," and his west bank palace at Thebes was called "The House of the Dazzling Aten."

Akhenaten, who came to the throne as Amenhotep IV, began his reign steeped to some extent in orthodoxy. A rock-cut stela in the sandstone quarries at Gebel el-Silsila shows him before Amun (although the image of the god was later defaced, and the inscription celebrates his new temples for the Aten at Karnak). At the Third Cataract in Nubia, he founded a new city to the god Amun. But he soon began to bring his new religion to prominence. By the third year of his reign, the king had begun a series of temples dedicated to the solar cult at Karnak. Called the Aten for short, the god worshipped here was given an elaborate name which effectively syncretized several sun gods: "The Living One, Re-Horakhty who rejoices in the two horizons in his name, which is Shu (illumination), which is from the Aten (the solar disk)." This name was divided into two parts that were placed inside cartouches, giving the

This limestone stela, now in Berlin, shows Akhenaten and Nefertiti playing with three of their six daughters in the kind of intimate scene unique to the Amarna Period. Found in a private house, the stela served as a cult focus, probably in a garden shrine.

god royal as well as divine status. At first, the god was shown with a hawk's head, but soon this image was replaced by a solar orb whose rays ended in human hands, extending ankh signs to the king.

One of the more intriguing co-regency theories (based to a large extent on historical and iconographic art analysis) equates Amenhotep III after his first Sed Festival with Atum-Re as the Aten and Amenhotep IV/Akhenaten with Atum-Re's firstborn child, Shu. This father-and-child pair are said in Egyptian religious texts

to re-create one another at dawn; thus each is essential to the other's existence, providing theological justification for the co-regency. According to this model, Queen Tiye was then identified with the consort of Re, Hathor, whose costume she often wears, and Nefertiti was Tefnut, twin sister and consort of Shu.

Like all Egyptian kings, Akhenaten was the high priest of his god. However, in a departure from previous royal iconography, cultic depictions show him with his family by his side, basking in the life-giving rays of the Aten. Even more remarkably, in one of the Karnak temples his great wife Nefertiti appears as the sole actor, taking on a role previously reserved for the king. Akhenaten and Nefertiti were also portrayed as deities in their own right, as members, with the Aten, of a divine triad. The six daughters that Nefertiti bore to her husband were important members of the divine family. In another radical departure from traditional Egyptian iconography, the girls are shown climbing on their parents' laps, bathing in the rays of the sun that shine down upon the idyllic intimacies of the royal family.

At least officially, it was only through the royal family that the Aten could be worshiped. A number of stelae found in private houses represent Akhenaten, Nefertiti, and increasing numbers of their daughters under the rays of the orb. These stelae, along with small statues, were used as cult foci, indicating that the inhabitants of Amarna prayed directly to the divine grouping of the Aten and the royal family.

When he decided to build a new religious capital dedicated to his god, Akhenaten looked for a pure site, untainted by association with any other cults. He chose a location in Middle Egypt where the eastern floodplain was narrow and a bay of cliffs enclosed a semicircle of low desert. A wadi cutting east to west through the center of this bay created a physical image of the hieroglyph for horizon, through which the sun rose each morning. The city, which was called Akhetaten, "Horizon of the Aten," was laid out parallel to the river, its boundaries marked by stelae carved into the cliffs ringing the site, twelve on the east bank and three on the west. Most of the agricultural fields were located on the western floodplain, much wider than the east.

The king himself took responsibility for the cosmologically significant master plan of Akhetaten (now known as Tell el Amarna after an Arab tribe that settled here), arranging it as a large-scale ceremonial stage for royal display. The city took the form of a large crescent, about 8 miles (10 km) long from north to south and 3 miles (5 km) from east to west. At its peak, the city might have housed about 20,000 inhabitants.

The central part of the city was the site of an immense temple to the Aten. This Great Temple covered an area of about 2,460 by 820 feet (750 by 250 m). Its plan is oddly narrow, and it may also have been a processional route. In contrast to the typical Egyptian temple, this and other Aten temples were open to the sky and full of sunlight. Most of the interior consisted of open courts filled with offering tables and lined with storage magazines. Food was piled on these altars for the delectation of the god and then redistributed to the inhabitants of the city. It is assumed that there were no divine images, but that the sun itself served as the focus of the cult. Near this temple was a formal reception palace where the king could meet officials and foreign dignitaries; nearby were administrative buildings, including the royal archives.

South of the Great Temple and west of the Royal Road that ran north to south was an enormous palace, one of the largest buildings known from the ancient world. Covering a total of 162,000 square feet (15,000 sq. m), it was built of limestone and surrounded by a mud-brick wall. Another royal enclosure, with gardens, pools, storerooms, and a king's house, stood across the Royal Road. This dwelling may have had a "Window of Appearances" overlooking a courtyard, from which the king and queen could greet their subjects and hand down golden rewards to those who had served them well. The Small Aten Temple, an abbreviated version of the Great Temple, was near this complex.

North of the Central City were two more royal palaces. One of these, the North Palace, seems to have been ceremonial in nature; the other, the North Riverside Palace, was most likely the principal home of the royal family. When they were resident at Amarna, Akhenaten and Nefertiti processed along the Royal Road from their northern palaces to the Central City, mirroring the journey of the sun across the sky and the festival processions in which divine images were taken from one cult temple to another.

A number of temples at Amarna were for the use of specific royal women. The best preserved of these is the Maruaten, built for Meritaten and the king. This vast enclosure surrounded a sort of water garden with altars and kiosks, all seemingly for the pleasure or divine cult of the king and his daughter-consort.

As time went on, Akhenaten's theology seems to have become more radical. In Year 9 of his reign, the name of the Aten was changed, and all mention of the gods Horakhty and Shu disappears. The new name was "The Living One, Re, Ruler of the Horizon who rejoices in the horizon in his name, which is Sunlight, which comes from the Aten." It is at this time that what many scholars identify as monotheism emerges. Divinities such as Khepri (the sun at dawn), Horakhty, and Atum were no longer considered aspects of the sun; only the Aten was identified with sunlight. Slowly, many old gods disappeared from the state pantheon: first the gods of the dead, such as Osiris, then others.

At some point late in his reign, Akhenaten sent out an army to hack away the name of Amun wherever it appeared (even in the name of his own father). Other divinities were similarly persecuted, and the word for god was erased wherever it was plural. The king did not ban all other gods entirely: Finds at Amarna indicate that minor deities, such as the household god Bes, were still honored. But temples to Amun and his associated gods were closed and their worship forbidden.

Akhenaten left behind a record of his faith in the form of a sun hymn, found in its fullest form in the tomb of one of his courtiers, Aye, at Amarna. This poem, written by the king himself, praises the Aten as creator and protector of the world. (Its influence can be clearly seen later in Psalm 104 of the Bible.) It is a paean to the beauty and grace of nature, and states that the king alone has access to the great god. It also identifies the Aten as a universal deity, a god for all countries. The following is a small portion:

> Splendid you rise, O living Aten, eternal lord!
> You are radiant, beauteous, mighty,
> Your love is great, immense.
> Your rays light up all faces,
> Your light here gives life to hearts,
> When you fill the Two Lands with your love.
> August God who fashioned himself,
> Who made every land, created what is in it,
> All peoples, herds and flocks,
> All trees that grow from soil;
> They live when you dawn for them,
> You are mother and father of all that you made.
> *(Translation by Miriam Lichtheim)*

In the mortuary realm, Akhenaten moved decisively away from the beliefs of his predecessors. His religion focused on life and day rather than night and death. Instead of being buried in the Valley of the Kings and associating himself with the setting sun, Akhenaten had his tomb carved into the cliffs of the eastern wadi near Amarna, so that he would spend eternity in the realm of the rising sun. In his funerary equipment, he avoided all mention of Osiris. Instead of the four protective goddesses that traditionally protected the deceased, he had Nefertiti, extending her arms to keep him safe, carved onto his sarcophagus. His courtiers were also buried in the eastern cliffs, decorating their tombs primarily with images of the royal family and hymns to the Aten.

## After Akhenaten

The Atenist heresy did not long (if at all) outlive its creator. Egypt's traditional religion was too deeply rooted and soon after Akhenaten's death the country under Tutankhamun rejected the new god and moved rapidly back into the arms of Amun-Re. Only a few years into his reign, Tutankhaten (Living Image of the Aten) changed his named to Tutankhamun (Living Image of Amun) and his queen, Ankhsenpaaten, became Ankhsenamun. During his rule of almost ten years, the young king worked hard (perhaps guided by his principal advisors, the general Horemheb and the elder statesman Aye) to restore the worship of Amun and the other gods who had been neglected under Akhenaten. He rebuilt their temples and replenished their treasuries, and left Amarna to return to Memphis and Thebes.

After Tutankhamun's untimely death, his elderly successor Aye, who reigned for less than four years, continued his policies of reconciliation. Aye also died without an heir, and general Horemheb took over the throne of the two lands. Horemheb reigned for at least 13 years, reaffirming the might of Amun but balancing it with the other great state gods, especially Re and Ptah. Taking credit for many of the policies initiated under Tutankhamun, Horemheb began the process of erasing the memory of the Amarna Period, claiming to be the direct successor of Amenhotep III. He too died without a surviving son, and with his death the 18th dynasty came to an end. To ensure a smooth transition of power, Horemheb appointed his army commander and vizier heir to the throne. This man, Ramses I, who was from the Delta, founded the 19th dynasty.

Light enters the Amarna tomb of Akhenaten's official, Parennefer.

## 30  Model of a Roll of Cloth
Faience
Length 10 cm
Thebes, Valley of the Kings (KV 55)
JE 39645

One of 16 such models found in Tomb 55, the rolled cloth or papyrus seen here was clearly an important element of the funerary equipment. Similar rolls were found in the tombs of Amenhotep II and Tuthmosis III and IV, most of them uninscribed but several bearing the names of the king in whose tomb they were found. These are often identified as papyrus rolls, placed within the tomb either to provide magical writing equipment for the afterlife or as a substitute for real scrolls containing spells to guide the deceased safely to the Hereafter. These models might also represent rolls of cloth. Linen was an essential part of the burial equipment, needed to wrap the mummy and protect the body from harm. This ceramic model could have served as a backup for the actual cloth, which was more fragile.

The vase in the center (right) is one of 25 ritual vessels from the tomb of Tuthmosis IV. Of blue glazed faience, its pieces were found scattered among different chambers of the tomb. Identifiable through its shape as a *nemset,* it would have been used for libations during important rituals such as the Opening of the Mouth (a ceremony that magically restored the senses to the mummy and to any images of the deceased). The inscription on the front gives the throne and birth names of the king as "beloved of Osiris, the great god of the west." Flanking this are rekhyt birds, symbols of the Egyptian populace, on baskets (the hieroglyph for "all"); this can be read as "all the Egyptian people worship Tuthmosis IV." The lid is shaped and decorated like a lotus blossom, a potent symbol of rebirth.

Flanking the vase are faience ankhs. The ankh on the left is one of 37 found in the tomb of Tuthmosis IV. Below the crosspiece is the throne name of the king, Menkheprure, above a papyrus blossom on a long stem. The right-hand ankh, which is hollow and has a hole on top, was found in Amenhotep II's tomb. On the crosspiece is the king's throne name, Aakheprure. By pouring water through the symbol for life, the priests who performed libations during important funerary rituals would help to ensure the eternal existence of the king.

## 27  Ankh Sign (left)
Faience
Height 24 cm; width 12.6 cm
Dynasty 18, reign of Tuthmosis IV
Thebes, Valley of the Kings, tomb of Tuthmosis IV (KV 43)
CG 46359

## 31  Model of a Ritual Vessel (center)
Faience
Height 24 cm; diameter 7.7 cm
Dynasty 18, reign of Amenhotep II
Thebes, Valley of the Kings, tomb of Amenhotep II (KV 35)
CG 46204

## 28  Vessel in the Shape of an Ankh (right)
Faience
Length 23.4 cm; width 10.9 cm; thickness 2.7 cm
Dynasty 18, reign of Amenhotep II
Thebes, Valley of the Kings, tomb of Amenhotep II (KV 35)
CG 24372

Made of blue faience, this elegant libation vase is one of several similar vessels found in Amenhotep II's tomb. At 24 cm high, it is a functional piece, designed for use both in the funeral ceremonies and in the afterlife. This example is decorated in black paint with a band of stylized lotus flowers drawn around the neck and the king's throne name, Aakheprure, written on the body. It would have been used to pour water over the deceased in order to purify and prepare him or her for the journey to the afterlife.

The vase was found in a number of fragments. Its shape, with a short, narrow neck topped by a flat lip, gently rounded shoulder, and long ovoid body tapering to a slightly flaring foot, is very ancient, dating back at least to the Old Kingdom. The hieroglyph *hes*, used in words connected with praise, is a two-dimensional depiction of this vase. Heset vases are seen often in Egyptian art, held by the narrow portion just above the foot by priests who pour water over the heads of divine figures.

29  Model of a Ritual Vessel
Faience
Height 24 cm; diameter 7.7 cm
Dynasty 18, reign of Amenhotep II
Thebes, Valley of the Kings, tomb of Amenhotep II (KV 35)
CG 3882a

(see p. 124) along the processional way so that they could participate perpetually in the divine cult.

This statuette was discovered in the northern cemetery at Abydos, between the great Osiris Temple and the cult enclosures of the Early Dynastic Period. It is inscribed for a vizier and high priest of Amun named Ptahmosis, who was appointed to his position late in the reign of Tuthmosis IV and continued his service into the rule of Amenhotep III. This official is also known from a stela now in France and a statue in Brooklyn; his tomb, which was probably on the west bank at Thebes, has not yet been identified.

The statuette is a masterpiece of faience-working. The hands and face are turquoise blue, an indication of divinity. Its long tripartite wig is colored gold with violet-blue lines to indicate strands of hair. Around the neck is a broad collar. The eyes are long, filling most of the width of the broad face, with pupils inlaid with alabaster and obsidian. Painted straps in violet faience and a small hole in the chin indicate that the figure once wore a false beard. Across the chest, under the hands that emerge from the mummy wrappings, is a vulture representing the sky goddess Nut, whose name is written below her outstretched wings. On the back, below the ends of the wig, are two jackals, recumbent on shrines, facing outward. They are labeled with the principal epithets of the god of mummification, Anubis, "he who is in the place of embalming, lord of the Sacred Land, who is before the divine shrine." Between the Anubis figures are a shen sign (representing the circuit of the sun and eternity) and an incense burner.

The remainder of the figure is covered with hieroglyphic texts in dark violet faience against the white of the mummy wrappings. The principal text is the shabti spell, Spell 6 from the Book of the Dead. This promises that the figurine will work in the Afterlife on behalf of the deceased, should he be called upon to do corvée labor.

Abydos was the burial ground of the earliest rulers of Egypt, and was associated with the great god Osiris as primeval king. This vast site, sacred for all of pharaonic history, held a series of temples dedicated to this god as "Foremost of the Westerners" (the blessed dead). Each year, Osiris's cult statue was carried in a sacred bark from its permanent home in the temple down a great wadi to an Early Dynastic royal tomb identified in the Middle Kingdom as the burial place of the great god. The festival, which included mystery plays, served to reenact the death and resurrection of Osiris, who had been murdered by his brother, Seth, then brought to life just long enough to sire a son, Horus. He then descended to the Netherworld, where he became lord of the dead. By participating in these celebrations, both royalty and the elite could themselves become blessed spirits, like Osiris, effective in the Afterlife. Thus an essential element of the elite and royal funeral from at least the Old Kingdom on was a journey, whether real or symbolic, to Abydos. A number of tombs were built at Abydos over the ages, and many of those who could not be buried there left cenotaphs (small chapels), stelae, or deposits of small funerary figurines known as shabtis

## 32  Shabti of Ptahmosis

Polychrome faience
Height 20 cm; width 6.8 cm; depth 4.2 cm
Abydos, Northern Cemetery
CG 48406

33   Funerary Figurine of Resi
Wood, partially gilded and painted
Height 32.5 cm; width 7.5 cm
Dynasty 18, reign of Amenhotep III
Medinet el-Ghurob, tomb no. 22
CG 814

A masterpiece of woodcarving, this elegant statue dates to the reign of Amenhotep III and exemplifies the artistic sophistication of the period. It was found at Medinet el-Ghurob in the Faiyum, site of an extensive royal harem to which older queens retired. When discovered, this piece lay on the breast of a mummy that turned to dust the moment it was exposed to air. Clearly treasured by its owner, the statue represents a woman standing on a wooden base, her left foot slightly in front of her right and her toes turned outward. She wears a flowing, pleated garment, fringed along one edge. Its elaborate folds cling to her curves, outlining her body and imparting a sense of movement to the figure. This sense is enhanced by the subtle shifting of the figure's center of gravity: She appears to have her weight on her back leg, ready to step forward.

The garment, which is tied below the breasts, covers one shoulder and leaves the other bare. Her right arm hangs by her side; in the left, she holds a partially gilded lotus blossom between her breasts. On her head is a full wig divided into tiny braids and painted black; this falls over her shoulders to the top of her breasts. A wide band, once gilded, sits atop her braids. In the back, three fatter braids fall over this band. At her forehead, a narrow strip of paint representing her natural hair is visible. Her wig hides most of a gilded broad collar; her other jewelry consists of a gilded armband on the left and traces of a similar band on the right. On the base is an offering prayer to "the revered one, Lady Resi."

The exquisite elegance of the body is matched, if not surpassed, by the serene beauty of the face. It is round, with full cheeks and delicate features. The inlaid eyes are large, wide-set, and almond-shaped, topped by thin, arching eyebrows that were once inlaid. The nose is small, narrow at the bridge and wider at the tip, with small but distinct nostrils. The full mouth turns down slightly at the outer corners, and the chin is small but determined. The overall effect is that of a beautiful woman.

Calcite
Height 69 cm; width 38 cm; depth 27 cm
Dynasty 18, reign of Tuthmosis I; reworked in reign of Tutankhamun
Temple of Amun, Court of the Cachette
CG 42052

Discovered in the Karnak Cachette, this divine triad depicts the god Amun flanked by a king and queen, originally Tuthmosis I and his principal queen Ahmosis, all seated on a block throne. The high slab behind them suggests that this piece was set against a wall, presumably at Karnak. Both king and queen have one arm around the god, who embraces the queen with one hand and holds an ankh sign in the other. The king holds a round shen rope, symbol of the sun's circuit, in his right hand. The god wears his traditional outfit of kilt, curled beard (much of which is missing), and leather bonnet topped with plumes. The queen is clad in a tight-fitting dress, a long tripartite wig, and a low crown topped by feathers. The king wears the royal shendyt kilt, the nemes headcloth, and ram's horns surmounted by a sun disk and two ostrich plumes, symbols of maat. A column of text to the left of the king reads: "The good god, Aakheperkare [the throne name of Tuthmosis I], beloved of Amun-Re." To the right of the queen is the title: "King's wife, Ahmosis, beloved of Amun."

Two sets of reliefs, one dating from the reign of Hatshepsut (the daughter of the royal couple depicted here), and the other from the reign of Amenhotep III, show the divine birth of the king. In each, the scenes and their accompanying inscriptions claim that Amun has come to earth, inhabiting the body of the ruling pharaoh in order to impregnate the queen. Thus the king is both an incarnation of Amun himself, and, as son of the previous pharaoh, the divine offspring of the god. Since Tuthmosis I does not appear to have been of royal blood, this statue group may be designed to help him legitimize his rule by depicting him as the son of Amun.

The upper part of this statue was destroyed, most likely during the reign of Akhenaten, when images of Amun were proscribed. Tutankhamun's sculptors restored it and changed the face of the god into the likeness of the young king.

## 35  Statuette of a Leonine Goddess

Wood coated with bitumen
Height 54 cm; width 17.2 cm; depth 33.8 cm
Dynasty 18, reign of Amenhotep II
Thebes, Valley of the Kings, tomb of Amenhotep II (KV 35)
CG 24620

Found in the sarcophagus chamber of Amenhotep II's tomb, this lioness goddess was carved from ten separate blocks of light reddish wood and coated with bitumen. She wears a tripartite wig and is enveloped in tight wrappings. Her eyes, now missing, were likely once inlaid with semiprecious stones. Similar figures were found in the tombs of Tuthmosis IV and Tutankhamun, the latter gilded, with a sun disk on its head, and wearing a net dress. Tutankhamun's lioness is labeled as the goddess Sekhmet, who protected both sun god and king, and guarded the head of the deceased. In her mummiform guise, she wielded a knife against the king's enemies during his nightly journey. An incarnation of Hathor, daughter and wife of Re, Sekhmet was fierce in defending those she loved and was an ideal symbol of strength and fury turned to protection.

Beautifully painted in still-vibrant colors, this winged, human-headed cobra most likely represents the goddess Meretseger, another important protectress of the king. The statue was carved in four parts: the base and lower body; the upper body; and the two wings. The sledge-shaped base is painted the green of fertility, and the serpent's coiled body is white with a dark blue line that follows the contours of the tail. The raised hood of the upper body imitates the red, green, blue, and white of semiprecious stones such as carnelian and lapis lazuli. A broad collar covers the awkward join between snake body and human head. The goddess's face is the yellow traditionally used for female skin. Her wig is blue, and her eyes and eyebrows are outlined in black. Her blue wings reach forward in a protective embrace.

The hooding cobra is identified from early in Egyptian history as a representation of Wadjet, the tutelary goddess of Lower Egypt, and is also associated with Re. As with the lioness, this is an example of a dangerous creature associated with a protective deity. Placed on the front of the king's crown, the deadly cobra symbolically protects the king, magically spitting fire (venom) at his enemies. By the New Kingdom, most female goddesses, including Meretseger, a deity also associated with the Theban cliffs in which the king's tomb was hidden, could be represented in the form of the cobra.

## 36  Serpent Goddess

Painted sycamore wood
Height 44 cm; length 65 cm; width 16 cm
Dynasty 18, reign of Amenhotep II
Thebes, Valley of the Kings, tomb of Amenhotep II (KV 35)
CG 24629

Limestone
Height 26 cm; width 16.7 cm; depth 3.9 cm
Amarna, Great Temple of the Aten
JE 59296

wife, and father-in-law (whether deceased or still living) formed a divine trio.

From the back of Nefertiti's crown flutter two streamers. This is a new convention introduced by Akhenaten as part of his naturalistic style. Nefertiti's face is a modulated version of the early style of the reign, with a long face, slender, long neck, full lips, a narrow eye, and a large ear pierced for one earring.

The figure on the reverse (left) has one knee on the ground and the other up and forward in a kneeling posture. Her arms are raised before her in an attitude of prayer. Only one sleeve of her garment is visible; her body is in the middle Amarna style, with heavy thighs, a narrow waist and chest, and elongated fingers. She wears a version of the short Nubian wig often seen on Amarna's royal women as well as on men of this era. (I was originally a military wig worn by Nubian recruits.) This figure cannot be identified with certainty, although she resembles images of Akhenaten's "greatly beloved wife," Kiya. She does have the elongated head of the Amarna princesses, so she also might be one of the daughters. The eldest daughter, Meritaten, wears this wig in reliefs from the middle part of the reign.

D iscovered during excavations in the Great Temple of the Aten at Amarna, this piece depicts Nefertiti's head and shoulders in profile on one side and a kneeling queen or princess on the other. These and similar reliefs may have been sculptor's models, patterns that guided the artisans carving the walls of the temple; or else trial pieces, practice sketches executed by apprentice sculptors. Nefertiti is shown in her typical high cylindrical crown (worn only by her) from which hang two uraei, a headdress which identifies her with Tefnut. This goddess and her twin Shu were the offspring of Atum and the first sexually differentiated pair in the Heliopolitan cosmogony. Shu was linked with Akhenaten, and Amenhotep III was considered an incarnation of Atum; thus husband,

### 38 Funerary Figurine of Akhenaten

Red quartzite

Height 14 cm; width 7.8 cm; thickness 4.8 cm

Amarna, Royal Wadi

JE 96830 and 96831

The Royal Tomb at Amarna was thoroughly robbed in antiquity, but bits and pieces of funerary equipment were still to be found in the area in the 20th century, both within the tomb and scattered about outside. The tomb may originally have contained up to 400 funerary figurines like the one illustrated here. In 1934, the Antiquities Service conducted excavations in the Royal Wadi, reacting to reports of illegal digging. The head of this funerary figurine was one of the pieces found. The torso, taken by the illicit diggers, was recovered in 1937 from an antiquities dealer who had brought it to the Antiquities Service for export approval. The museum staff recognized that it joined with this head, and the Service bought it from the dealer.

The statuette, known as a shabti, shows the king in the nemes headcloth, a uraeus on his brow and the wrapped "pigtail" of the headcloth hanging down his back. A false beard adorns his chin. His features are those of a young man, recognizable as Akhenaten's but lacking the exaggeration of the early Amarna style. His arms are crossed at his chest in the mummiform pose traditional for such statues, but rather than the symbols of kingship or agricultural tools that would normally be expected, he grasps an ankh in each hand. The beginning of a vertical inscription begins below his hands: "King of Upper and Lower Egypt, Neferkhepr[ure Waenre]." The texts on Akhenaten's shabtis are unique in that they do not associate the king with Osiris.

Found in the debris of the Great Palace at Amarna, this relief comes from a balustrade that lined a ramp leading to the central hall. The principal relief decoration depicts Akhenaten, Nefertiti, and their eldest daughter Meritaten, their relative importance indicated by their sizes, making offerings to the Aten. The god in return extends ankh signs to the king and queen. The king wears the tall crown of Upper Egypt and a knee-length, flowing kilt with the royal bull's tail; on his chest, arms and prominent breasts are carved six sets of cartouches containing the names of the Aten. Nefertiti and her daughter are dressed in flowing, floor-length robes that expose their heavy-thighed, narrow-waisted bodies. Nefertiti's head is covered by a khat headdress, usually worn only by kings; her daughter's head is adorned by the side lock of youth, leaving her elongated skull visible (see cat. 5). The entire family wears sandals, indicating that they are outside, possibly on the way to the nearby Aten Temple to present offerings to their god. The rounded top is adorned with cartouches of Akhenaten and Nefertiti.

The concept underlying this scene can be traced to traditional temple iconography. One of the primary functions of these sorts of cultic representations was to illustrate and thus magically ensure the reciprocal relationship of god and king. Images, reinforced by hieroglyphic captions, show the king making offerings of various sorts (food, drink, and incense, for example) to the god who, in return, presents the pharoah with symbols of life, stability, health, and the ability to rule. In a radical departure from previous iconography, not only Akhenaten, but also his wife Nefertiti, offers ritual vessels to the Aten while their daughter Meritaten shakes a sistrum—a sacred rattle (see cat. 75). In front of the royal couple are two offering stands bearing marsh plants.

This balustrade was carved before the ninth year of Akhenaten's reign. The bodies of the royal family are in the early, more exaggerated style of Amarna art, and the cartouches of the Aten contain the earlier form of his name, incorporating the names of the gods Re-Horakhty and Shu.

34 **Balustrade Showing Akhenaten and Family under the Aten**
Crystalline limestone
Height 102 cm; width 51 cm; depth 15 cm
Amarna, Great Palace
TR 30.10.26.12

T his colossal head represents Amenhotep IV with the exaggerated features of this period: an elongated face, narrow slanted eyes, a long, slightly bulbous nose, thick lips, and a jutting chin. The king wears the nemes headdress topped by four ostrich plumes, emblems of the goddess Maat. Worn in this fashion, the feathers identify the king as an incarnation of Shu, god of the air and son of the Heliopolitan creator god Atum.

French archaeologist Henri Chevrier discovered this head in the mid-1920s, in an area east of the Amun Precinct at Karnak. To date, parts of about 28 colossal figures of this king have been found in the area. These were once set in front of the pillars of a colonnade that was part of a complex of temples to the Aten built here by Amenhotep IV early in his reign (before he changed his name to Akhenaten).

Some of the other colossal figures are more complete and are in the "Osiride" pose associated with the god of the dead, feet together and hands crossed over the chest. Their bodies also display the early Amarna style, with narrow shoulders, wide hips, a sagging belly, and long, spindly limbs. Some are adorned with stone-carved jewels bearing the cartouches of the Aten.

These figures wear various headdresses and costumes. One type is either naked or in a tight-fitting garment, making it clear that no male genitals are present. For a long time, this was seen as evidence for the androgynous nature of both Akhenaten and his god; this may still be the correct analysis. However, recent interpretation has suggested instead that this is a figure of Nefertiti, rather than her husband, and that she is seen here as an incarnation of the goddess Tefnut, twin sister and wife of Shu. Others of these figures wear the double crown and can be identified as the god Atum, patriarch and creator god at Heliopolis. Mythologically then, the figures of Akhenaten and Nefertiti may represent Shu and Tefnut as part of a triad whose third member was the Atum, perhaps to be identified with the senior king (if there was a co-regency), Amenhotep III. A fourth member of the divine family might have been Queen Tiye as the goddess Hathor.

40  Head of Colossal Statue of Amenhotep IV
Limestone
Height 148 cm; width 84 cm; depth 55 cm
Dynasty 18, reign of Amenhotep IV

SENNEDJEM REAPING WHEAT, FROM HIS TOMB AT DEIR EL MEDINA

# Death, Burial, and the Afterlife

*The ancient Egyptians dedicated much of their resources to building tombs and endowing mortuary cults. Their focus, however, was not on death; the reward for a life well lived was unending existence in the Fields of the Blessed as a transfigured spirit who accompanied the sun god in his daily voyage from death to resurrection.*

The world beyond the grave was in many ways an idealized version of life on earth. The path from death to the eternal afterlife was fraught with danger, and the journey was repeated in an undying cycle. After the funeral, the deceased joined the sun god on his journey across the earthly sky during the day and through the Netherworld during the night. During the dangerous hours after sunset, corresponding to the period after death, sun god and deceased worked to repel the demons that haunted the beyond so that they could join with Osiris and be reborn the next morning. This in turn helped to reiterate the moment of creation and maintain the proper order of the cosmos.

The proper rites and equipment were essential for the success of this cycle. At the moment of death, the ba and ka—two parts of the person's total identity—separated from the body; it was only through the properly executed funerary rites that the ba, ka, and

body could come together again, allowing the deceased to become an *akh*, an effective and blessed spirit.

The ka was the life force, perhaps the most crucial part of a person's identity. In order to function in the afterlife, the ka in its tomb, like a god in his or her temple, needed food, drink, incense, clothing, and perpetual ritual care. The ba can be understood as the soul or personality. Represented as a bird with a human head, it could leave the tomb and affect the lives of loved ones left behind on earth. The properly mummified body was the physical vessel in which these aspects of the person would dwell for eternity. If something happened to the mummy, statues and other images of the deceased could serve as substitutes. So that the deceased could be called by the gods, it was essential that his or her name be remembered forever.

## The Realm of the Dead

The traditional Egyptian tomb, royal or private, consisted of two main parts: the burial itself, generally located below ground; and the cult temple or chapel above. The chapel was the ka's eternal dwelling place, where offerings were made and rituals performed. The decoration of this chapel was designed to magically

Osiris, Lord of the Dead, is shown in this painted limestone relief wearing his characteristic white crown (representing dominion over the Nile Valley) flanked by the ostrich plumes of maat. His green skin symbolizes the rejuvenated earth that emerged after the annual flood.

reproduce these offerings and rituals for eternity in case the actual cult fell into abeyance.

The body was placed in the burial chamber along with actual and model offerings. This part of the tomb was then sealed so that the body would be safe forever. Where possible, cemeteries were located on the west bank of the Nile, linking the dead to the setting sun. Hundreds of tombs were carved into the cliffs at Thebes, where a narrow strip of low desert gives way rapidly to the rocky hills.

Private tombs of the New Kingdom follow the usual pattern for Egyptian mortuary monuments, with tomb chapel above and burial chamber below. However, in the early 18th dynasty, the royal tomb and its associated cult temple were separated. This was not unprecedented for royal tombs: In the 1st dynasty (around 2950 B.C.) the tomb of the king was physically separated from his cult center. After this time, however, it was usual for the king's tomb and cult place to be merged into one complex. The rulers of the Old and Middle Kingdoms were buried under pyramids, surrounded by temples for their mortuary cult and the tombs of their families and officials. By the New Kingdom, these immense symbols of might and power stood silent and empty, victims of the vandals who took advantage of waning royal power to steal their grave goods.

The kings of the 18th dynasty buried at Thebes built mortuary temples in the low desert at the edge of the cultivation. In these temples, the deceased kings were associated with various gods, especially Re, Amun, and Osiris, and worshiped as divine. The images carved on temple walls correspond in part with scenes found in the temples of the state gods; like the divine temple, the royal mortuary temple was a model of the created cosmos.

In lieu of a man-made pyramid, New Kingdom pharaohs hid their burials beneath a pyramid-shaped mountain. Shadowed by the peak known today as el-Qurn ("the Horn") were a series of canyons that cut through the cliffs of the remote high desert. The kings chose to carve their tombs in the folds of two of these wadis, which are now called collectively the Valley of the Kings. This major architectural shift served to protect their treasures from the thieves who had violated the burials of their predecessors. Perhaps more importantly, the hills of Thebes were imagined as both the

Netherworld through which the king had to pass each night and the womb of the great goddess from which he was reborn.

The purpose of the royal tomb was to protect the royal body and, in conjunction with the cult temple near the floodplain, to guarantee the eternal life of the king and the continuance of the universe. The soul of the deceased king would hear rituals and receive offerings within the mortuary temple, then return to the body within the tomb, symbolically slipping below the horizon to brave the dangers of the night world and join with Osiris before being reborn at dawn.

## Architecture and Decoration of the Royal Tomb

The kings from Thutmosis III through Amenhotep III were buried in tombs that followed the same basic plan. Carved into the rock, its entrance in the cracks and crevices of the valley walls or floor, was a long corridor that descended steeply through a series of ramps and stairways to a deep well shaft, known as the Hall of Waiting. This functioned as a hindrance to tomb robbers, as a place to collect the floodwaters that periodically poured through the valley, and as a symbolic burial shaft.

Beyond the well shaft was a small rectangular pillared hall set at a 90 degree angle to the corridor. This led to a larger pillared hall, the burial chamber; in the case of Thutmosis IV and Amenhotep III this was on yet another axis. Early examples of this hall are oval, in the shape of the royal cartouche. At the far end lay the sarcophagus itself, the eternal resting place of the royal mummy. Much of the burial equipment was placed in this chamber; small storerooms carved to either side of this hall held additional grave goods.

Identification of the 18th dynasty royal tomb as a model of the Netherworld, its turns and twists mirroring the winding waterways of the Beyond, was enhanced by its decoration. Scenes and texts painted on the walls and pillars created an image of this world and the successful night journey of the sun god through it. This in turn guided the king on his journey to the Afterlife and ensured his transformation into a god.

Colossal quartzite figures of Amenhotep III (nicknamed the Colossi of Memnon) stand like sentinels before the site of his dismantled mortuary temple on the west bank of Thebes. Behind these statues rise the rocky hills of the high desert, guardians of the royal tombs.

Chosen from a group of writings known collectively as netherworld texts, the scenes on the tomb walls and their associated labels developed out of the Pyramid Texts, older religious writings that had appeared first in Old Kingdom royal burial complexes. In the Middle Kingdom, these spells reappeared in a new form, as Coffin Texts inscribed on the inner walls of elite coffins. By the New Kingdom these mythological texts, with their associated illustrations, were painted on the walls of royal tombs and written on papyri. Not just collections of spells, as are found earlier, the New Kingdom texts are more coherent compositions that provide detailed images of the world beyond the Earth.

These texts have been grouped into several "books," each of which follows its own development. The principal corpus of scenes in 18th dynasty royal tombs comes from the *Imy-Duat,* or *What is in the Netherworld.* Although this book may have existed earlier, it is first attested in the early 18th dynasty, and then appears in almost all royal tombs of this era. The most complete copies were inscribed in the tombs of Tuthmosis III and Amenhotep II, whose burial chambers look as if they are covered with a large, unrolled papyrus bearing scenes and texts from this book.

Carefully composed with an introduction, a conclusion, and 12 chapters corresponding to the 12 hours of the night, the book describes the trip of the sun god through the Netherworld. Texts and images are arranged in three registers, with the central band representing the underworld river on which the sun travels in his bark and the upper and lower registers illustrating the riverbanks. The sun god is accompanied and guided by Hathor, who is responsible for renewing the

Aerial perspective of the West Bank at Thebes with Deir el Bahri
in the foreground and the Valley of the Kings behind.

Two separate vignettes can be seen on this funerary papyrus: the weighing of the heart on the left and the ba bird leaving the tomb on the right.

world each day. Horus steers the solar bark; various other deities also join the sun god on his journey. The topography and inhabitants of the Netherworld are depicted quite specifically in the book, with measurements and labels given for some features of the landscape and with most figures, no matter how obscure, identified in some way.

The first chapter shows the sun descending to the Netherworld as it sets in the west. In the second and third hours the river is bordered by fertile fields, and other boats accompany the sun god's bark. Osiris is prominent in the fourth hour, during which the solar bark is towed through the hilly desert of Ro-setau, a land filled with dangerous serpents. The solar bark itself turns into a fire-breathing serpent, and the other boats are forced to turn back. The hills of sand continue through the fifth hour, along with the cavern of the

mortuary god Sokar. Below this, evildoers are punished in the Lake of Fire.

The sun reaches the lowest point in the Netherworld during the sixth hour. The body of the god lies here, surrounded by the primeval waters; here the ba of Re is reunited with his body and with Osiris, so that the process of rebirth can begin. In the seventh hour, the most dangerous time, Isis is shown standing on the prow of the sun god's boat, protecting him from the evil snake Apophis with her magic. This serpent is the enemy of the sun, and tries to keep him from continuing on through the Netherworld. Osiris appears also and claims victory over his enemies. The eight and ninth hours are concerned with provisioning the sun god (and thus the deceased king) with cloth and food. In the tenth hour, the primordial waters of the Nun begin the process of regeneration, leading to the eleventh hour, when the sun is prepared for the dawn. The last chapter depicts the sun in the shape of a scarab beetle rising in the east. The *Imy-Duat* text also incorporates the funeral, the

Khepri, the scarab beetle, pushes the sun disk onto the horizon of dawn in a scene from the tomb of Amenhotep II, representing the 12th hour of the night in the book *What is in the Netherworld.*

arrival of the body at the tomb, and its union with the sun.

The tomb of Tuthmosis III included a new book known as the *Litany of Re,* whose principal purpose was to identify the deceased king with Re. It begins by listing 75 names for the sun god and constitutes something of a hymn of praise to the great ruler of the sky. New books were introduced in the later New Kingdom, but do not appear in the 18th dynasty before Tutankhamun.

The nonroyal tombs in the Valley of the Kings were left undecorated (as were the burial chambers of most 18th-dynasty private tombs); these, like the royal tombs, consist only of burial chambers with no associated chapels. Elaborate funerary papyri, examples of which were buried with Maiherpri and Yuya and Tjuya, most likely functioned in lieu of the scenes and texts found in royal sepulchres. Elsewhere in the Theban necropolis, and at other sites of this period, the chapels of elite mortuary monuments (corresponding to the royal memorial temple) were beautifully adorned with images and inscriptions relating to the life on earth, funeral, mortuary cult, and eternal existence of the deceased.

## Burial Equipment

The most essential item for the burial was the mummified body of the deceased. After death, the body stayed at the embalmers for at least 70 days to be prepared for its eternal home. The process of desiccation took 40 days. First, the embalmers removed the viscera—liver, lungs, stomach, and intestine—through an incision in the flank. These viscera were dried, wrapped, anointed with molten resin, and placed in special canopic containers, which consisted of either four jars or four compartments within a chest. Each of these containers was identified with one of the "sons of Horus": Duamutef (jackal-headed protector of the stomach); Hapy (baboon-headed god of the lungs); Imsety (human-headed patron of the liver); or Qebehsenuef (falcon-headed protector of the intestines). These gods were paired with the protective goddesses: Duamutef with Neith (goddess of war and hunting), Hapy with Nephthys (sister and protector of Osiris), Imsety with Isis (sister and wife of Osiris), and Qebehsenuef with Selket (another protective goddess). In the 18th dynasty, royal canopics had stoppers in the form of human heads representing the deceased, and private jars were topped with images of the four sons of Horus—at first human-headed, and later with heads corresponding to their animal totems.

The heart was either removed, desiccated, and placed back in the body, or else simply left in the chest cavity. The drying agent, natron, was basically a combination of salt and baking soda that occurs naturally in Egypt. The body was laid in a bed of this material, which was also stuffed into its internal cavities. When the tissues had been stripped of water, the process of bandaging began. Supervised by a priest identified with Anubis, god of embalming, this elaborate ritual involved yards of linen bandages. Amulets and charms, frequently made of gold or semiprecious stone, were placed on the body among the bandages. These charms helped to protect the deceased during his or her journey to and existence in the Afterlife. Funerary texts often list the amulets to be used, and even specify their material and color. Mummies, especially royal ones, were also adorned with jewelry and personal effects such as daggers and diadems. As the mummy was wrapped and the amulets put into place, special spells were chanted.

Elaborate sets of nested coffins and sarcophagi were also crucial for both elite and royal burials. Kings were placed in a series of three anthropoid coffins that were then housed in a large rectangular sarcophagus of stone. A series of concentric shrines were built around the sarcophagus, further shielding the body. People of high status could also have up to three coffins within a sarcophagus. Funerary masks, images of the head and

The burial chamber of Amenhotep II, its walls decorated with excerpts from the Netherworld texts, is still dominated by the king's elegant quartzite sarcophagus. The king's mummy was found inside when the tomb was discovered in 1898.

shoulders of the deceased, were placed over the head to provide extra protection for this vital part of the body. Coffins and sarcophagi were adorned with magical spells and images of protective gods and goddesses. Only Tutankhamun's shrines have survived; these are decorated with protective deities and Netherworld texts.

Also made specifically for the burial were sets of funerary figurines known as shabtis. These first appear during the Middle Kingdom, a development from servant figures first placed in the tombs of the later Old Kingdom. Shabtis were meant to perform menial tasks for the tomb owner in the afterlife. Also known as shawabtis and, in the Late Period, as ushabtis ("answerers"), they are seen first in single examples. During the New Kingdom, their numbers gradually increased until there were over 400 in each tomb: 365 workers for each day of the year plus overseers. Royal shabtis appear first at the beginning of the 18th dynasty; the tomb of Amenhotep II is the first from which a large number, 88 in all, has been preserved. Most shabtis were inscribed with Spell 6 from the Book of the Dead, in which they promise to serve in the place of their masters should they be called upon to work in the fields of the Afterlife.

Royal burials also required certain additional objects, such as figures of the king, gods, and other divine beings that served ritual functions. In addition, there were items such as strange wooden trays in the shape of the god Osiris, planted with seeds that would sprout after the tomb had been closed and symbolize resurrection, and Anubis fetishes, figurines in the shape of poles with animal skins tied around them, thought to imitate prehistoric cult objects. Royal burials also included multiple amulets and ritual vessels.

Private tombs of the New Kingdom often contained papyrus copies of another of the Netherworld texts, the *Book of Coming Forth by Day* (also known as the Book of the Dead). This was a collection of spells containing information the deceased needed to combat the dangers of the Netherworld. Broken into 12 chapters, it was further divided into 192 spells that, for example, list the secret words required to pass all gates and barriers and the names of the demons to be faced. No single papyrus has been found that contains all of these formulae, as each person chose what he or she liked from the total repertoire.

One of the most important episodes in this book was the Judgment of the Deceased. This took place before the god Osiris, king of the Netherworld, and a council of 42 judges. When the deceased arrived at the Hall of Judgment, he would recite the "negative confession," in which he would claim not to have committed transgressions against humans or gods. His or her heart—thought to be the seat of intelligence—would be weighed against the ostrich plume of Maat. If the scales balanced, the deceased would continue into the realm of the blessed, the Fields of Iaru. If not, the heart would be swallowed by the monstrous Eater of the Dead—a composite creature with the head of a crocodile, the forepart and mane of a lion, and the hindquarters of a hippopotamus—and the unfortunate sinner would die forever.

Also essential for the Afterlife were items used in life and needed for eternal survival and pleasure. Food and drink could take the form of offerings made in the tomb chapel or mortuary temple, or could be mummified meat, spices, jars of wine, and other foodstuffs placed in the tomb chambers. For the elite, images of food or its production on the tomb walls might supplement the offerings themselves. Clothing, weapons, furniture, and other objects used by the living were also important to the burial. These could include actual chairs, beds, bows and arrows, games, chariots, boats, and so forth, or could be models or dummy versions made especially for the tomb. Incense, oils, and unguents of various sorts were also essential.

## Journey to the Afterlife

After the body had been prepared and the burial equipment produced and gathered, the funeral ceremonies began. The mummy was placed inside a shrine and transported to the burial site known as the "beautiful West." Upon arrival at the tomb, the essential rite of the Opening of the Mouth was performed. The mummy was set upright and purified with libations, incense, and natron. The principal rites involved several officiants, including the heir, touching the mummy's mouth with ritual implements while pronouncing spells to restore its senses. This rite may originally have been a reenactment of the moment of birth,

Women mourn the 18th-dynasty official Ramose, vizier under Amenhotep III and Amenhotep IV, as the funeral procession arrives at his tomb.

when the midwife clears the newborn baby's mouth and it takes its first breath. In other ceremonies, a bull was butchered, and the heart and foreleg presented to the mummy. Other offerings, such as clothing and eye-paint, were also given to the deceased, and the mummy was anointed with seven special oils. When the ritual was complete, the mummy was considered an effective being, able to eat, drink, see, hear, and receive the cult. This rite was also carried out on statues and other images of the deceased.

At some point during the funeral, mourners held a great banquet, possibly outside the tomb, perhaps under some sort of portable tent. This banquet might have taken place after the actual burial, but also may have occurred just after the Opening of the Mouth, so that the deceased could magically join the party.

After the Opening of the Mouth, the mummy was carried into the tomb, draped with floral garlands, and placed inside its nest of coffins. As each lid was closed, the family recited prayers and the priests poured fragrant unguents over the body and coffins. The heavy top of the sarcophagus was lowered, and then, for kings, the door of each gilded shrine was closed and sealed. Appropriate incantations and gestures would have accompanied each stage of this process.

Any funerary equipment not already in place was then placed in the tomb, and the last priest swept away the footprints and prepared to close the tomb. Its door way stamped with the seals of the necropolis, the tomb would theoretically remain inviolate for eternity.

The mortuary cult, which served to keep the deceased well fed and properly attended, would have been carried out by the deceased's family or by special priests. For private people, this would have taken place within the tomb chapel; for royalty, it would have been carried out in the mortuary temple.

This miniature mask was discovered by Theodore Davis some time in the early part of the 20th century, probably in a small pit in the Valley of the Kings labeled KV 54. The material found here included a number of large earthenware pots filled with scraps of linen, broken pottery, reed brooms, wreaths of dried flowers and leaves, small cloth bags filled with natron, a scrap of cloth dated to year 6 of Tutankhamun, and a small mask, said to be gilded. Davis subsequently gave most of this material to the Metropolitan Museum of Art, where it was studied and catalogued. A miniature mask was included with the materials sent to the Metropolitan, but it was colorfully painted, not gilded. It is likely that Davis took the gilded mask displayed here from the jar and substituted the painted one; the original mask, along with a miscellany of objects from the Valley of the Kings, was later given to the Cairo Museum.

Egyptological analysis proved that the material from KV 54 represented the remains of the funerary banquet celebrated by Tutankhamun's chief mourners, along with scraps of linen and natron collected from his embalming. These objects would have been given ritual burial, as they were sacred and could not simply be abandoned. This mask was probably meant to be used for one of the two female fetuses found buried with the young king. These were discovered, each within its own set of miniature anthropoid coffins, inside a plain wooden chest (above). The larger of the two had reached seven months gestation; she was either stillborn or died soon after birth. She appears to have suffered from genetic abnormalities, including spina bifida. This baby was properly mummified, at least to the extent of having her viscera removed and brain extracted, and was carefully wrapped. The smaller appears to have been miscarried at about five months; she was mummified with her viscera still in place.

Over the head of the smaller child (whose mummy was much too small for its coffin) was a gilded miniature mummy mask almost identical to the one shown here, but the larger child had no mask. It is most likely that this mask was brought to the tomb, then ritually discarded when it was discovered that it did not fit the larger fetus.

41  Small Gilded Funerary Mask for a Fetus
Cartonnage; gold
Height 13.8 cm.; width 10.7 cm.; depth 10.5 cm.
Dynasty 18; reign of Tutankhamun
Thebes, Valley of the Kings (KV 54 "Embalming Cache")
JE 39711

This exquisite mask, a masterpiece of the jeweler's art, was fitted closely over the lady Tjuya's head, shoulders, and upper chest to preserve and echo her features for eternity. At some point, most likely during the funeral ceremonies, the body was covered with a very fine linen pall and then anointed with resin. Much of the mask was covered with this pall, which had adhered to its surface. Some of this has been removed, but a significant amount, especially on the hair, remains. The ears of the mask are still filled with resin.

Although the basic material (stiffened cloth bandages known as cartonnage) differs, the design is very similar to the upper part of Tjuya's gilded outer coffin (cat. 43). As on the coffin, Tjuya wears a long wig and a broad collar of gold and glass. The eyes are inlaid with obsidian and calcite (with a green faience backing), and the cosmetic lines and eyebrows are inset in dark blue glass. A floral diadem in low relief adorns Tjuya's brow, with a lotus blossom directly over the center of her forehead.

The general outlines of the face are similar to those of the outer and inner coffins, but with subtle differences. The face in each case is wide, with a small rounded chin. The eyes are narrow and almond-shaped, tilted up at the corners. The nose here is fine, with a thin bridge to the nose; the mouth is wide, and bears a slight smile.

Funerary masks can be traced back to the early Old Kingdom, when the outer bandages wrapping the body were coated with a layer of plaster. The features of the deceased were modeled in realistic detail and then painted. Toward the end of this era, the plaster coating of the rest of the body was dropped and helmet masks came into use. Made of cartonnage, these fit over the entire head and were shaped and painted in the likeness of the face underneath. Later, some masks were extended in front and back, eventually becoming full anthropoid coffins. For a while, these coffins replaced the separate mask, and then burials that included both mask and anthropoid coffins appeared. In addition to its mask and nest of coffins, Tjuya's body rested within an elaborate cartonnage "cage" decorated with figures of mortuary deities. Armed with mask, cage, coffins, and sarcophagus, Tjuya's body was well protected for her journey to the Afterlife.

42  Gilded Funerary Mask of Tjuya
Gilded cartonnage
Height 43.1 cm; width 31.1 cm; depth 29.5 cm
Dynasty 18, reign of Amenhotep III
Thebes, Valley of the Kings, tomb of Yuya and Tjuya (KV 46)
CG 51009

43  Gilded Coffin of Tjuya
Gilded wood
Length 218.5 cm; width 67.5 cm; height 100.8 cm
Dynasty 18, reign of Amenhotep III
Thebes, Valley of the Kings, tomb of Yuya and Tjuya (KV 46)
CG 51006

Tjuya's mummy was found inside two nested anthropoid coffins that lay within a large shrine-shaped sarcophagus. This assemblage was farther inside the tomb than the sarcophagus of her husband, suggesting that she had predeceased him and been buried first. Robbers had disturbed her coffins and rifled her mummy. The base of the sarcophagus, set on a sledge, was still in place, with the runners facing west. This sarcophagus was predominantly black, with figures and bands in gold. The outer coffin, shown here, had been opened and the lid thrown into one corner. The innermost coffin was still inside the sarcophagus.

Despite the rough treatment accorded it by the thieves, this is perhaps the best preserved and most beautiful of the coffins found in the tomb. It is almost entirely covered with reddish gold. The exterior depicts Tjuya wearing a tripartite wig, its strands indicated with impressed lines. Her face is broad, with a small chin, a wide-bridged nose and a dainty, faintly smiling mouth. Her eyes were inlaid with obsidian and calcite set into blue glass, with red in the corners to indicate capillaries. The flowers and petals that form the beads of her broad collar are of gold and inlaid glass in dark blue, turquoise, and red, with the falcon-headed

fasteners at each side in black glass. Her clenched fists, empty of any implements or regalia, are crossed on her breast (right over left), and she wears an inlaid bracelet of dark blue, turquoise, and red on one wrist.

Figures and texts in raised relief adorn the body of the coffin. The sky goddess Nut, her wings outstretched to protect Tjuya, dominates the front of the lid. Two vertical bands below and four horizontal registers that wrap around the entire coffin allude to mummy straps (strips of linen that helped hold the mummy together) while providing space for inscriptions and dividing the surface into image fields. Some of the texts are spells designed to protect the body, and the others name Tjuya as honored before various gods; many of Tjuya's titles appear in these inscriptions.

On the trough of the coffin, between the "bandages," are depictions of various gods, including Thoth, god of wisdom; Anubis, patron of embalming; and the four sons of Horus. The coffin is also protected at the head by Nephthys and at the foot by Isis. In Egyptian mythology, these goddesses were responsible for both reviving and mourning their brother Osiris, and served as guardians of the body. Below Isis are two *djed* pillars, symbols of stability. The inside of the coffin was simply colored black.

**59 Shabti of Tjuya** (opposite)
Wood, gessoed and gilded
Height 21.7 cm; width 8.1 cm; depth 5.1 cm
CG 51039

**44 and 45 Shabti Boxes** (above, in background)
Painted wood
A. Height with lid 36.9 cm; width 11.6 cm; depth 11.5 cm
CG 51042
B. Height with lid 36.4 cm; width 11.0 cm; depth 10.2 cm
CG 51044

**60 Shabti of Yuya** (above, left)
Wood, gessoed and painted/gilded
Height 23.5 cm; width 7.5 cm; depth 4.8 cm
CG 51030

**61 Shabti (on Stand) of Yuya** (above, right)
Wooden core; sheet copper, partially gilded
Height 25.3 cm; width 7.2 cm; depth 4.6 cm
CG 51033

Dynasty 18, reign of Amenhotep III
Thebes, Valley of the Kings, tomb of Yuya and Tjuya (KV 46)

Thirteen tall rectangular boxes painted with a niched pattern in bright primary colors, designed to hold single shabtis, were found in the tomb of Yuya and Tjuya. This vaulted shape and niched decoration go back to early sarcophagi, which in turn refer to the mythical sanctuary of the north, an early religious building made of perishable material of which only iconic representations have survived. This shape is also linked to the chest in which Osiris was buried, and to a structure where the deceased waits in the Netherworld to be awakened by the sun god.

Fourteen shabtis belonging to Yuya and four bearing the name of Tjuya were found in the tomb. Although none of these figures held agricultural tools, a collection of model implements was found nearby, including copper baskets, wooden yokes, hoes, picks, and one brick mold,

This gilded wooden shabti (59) of Tjuya's and the painted wooden shabti of Yuya's (60) are similar in form and iconography. Each wears a long tripartite wig and crosses empty hands at the chest. One of the most unusual shabtis found in the tomb was this third example (61), belonging to Yuya. Its body is made of a sheet of copper wrapped around a wooden core, the seams visible on both sides and lined with rows of copper nails. This figure holds a sekhem scepter and a folded cloth handkerchief, both ancient symbols of authority. Its body is made of a sheet of copper wrapped around a wooden core, the seams visible on both sides and lined with rows of copper nails. Head and wig are

carved from the wooden core, and the face is made from a separate piece of metal. The broad collar is plastered and gilded with yellow gold; the gilding of the necklace with heart pendant is of a redder alloy. In its hands, this figure holds a sekhem scepter and a folded cloth handkerchief, both ancient symbols of authority. All three shabtis are inscribed with Spell 6 from the Book of the Dead, in which the figure agrees to work for the deceased in the Afterlife.

**46 and 47  Lid and Base of Canopic Jar of Tjuya**
Calcite
Lid: Height 16.5 cm; diameter 17.6 cm
Vase: Height 32 cm; diameter of shoulder 21.6 cm
Dynasty 18, reign of Amenhotep III
Thebes, Valley of the Kings, tomb of Yuya and Tjuya (KV 46)
Lid: CG 51018
Body: CG 51021

them upright. The viscera themselves can be considered both as images of the four sons of Horus, each protected by a goddess and images of Tjuya herself.

All of the canopic stoppers, like the one illustrated above, depict one of the sons of Horus in a shoulder-length wig, the eyes outlined in black, the pupils painted black, and the irises white. An inscription on the front of this jar contains the spell: "Words spoken by Selket: My two arms will embrace what is inside, extending protection around Qebehsenuef (god of the intestines) who is therein, the one revered before Qebehsenuef, the Osiris, king's ornament, lady of the house, Tjuya." Thus the goddess Selket promises to protect the viscera inside, in this case the intestines identified with Qebehsenuef. The stopper wears a short rectangular beard; the other two stoppers (for Imsety and Duamutef) are beardless.

Within her canopic chest were Tjuya's four calcite canopic vases, each one containing a mummified package of viscera that had been carefully wrapped and shaped into the semblance of a human body. The packages were topped with gilded and painted masks of cartonnage, echoing in miniature the mummy and its mask. The masks (one of which is shown at left) represent Tjuya herself, wearing a broad collar and a long tripartite wig that comes down over her shoulders, just as she does on both anthropoid coffins and the mummy mask. The packages of viscera, one of which was found to contain a mummified liver, were packed with sawdust to keep

**48  Small Mask for Bundled Viscera of Tjuya**
Gilded cartonnage
Height 9.2 cm; diameter 7.2 cm
Dynasty 18, reign of Amenhotep III
Thebes, Valley of the Kings, tomb of Yuya and Tjuya (KV 46)
CG 51021

49 Four Dummy Vessels on a Stand
Limestone; wood
Vessels: Height (with lid) 24.6 cm; diameter 8.5 cm
Stand: Height 6 cm; width 38 cm; diameter 7.7 cm
Dynasty 18, reign of Amenhotep III
Thebes, Valley of the Kings, tomb of Yuya and Tjuya (KV 46)
CG 51102

Vessels of various shapes and sizes, holding wine, oils, grain, and other foodstuffs, were among the first grave goods to appear in Egyptian tombs. Labels from the Early Dynastic Period tell us that oils and unguents used for ritual and cosmetic purposes were important commodities, and indeed, such materials formed a significant part of the funerary furnishings throughout Egyptian history.

In addition to actual vases holding real substances, dummy vases, with no internal space for contents, were sometimes found in tombs. This "dummy" concept goes far back into Egyptian history. In the mortuary complex of Djoser at Saqqara, for example, many of the buildings themselves are dummies, life-size models of important structures with false entrances and no interior rooms. In the land of the dead, the idea was as important as the actuality—a model or even just a name could easily substitute for the real thing.

These four dummy vases, affixed to a painted wooden base, were found in the tomb of Yuya and Tjuya. Each is completely solid, with only a small hollow 1.5 inches (4 cm) deep in the top. Although the four shapes are subtly different, they share the same profile, with a round base curving up to an ovoid body and a conical neck topped by a wider ring at the mouth. Three have handles, each slightly different, and the forth is fronted by the head of an ibex. Disc-shaped lids, each surmounted by a different animal, close the vessels.

The stone of the vessels has been painted white. An offering prayer painted in blue on a yellow field, with red vertical lines delimiting the short columns of hiero-glyphs, states that the vases are offerings from Osiris to the deceased (Yuya). The animals are also painted, and comprise two calves' heads (one on either end), one dappled black and one spotted red; an ibex calf; and a frog. All of these animals are linked with regeneration and resurrection; the colors black and red are associated with the fertile floodplain and the barren desert, respectively.

This is one of two sets of dummy vases found in the tomb. In addition, the tomb contained a number of free-standing dummy containers (see cats. 20-22).

This unusual figurine, carved from a block of pure white limestone, represents a mummy lying on a lion-footed bed. Such beds were commonly used to transport the deceased and to support the coffin within the tomb. In Tutankhamun's burial chamber, for example, the inner nest of coffins rests on a lion-footed bed within the outer sarcophagus. This type of bed is thought to represent the womb of the king's mother in the form of a protective lioness. The niches that fill the space beneath the bed have been painted with a colorful palace façade pattern seen often on cult objects.

The mummy's arms, which can be seen faintly through the wrappings, are crossed at chest level. The figure wears a long tripartite wig, the ends tipped with yellow paint, and a broad collar of golden yellow. Facial features have been picked out with paint.

Carved in high relief at the level of the pelvis is the figure of a human-headed bird, its wings outstretched to cover the body. Instead of talons, the bird has human hands. This bird represents the ba, one of the aspects of the deceased. In this form, the spirit of the dead person could leave the tomb and be active in the realm of the living, able to eat, drink, and have sexual relations. The figure as a whole may be a reference to Spell 89 of the Book of the Dead, the spell for allowing a soul to join its body in the land of the dead, which can be illustrated by a ba bird resting on a mummy.

This bird can perhaps also be seen as an image of the goddess Isis, and the entire figure may make reference to the Osiris myth. According to this legend, Osiris (mythical proto-king of Egypt) was murdered by his brother, Seth. Osiris's sister-wife, Isis, was able to bring her husband back to life just long enough to become pregnant with a son, Horus. To achieve this end, Isis transformed herself into a kite, hovering above the temporarily vivified Osiris to receive his seed.

At the foot of the bed is a projection of uncertain function in the shape of a flattened cylinder, a hole 0.2 inches (5 mm) deep on its upper side. The excavator suggested that this was meant to hold offerings of some sort. It may also be a receptacle to collect mummification fluids, meaning that the bed would represent an embalming table on which the mummy is lying. The mummy and bed are attached to a wooden pedestal with tenons.

This unusual type of figure is seen for the first time during the reign of Amenhotep III; a similar, but not identical, example was found in the tomb of Tutankhamun, donated to the burial by the royal treasurer, Maya. Figures of mummies on beds, although never common, are found throughout the 19th dynasty. Some examples are inscribed with the shabti spell, and others were placed in small coffins next to small models of beds.

50  Funerary Figurine on a Bed

Painted limestone; wood
Length 30 cm; width 16 cm; width 9 cm
Dynasty 18, reign of Amenhotep III
Thebes, Valley of the Kings, tomb of Yuya and Tjuya (KV 46)
CG 51103

52  **Ankh (Life) Symbol**  (left)
Faience
Height 42 cm; width 21 cm
Dynasty 18, reign of Amenhotep II
Thebes, Valley of the Kings, Tomb of Amenhotep II (KV 35)
CG 24348

51  **Djed (Endurance) Symbol** (center)
Painted wood
Height 51 cm; width 21 cm
Dynasty 18, reign of Amenhotep II
Thebes, Valley of the Kings, Tomb of Amenhotep II (KV 35)
CG 24437

These three large models from the tomb of Amenhotep II represent the hieroglyphs for life, stability, and prosperity. These were fundamental elements of a common formula for wishing someone well. Temple scenes frequently depict gods handing the king one or more of these symbols, and inscriptions found in such contexts ask for them as boons, sometimes along with health and happiness, or simply list them following the royal name.

The ankh, symbol of life, was once thought to depict a sandal strap but is now interpreted variously as the ceremonial tie for a girdle, a variation on the royal cartouche, or a sexual symbol linking the male and female. This is the most potent and frequently seen of the three symbols. Egyptian art often shows gods offering life to kings; an extreme example of this is seen in the Amarna period, where the rays of the Aten, or globe of the sun, end with hands holding ankhs to the noses of the royal family.

The djed pillar can be traced to the Predynastic Period, and is thought originally to have represented a column or post wrapped with some kind of plant, perhaps sheaves of grain or a sacred tree. The pillar was closely linked to Osiris, god of the dead. In later periods, it came to be associated with the god's backbone; thus, djed pillars are also seen decorating the troughs of coffins, in line with the backbone of the deceased. The raising of the djed pillar as a symbol of endurance or stability was an important ritual carried out during the Sed Festival, the feast of renewal first celebrated by each king after 30 years of rule. Through his association with this ancient object, the king helped to guarantee the fertility of the soil and the continuance of the agricultural cycle. The djed pillar is also linked with Ptah and Sokar, both Memphite gods who were joined during the New Kingdom into a composite deity. This example is of wood, painted blue, green, red, and yellow.

The *was* scepter, with its forked bottom, may be modeled on a shepherd's crook. The head on top, presumed to be a canid of some sort, has never been identified satisfactorily—suggestions include a donkey, a jackal, a gazelle, or even a giraffe. Was scepters are traditionally carried by gods and certain goddesses, and also appear in Egyptian art as supports holding up the sky.

53  **Was (Prosperity) Symbol**  (right)
Faience
Height 40 cm
Dynasty 18, reign of Amenhotep II
Thebes, Valley of the Kings, tomb of Amenhotep II (KV 35)
CG 24396

54  Canopic Chest of Tjuya
Wood covered with bitumen and gold
Height 64.5 cm; width 52.5 cm; depth 72.5 cm
Inner compartments 23 cm square
Dynasty 18, reign of Amenhotep III
Thebes, Valley of the Kings, tomb of Yuya and Tjuya (KV 46)
CG 51013

This elaborate wooden box, which contained Tjuya's canopic jars, was found at the foot of her outer sarcophagus. It takes the shape of a shrine, a typical box form that traces its lineage back to the earliest religious architecture of Egyptian history. Like the sarcophagus, it sits on the sledge that would have carried it to the tomb. Black bitumen, representing fertility and rebirth, covers the wooden surface. The figures have been added in gold, the color of divinity. The box and its decoration were designed specifically to protect the viscera from physical or spiritual harm.

On front of the sloping lid is a shen ring, the hieroglyphs for water, and an incense jar. These are flanked by wedjat eyes, recumbent Anubis jackals atop shrines, and the signs for the eastern and western deserts. On the upper surface of the lid is a figure of the sky goddess Nut, arms and wings outstretched, along with two columns of text. Knobs on the top and front would have been used to close the box.

A dado of engraved niches (known as a palace façade) in gold runs around the bottom edge of the shrine; gilded frames around the edges of each side provide spaces for texts. Within the fields formed by these frames are deities: on the front, Isis and Nephthys; on the back, Selket and Neith; on the right, Duamutef and Qebehsenuef; and on the left, Hapy and Imsety. The gilded frames bear the names and titles of Tjuya along with spells spoken by these eight gods and goddesses, promising to protect the contents of the box.

Elegant in its simplicity, yet rich in decorative detail, this beautiful chair is one of the greatest treasures found in the tomb of Yuya and Tjuya. It was given to them by their granddaughter, Sitamun, who is represented twice on the back. Sitamun was the daughter of Amenhotep III and Tiye, and became queen to her father late in his reign.

Crafted of one wood and veneered with another, more precious one (perhaps walnut), the various pieces of this chair are joined with mortices and tenons. The legs are in the shape of lion's limbs, ending in paws that rest atop trapezoidal pieces plated with silver. The seat of the chair, given extra support by a piece of wood placed underneath, is of braided string woven in a herringbone pattern.

The low back and arms are decorated with gold. In front of each arm is the bust of a queen, her low crown also covered with gold. The outer face of the left armrest is decorated with three dancing figures of the grotesque god of amusement and protector of the household, Bes. The outer Bes figures hold tambourines; the central one grasps a boomerang. On the right armrest are two additional figures of Bes, one with a tambourine and the other with two knives;

**55   Chair of Princess Sitamun**
Wood, partially gilded and silver-plated
Height 77 cm; width 52 cm; depth 63 cm
Dynasty 18, reign of Amenhotep III
Thebes, Valley of the Kings, tomb of Yuya and Tjuya (KV 46 )
CG 51113

between them is Tawaret, a blend of hippopotamus, lion, crocodile, and human who served as goddess of childbirth. This figure is unusual in that the goddess has a leonine rather than her usual hippopotamus head. On the inner surface of each arm are four female offering-bearers with rosette or lotus flower crowns carrying platters heaped with rings of gold.

The decoration on the inner part of the backrest consists of two identical and symmetrical scenes. In each, the princess sits on a chair similar in shape to the one shown here, which in turn rests on a papyrus mat. In one hand she holds a menat necklace, in the other a sistrum, both implements associated with the cult of Hathor. On her head is a clump of marsh plants; the inscription above identifies her as "Daughter of the king, whom he loves, Sitamun." An attendant stands in front of her chair, offering her a broad collar on a platter. According to the accompanying inscriptions, she is "bringing gold from the southern foreign lands," a reference to Nubia. Protecting the princess is a winged sun disk, an image of Horus of Idfu. The back of the chair is marked with a feather pattern in silver and reinforced with three struts. Patterns of wear indicate that the chair was used before it was placed in the tomb.

The decoration of this chair, which includes many figures of the household deities Tawaret and Bes, suggests to some scholars that it was used in the princess's private apartments. Alternatively, it may have had a ceremonial function, as it refers to the bringing of gold as tribute from Nubia and may have been made for a state occasion such as a Sed Festival.

## 56 Head of a Cow

Painted wood

Length 20.3 cm; width 19.7 cm; depth 22.5 cm

Dynasty 18, reign of Amenhotep II

Thebes, Valley of the Kings, tomb of Amenhotep II (KV 35)

CG 24631

Among the objects placed in royal tombs were ritual figures, images of gods and other divine creatures whose job it was to protect the king on his journey to the afterlife. This simple, yet beautifully modeled head of a bovine (left) most likely represents the Celestial Cow, one of the deities charged with insuring that Amenhotep II reached his eternal destiny. Mentioned in texts as far back as the Old Kingdom, this creature is featured in a myth preserved for the first time on the outermost of the golden shrines protecting Tutankhamun's sarcophagus. In this story, humankind rebels against the aged sun god Re, who renounces the earth and is carried to the sky by the Celestial Cow. This cow also represents the heavens themselves, which were in turn associated with the watery void of the Nun out of which the universe was created, a metaphor for the womb of the great mother goddess from whom the sun god was born. By placing this figure in his tomb, Amenhotep II magically helped to ensure his own daily rebirth.

The head is carved from a single block of wood, with the ears, the horns, and part of the neck attached separately. The eyes are painted in black and white to resemble the wedjat, the wounded eye of Horus. The short horns are painted grey. A similar sculpture, gilded and with longer horns, but with the same special treatment of the eyes, was found in the tomb of Tutankhamun. Both are designed as heads only, and are not meant to be attached to a larger statue of a cow.

Made of imported cedar from Lebanon, the other cow's head (above) is part of the repertoire of ritual figures from Amenhotep II's tomb. It was carved in two pieces, with the ears and short, stumpy horns (indicating that this is a calf) attached separately. A short mane is depicted running down the animal's spine; hairs are indicated around the muzzle and on the top of the head; and the insides of the ears, the throat, and ovals around the large, eloquent eyes have been painted pink. The hide is painted with black and white splotches. The head is designed to stand alone, not to be attached to a body.

This head is unique, and appears neither in the funerary equipment of other royal tombs (including Tutankhamun's) nor the wall decoration of later sepulchres. It is most likely connected with the Celestial Cow. In mythological texts, the reborn sun god can be described as the offspring of the Celestial Cow, and sometimes specifically as a calf. By placing this image in his tomb, the king was most likely expressing the hope that he be reborn each day.

## 58 Head of a Bovine Goddess

Painted wood

Height 46.5 cm; width 44 cm

Dynasty 18, reign of Amenhotep II

Thebes, Valley of the Kings, tomb of Amenhotep II (KV 35)

CG 24630

## 57 Panther Base for a Statuette of Amenhotep II

Coniferous wood and resin
Height 27 cm; length 70 cm
Dynasty 18, reign of Amenhotep II
Thebes, Valley of the Kings, tomb of Amenhotep II (KV 35)
CG 24621

This elegant panther was carved of coniferous wood and covered with a layer of resin. The legs and tails were worked separately and attached to the body with tenons. A master craftsman gave this powerful creature a sinuous strength and a sense of movement: Even in its damaged condition, the muscles seem to flow beneath the supple skin. It is one of two panthers found in KV 35. Similar pairs were found in the tombs of Tuthmosis III, Tuthmosis IV, and Tutankhamun, and a single panther was discovered in the tomb of Horemheb. As indicated by the tenons on the back of this example, these panthers were originally parts of larger figural groups. Comparable figures (left) from the tomb of Tutankhamun show the king wearing the white crown of Upper Egypt, holding a staff and a flail, and standing on a rectangular platform that rests on the back of the panther.

In religious contexts, the panther seems to be connected to the sun, perhaps helping to guarantee its daily journey through the sky. The groups from Tutankhamun's tomb have been interpreted as hunting pairs, possibly forming a set with two figures of the king on a papyrus skiff, symbolizing the hunt in the marshes. The panther can serve, like other felines, as a mother goddess, and thus protect the king. When seen carrying the king on its back, the panther could also represent the fierce goddess Mafdet, who traveled with the king to the beyond and killed snakes and scorpions that tried to prevent him from completing his journey. In the Netherworld texts, Mafdet helps the sun god to kill the great snake Apophis. By placing this figure in his tomb, Amenhotep II was placing himself under the protection of this powerful goddess and acting to aid the sun god and thus insure the perpetuation of the cosmos.

## 62 Shabti of Tuthmosis IV

Faience

Length 18.5 cm; width 5.5 cm; depth 3.3 cm

Dynasty 18, reign of Tuthmosis IV

Thebes, Valley of the Kings, tomb of Tuthmosis IV (KV 43)

CG 46161

beard. A uraeus serpent, symbol of royalty, protects the king's forehead. Like most shabtis, this figure is mummiform, its arms crossed over its chest and each hand holding an ankh sign, the symbol for life. The inscription on the body and legs, engraved and then filled with yellow coloring, is a variant of Spell 6 from the Book of the Dead. This is the most common inscription found on shabtis, and promises that the figure will work in the Afterlife in place of the king.

Eighty-eight shabtis (funerary figurines) of varying size, appearance, and material, were found in this king's tomb. Fifty-seven were made of serpentinite or calcite and inscribed with Spell 6. These all wear the nemes headcloth and hold ankhs in each hand. A sandstone example also wears the nemes and bears Spell 6, but has empty hands. The remaining thirty are of wood and faience and are distinctly different: They wear tripartite wigs and their hands are completely enveloped by their wrappings. Some bear Spell 6, but others are simply inscribed with the name of the king. Five additional shabtis were also found; these were dedicated to a son of the king's named Webensenu.

Many shabtis from the tomb are similar or identical to this one. Others wear the tripartite wig and a broad collar. In a new development from this reign, model tools frequently are painted directly onto the figures. Most of these shabtis carry hoes in each hand and have a seed basket hanging on their backs.

Thirty faience shabtis were excavated from the tomb of Tuthmosis IV, most in a chamber next to the hall that held the sarcophagus. The majority are of blue glazed faience, although several are white or violet. This (above) is one of the best examples. The blue is of a beautiful, luminous hue, and the glaze is remarkably even. Details are brushed on in black paint. The features are delicately modeled, eyes are large and slightly tapered at the outer edges, and the mouth is smiling gently. The king wears the royal beard (with a squared-off end) and the nemes headdress topped by a uraeus, and is in the typical mummiform pose. His empty hands emerge from the bindings to cross on his chest. Instead of the shabti spell, this piece bears the name and titles of the king: "The good god, Lord of the Two Lands, Menkheprure, true of voice, beloved of Osiris."

The serpentinite shabti (right) represents Amenhotep II in a striped nemes headdress and a divine

## 63 Shabti of Amenhotep II

Serpentinite

Height 22.5 cm; width 7.5 cm; depth 4.9 cm

Dynasty 18, reign of Amenhotep II

Thebes, Valley of the Kings, tomb of Amenhotep II (KV 35)

CG 24206

T his sun-dried clay brick, surmounted by a mummiform figure of date-palm wood in a tripartite blue wig, was found in a niche in the north wall of the sarcophagus chamber in the tomb of Tuthmosis IV. White cloth envelops the figure so completely that not even the hands are free. The face is yellow, perhaps suggesting that it is female, and the eyes and brows have been outlined in black. The word for northern, *meheyt*, is inscribed on the front end of the brick. On the top surface, arranged in six horizontal lines, is part of Spell 151 of the Book of the Dead: "One who is coming in order to grab, never will I let you grab (me); One who is coming in order to attack, never will I let you attack (me); It is I who will grab you; it is I who will attack you; I am the protection of the Osiris, king Menkheprure, son of Re, Tuthmosis, true of voice." The figure is thus designated as a protector of the king, identified as deceased because of his association with Osiris, ruler of the dead, and because he has earned the epithet "true of voice" a reference to his successful passage through the Hall of Judgment.

Niches in the south, east, and west walls of the same chamber contained three additional bricks topped by a "pedestal of the magical flame" (a reed torch), a jackal (a figure of Anubis, god of the dead), and a djed pillar (symbol of stability), respectively. The inscriptions on these objects also come from Spell 151, protecting the king against dangers that might attack from any of the cardinal directions.

It has been suggested that bricks were also used in childbirth: The pregnant woman squatted, each foot on two stacked bricks. After the baby was born, he or she was set on a platform made by placing the bricks together. Thus magical bricks may also refer to the moment of birth, helping to ensure the perpetual regeneration of the king.

Magical bricks were a standard part of the funerary equipment of royalty and the high elite during the New Kingdom. They appear during the reign of Tuthmosis III in a private context and die out after the 20th dynasty. The first royal examples come from the tomb of Amenhotep II.

64  Magical Brick of Tuthmosis IV
Statuette: painted wood
Height 18.3 cm; width 4.2 cm; depth 3.2 cm
Brick: dried clay
Height 5.5 cm; width 7.5 cm; depth 16.0 cm
Dynasty 18, reign of Tuthmosis IV
Thebes, Valley of the Kings, tomb of Tuthmosis IV (KV 43)
CG 46042

DISMANTLED CHARIOTS, RITUAL COUCHES, BOXES, CHESTS, AND OTHER FUNERARY FURNITURE LIE IN PILES IN THE ANTECHAMBER OF TUTANKHAMUN'S TOMB.

# The Discovery of Tutankhamun

*There are 62 tombs in the Valley of the Kings, most in the eastern of the two main wadis. Of these, approximately 26 were carved for kings, and the others, many of which are now anonymous, were made for highly favored courtiers. The necropolis police, hired by the royal house, were relatively effective until the late New Kingdom.*

**B**ut then, despite the best efforts of the kings and their officials, the royal necropolis was at first randomly, and then systematically, violated.

In the centuries following Akhenaten's revolution, the priests of Amun regained much of their former power. By the late 20th dynasty, they were strong enough to challenge the pharaohs for control of Egypt. The end of the New Kingdom was marked by a civil war that raged between the holders of the High Priesthood of Amun at Thebes, once a royal appointment and now a hereditary office, and the rightful descendents of the earlier kings, based in the north. Eventually the country was divided politically between the two houses, which were related to one another through blood and marriage. By this time, Egypt had lost its empire, and with it the access to great wealth and resources that it had enjoyed during much of the preceding centuries.

In the first years of this complex era, the High Priests of Amun decided to begin consolidating the burials of the New Kingdom pharaohs. This served two purposes: to protect the ancient dead, whose tombs could no longer be guarded effectively, and to collect materials to fund military campaigns and supply burial equipment for the current rulers. Under official orders, specially appointed scribes combed the Theban hills for royal and private tombs, leaving graffiti behind them. Under their supervision, the royal tombs, along with the mummies of the kings and queens, were methodically stripped of precious metals and other reusable materials left behind by earlier thieves. After they were stripped, the bodies were carefully rewrapped and labeled, in most cases with the name of the king or queen and date of the "restoration." They were then taken and reburied, along with leftover items such as funerary papyri and shabtis, in a series of caches meant to keep them safe from further predation.

## Early Explorations in the Valley of the Kings

The rocky hills of Thebes hid their secrets well: Over the centuries following the fall of the pharaohs, the tombs in the Valley of the Kings were lost from view. Little is known about explorations that may have taken place before 1708, when the first recorded European visitor, a French Jesuit priest named Claude Sicard, found ten of the royal tombs open. In the wake of

Howard Carter, with Arthur Callender and one of the Egyptian supervisors behind him, opens the doors of the golden shrines that surrounded the sarcophagus of the king.

(From left to right) Hortense and Arthur Weigall, Theodore Davis, and Edward Ayrton pose in the Valley of the Kings.

Napoleon's expedition to Egypt (1799-1801), a team of French scientists carried out intensive explorations in the Valley; these men copied a number of the wall reliefs and paintings in the accessible tombs and published them in their monumental *Description de l'Égypte*.

The early 19th century saw a surge of interest in the Theban necropolis, especially the royal valley, with Italian strongman and engineer turned adventurer-archaeologist Giovanni Belzoni leading the way. With the cracking of the hieroglyphic code in 1822 by Jean-François Champollion, the field of Egyptology was born and a new breed of scholars worked tirelessly to shed light on the lives of the ancient kings and their subjects. However, there were no rules or regulations governing their activities, and Europeans and Americans systematically pillaged the land, taking statues, mummies, and even the reliefs from temple and tomb walls. In the 1850s, an energetic and competent French scholar named Auguste Mariette founded the Egyptian Antiquities Service, and some important objects began to stay in Egypt.

One summer in around 1871, members of a native Egyptian family called Abd al-Rassul made a spectacular find: a cache of royal mummies from the Golden Age of Egypt. There are many versions of this story, but all agree that one of the three Abd al-Rassul brothers was tending his goats in the Theban hills when he stumbled across the hidden tomb. Many of the most famous kings of the New Kingdom were there, including Ahmosis, Amenhotep I, Tuthmosis I, II, and III, Seti I, Ramses II, and Ramses III. With them were some of their queens and princesses and the bodies of later priests and their families.

The Abd al-Rassul brothers kept their secret for about ten years, entering the tomb infrequently and selling only minor artifacts on the black market. However, by the early 1880s, the Egyptian Antiquities Department had gotten wind of the find, and one of the Abd al-Rassuls eventually led the authorities to the tomb. On July 6th, 1881, representatives from the Antiquities Service, including Kamal Pasha, the first great Egyptian Egyptologist, and Emile Brugsch, entered the cache and found approximately 40 mummies and coffins, along with shabtis, papyri, and other objects.

They cleared the tomb over the course of only two days, and on July 15, 1881, a steamer arrived to take the mummies and their trappings to Cairo. As the great kings and queens of the Golden Age sailed north to their new home, the people of Luxor lined the riverbanks to mourn their ancestors. Their reception in Cairo was not quite so dramatic, however—the customs register had no category for mummies, and so they entered the city as salted fish.

A second cache, this time containing 11 or 12 royal mummies, was found in 1898 in the tomb of Amenhotep II by Victor Loret, then head of the Antiquities Service. Tuthmosis IV, Amenhotep III, and many of the Ramesside kings who ruled near the end of the New Kingdom were there, and Amenhotep II still rested inside his massive sarcophagus. In a side chamber of this tomb were three unlabelled mummies. One, nicknamed "the Elder Lady," is thought by many to be Queen Tiye, although others have suggested that she is Nefertiti; the second is a young boy, perhaps the son of Amenhotep II known to have been buried in the tomb; and the third has recently and publicly been identified as Nefertiti, although there is no good evidence for this.

Work in the Valley of the Kings from 1902 to 1914 was dominated by a rich American businessman named Theodore Davis. In return for funding excavations, Davis expected a share of the artifacts. The first archaeologist he hired was Howard Carter.

Lord Carnarvon (second from left) and his daughter, Lady Evelyn Herbert, arrive at the Luxor train station on November 23, 1922. On Lady Evelyn's left is the governor of the province.

Born in London in 1874, Howard Carter was a sickly child. His father was a successful artist who trained his talented youngest son in the techniques of drawing and painting. When he was 17, Carter was hired to go with British archaeologist Percy Newberry to Middle Egypt as a copyist; while there, he developed a new style that became the standard for epigraphy in Egypt. Soon after this, he went to work with William Flinders Petrie at Tell el Amarna.

Over the next decade and a half, Carter became a trained archaeologist, learning the most current techniques of excavation, reconstruction, and recording. In 1899, the head of the Antiquities Service appointed him Chief Inspector of Upper Egypt; in 1902, Davis hired him to supervise excavations in the Valley of the Kings. In his first season, Carter found the tomb of Tuthmosis IV. He then began work on KV 20, a tomb long known but never properly excavated. Carter believed that this tomb belonged to the great female pharaoh Hatshepsut; it was quite possibly the first tomb in the valley, and may have been carved originally for Tuthmosis I.

In 1904, Carter was promoted to a new post in the north of Egypt, and his replacement as Chief Inspector of Luxor, James Quibell, took over as Davis's excavator. Fortune smiled upon the pair, and less than a year later, the tomb of Tutankhamun's likely great-grandparents, Yuya and Tjuya, saw the light of day for the first time in millennia. It would seem that Davis was not an easy man to work for, and Quibell and Davis soon ended their partnership. He was succeeded briefly by Arthur Weigall, and then by an experienced excavator named Edward Ayrton, whose methodical explorations of the valley led to a number of important discoveries, including the mysterious Tomb 55.

Among the small finds made by Ayrton were some tantalizing traces of Tutankhamun himself. First to emerge, in the winter of 1906, was a faience cup inscribed with the king's name. The next year, the team found a pit containing a number of large pottery jars filled with miscellaneous materials, including a miniature mummy mask (cat. 41). One lid was covered with a fringed scarf dated to year 6 of Tutankhamun.

Frustrated with Davis's refusal to publish properly, Ayrton resigned from his post in 1908, and Davis hired a man named Ernest Harold Jones. In 1909, Jones found another trace of Tutankhamun and his successor Ay: a small undecorated rock-cut chamber whose contents included pieces of gold foil from chariot fittings and an alabaster shabti. Jones died in 1911 and was replaced by Harry Burton, who made no major finds.

## Howard Carter and Lord Carnarvon

Despite the many fabulous finds made in the Valley of the Kings in the years leading up to 1914, both the tomb and the mummy of King Tutankhamun were still missing, which led Carter to believe that his tomb might still be intact. Davis's finds convinced him that the tomb was still hidden in the royal valley.

By 1922, Carter had been working for George Edward Stanhope Molyneux Herbert, fifth earl of Carnarvon, for over a decade. Their association had begun during a lean period for the archaeologist, several years after he had resigned from the Antiquities Service over an unpleasant incident with a group of drunken tourists at Saqqara. Lord Carnarvon was in Egypt for his health—he had been sickly since being injured in a car accident—and had recently taken up excavation at Thebes. His first season had yielded little of interest, but his second produced an important historical tablet (known as the Carnarvon tablet), which bore on one face a schoolboy copy of the Kamose stela from Karnak, describing this king's battle with the Hyksos. The next season, he hired Howard Carter, forming a partnership that would make history.

## The Search Begins

In their first years together, Carter and Carnarvon could not work in the Valley of the Kings, as the concession was still held by Davis. In late 1914, tired and sick, the 77-year-old American gave up the valley,

believing it had yielded all of its secrets. He died soon afterward, never knowing he had missed the greatest treasure of all by a matter of yards. Carter and Carnarvon lost no time in acquiring the concession. In early 1915, the team began systematic clearance of the tomb of Amenhotep III in the western wadi. Although this had been explored earlier, they found a number of miscellaneous artifacts. Over the next few years, the Great War forced Carnarvon to stay in England and kept Carter busy as a diplomatic courier. In 1916, Carter excavated an unused tomb built for Hatshepsut while she was Tuthmosis II's queen.

In 1917 Carter and Carnarvon were granted the concession to the eastern valley and began clearing the wadi down to the bedrock. One of their main goals, although they kept it to themselves, was to find Tutankhamun. Carter decided to concentrate his forces on the area where Davis had found materials relating to Tutankhamun. Well funded by Carnarvon, he was able to hire large crews of over a hundred men each for their winter seasons. Little of interest emerged between 1917 and 1922 from the sand and rubble that covered the valley floor, and Carnarvon began to lose hope.

In the summer of 1922, Carnarvon called Carter to his castle in England, and told him that he could not continue to support his work in the Valley of the Kings. Carter was not surprised, and offered to stake his own money for the next few months. Impressed by his dedication, Carnarvon agreed to finance one more season.

Carter arrived with a small team in the Valley of the Kings in late October 1922. They began work in the only place still unexplored, a triangular area below the tomb of Ramses VI covered by a bed of limestone chips and ancient workmen's huts.

On November 1, 1922, Carter quickly recorded the huts, and then ordered his workmen to sink a trench right through them. Three days passed in feverish activity, as Carter drove his men to make every moment count.

## Finding Tutankhamun

On the morning of November 4, 1922, a young boy arrived at the site with jars of water for the workers loaded on the back of his donkey. These jars had

Carter carefully cleans the hardened unguents from the innermost coffin of Tutankhamun, still resting inside the second coffin.

rounded bases, and had to be set into the sand to stay upright. The boy was making a hole for the first jar when his hand brushed against stone. Investigating further, he found the top of a step cut into the bedrock.

Soon afterward, Carter arrived at the excavation and found that the atmosphere had changed. The men usually sang as they worked, but this morning everyone was quiet and the air was heavy with anticipation. Carter directed his workmen to clear away the sand from the first step, revealing the beginning of a stairway of the type often found in 18th-dynasty tombs. Legend has it that Carter ran back to his tent, and arrived just in time to see the good-luck canary he had brought with him from England being eaten by a cobra! By late the next day, working feverishly, the workmen had uncovered a flight of steps leading to a doorway blocked with stones and plaster. Stamped on this

surface was the Jackal-and-Nine-Captives seal of the necropolis guards, but no royal name was visible.

At first it may have seemed that the blocking was intact, but close inspection revealed an area in the upper left-hand corner that had been replastered and resealed. This told Carter that robbers had violated the tomb in antiquity, but that something important remained to make it worth resealing. Making a small hole, Carter looked through into a descending corridor filled with rubble. Curbing his impatience, he ordered his men to refill the stairway and sent a telegram to Lord Carnarvon saying:

AT LAST HAVE MADE WONDERFUL DISCOVERY IN THE VALLEY, A MAGNIFICENT TOMB WITH SEALS INTACT; RECOVERED SAME FOR YOUR ARRIVAL; CONGRATULATIONS!

Lord Carnarvon and his daughter, Lady Evelyn Herbert, sailed as soon as possible from England. On November 24, after three weeks of suspense for Carter

Carter and Callender wrap one of the guardian statues of Tutankhamun, found next to the entrance to the Burial Chamber, in preparation for transport.

and his men, work began again. To the excavators' great delight, the name of Tutankhamun appeared almost immediately, stamped on the lower part of the doorway.

After the blocking had been recorded and removed, the workmen labored to clear dust and rubble from the corridor. The fill, which showed traces of at least two and perhaps three ancient robberies, contained fragments of wood and broken vessels of stone and pottery, along with mud sealings bearing the names of kings from Tuthmosis III through Tutankhamun.

At the end of the corridor was a second plastered doorway, again marred by evidence that the tomb had been breached and officially reclosed in antiquity. At 4 p.m. on November 26, Carter, with Carnarvon, Evelyn Herbert, architect Arthur Callender, and a small group of workmen standing anxiously by his side, made a hole in the doorway. Probing carefully with an iron rod, he found empty space beyond. After lighting a candle to check for the presence of noxious gases, he widened the hole and peered inside. It is hard to imagine the excitement that must have gripped the spectators. Carter records his reaction in the first volume of his popular publication, *The Tomb of Tut.ankh.Amen:*

> At first I could see nothing, the hot air escaping from the chamber causing the candle flame to flicker, but presently, as my eyes grew accustomed to the light, details of the room within emerged slowly from the mist, strange animals, statues and gold—everywhere the glint of gold. For the moment—an eternity it must have seemed to the others standing by—I was struck dumb with amazement, and when Lord Carnarvon, unable to stand the suspense any longer, inquired anxiously, "'Can you see anything?" it was all I could do to get out the words, "Yes, wonderful things."

Widening the hole, Carter inserted a torch. Caught in its light was a jumble of fabulous objects: four huge gilded couches with fantastic animal heads;

A life-size figure of Anubis as a super-jackal atop a gilded shrine guards the entrance to the Treasury. The king's canopic shrine is visible in the background.

boxes in all shapes and sizes; alabaster vessels; and much more.

Sometime after this first glimpse, Carter, accompanied at least by Lord Carnarvon and Lady Evelyn, made an unofficial exploration of the entire tomb. The first treasure-filled room was dubbed the Antechamber; to the west lay the Annexe, another storage area. In the north wall of the Antechamber, flanked by life-size figures of the king, was a blocked and plastered doorway breached at the bottom by a small robbers' hole. Carter enlarged this enough to gain entrance to the Burial Chamber beyond. This room was filled to within two feet of its walls with nested shrines of gilded wood: The first was open, but the second was intact. Beyond the Burial Chamber was the Treasury, guarded by a life-size super-jackal representing Anubis, god of the dead.

The tomb was formally opened on the morning of November 27, 1922. Official viewings were held over the next few days, attended by local officials, Pierre Lacau, then head of the Antiquities Service, and the journalist Arthur Merton, representing the *London Times.*

In early December, the Carnarvons sailed back to England, and Carter stayed behind to arrange matters for the next season. The tomb entrance was closed with timber and the stairway refilled. From Cairo came a steel gate and, most unusually for excavations of that era, a motorcar.

Carter assembled an expert team of English and American Egyptologists. Arthur Mace, his principal assistant, was invaluable for the first years of clearance and conservation. He was aided by Alfred Lucas, a chemist with the Antiquities Service. Chief photographer was Metropolitan Museum of Art archaeologist Harry Burton. For the many inscribed objects, Carter consulted the great British philologist, Sir Alan Gardiner, and American epigrapher Henry James Breasted. Arthur Callender, an architect and engineer who had long been a friend of Carter's, became part of his staff. These men were joined by Carter's first mentor, Percy Newberry, Newberry's wife, and by American draftsmen Walter Hauser and Lindsley Foote Hall.

Everything was ready by late December 1922. The team used a nearby tomb, that of Ramses XI, as a storeroom, and the tomb of Seti II as a photo and conservation lab; Tomb 55 became a darkroom. In line with the highest standards of the day, each object, both before and after it emerged from the jumble of treasures piled within the tomb, was carefully recorded and preserved before being packed for transport.

The first official press viewing of the tomb took place on December 22, and a frenzy immediately ensued. From the start, the public's interest was intense and unremitting. In January of 1923 Carnarvon gave the London *Times* a monopoly on breaking news. This turned out to be a mistake with far-reaching consequences.

The team cleared the Antechamber in two months. It was hard work, and progress was slowed by the many official visits and problems with the press, who were extremely frustrated by their lack of access to the tomb. Carnarvon returned to Egypt, but mostly seems to have gotten in the way and annoyed Carter—not an easy man at the best of times.

The Burial Chamber was officially opened on February 16, 1923. Carnarvon was nervous, afraid that the officials would notice the hole they had used to preview the chamber (now strategically hidden behind rushes, vessels, and a large basket), but all was well. Carter entered first, followed by Carnarvon and Lacau and then the others present, two by two. They came face to face with what seemed to them a solid wall of gold— the first of the massive gilded shrines.

The tomb was shut and sealed for the end of the excavation season on February 26, 1923. By the 14th of March, Carter was preparing to leave for Cairo. But then tragedy struck. A mosquito bite that Lord Carnarvon had cut open while shaving had become infected. On March 18, Evelyn wrote to Carter to tell him that her father (never robust since his car accident) was running a fever. By the next day, it was clear that he was seriously ill. Over the next few days, blood poisoning progressed to pneumonia, and Carter hurried to Cairo to support the family. In the dawn hours of April 5, 1923, the 57-year-old Lord Carnarvon died.

## Tutankhamun in Danger

After Carnarvon's death, Carter spent until mid-May in Luxor, packing the objects from the Antechamber for transport to Cairo, then went to England for the summer. In early October 1923 he was back in Egypt, ready to continue work. But there was trouble brewing and he was occupied until April of the following year dealing with competing newspapers, jealous colleagues, and a changing political climate.

The discovery of Tutankhamun had coincided with major political changes in Egypt. In April of 1922 the British Protectorate had been formally abolished. A new constitution was adopted, and Egyptian nationalism dominated the political landscape. The changed political situation had a significant effect on archaeology in Egypt. Before this time, artifacts discovered in Egypt were supposed to be the property of the Egyptian government, to be kept and displayed at home. If they were considered "duplicates" (not essential to the Egyptian collections), they could, at the discretion of the antiquities service, be awarded to their excavators. In addition to expecting a share of the artifacts they discovered, foreign excavators to some extent treated their concessions as their own to do with as they pleased; Carter, now on behalf of Lady Carnarvon, was no exception.

Carter did not want a constant stream of visitors, official and otherwise, interrupting the work at the tomb, and so he proposed that the team be allowed to work in peace for a time, and then to suspend activities when it was convenient to let visitors in. Arthur Merton was now part of Carter's staff, and the plan was for him to send bulletins to the *Times* in the evening and then to the Egyptian press the following morning. In this way, Cairo and London would announce any news at about the same time.

Negotiations commenced in October 1923. The Service announced that it would require an Egyptian inspector to be on hand at all times during work in the tomb. This seems absolutely necessary now, but it was new at the time, and contrary to the way Carter was used to working. Relations were so difficult that at one point, the Antiquities Service threatened to take over the tomb. Work continued, but slowly.

By the beginning of January 1924, Carter had decided that the team was ready to open the doors of the remaining shrines. On January 3, the doors of the inner shrines were opened, revealing a massive, beautifully carved sarcophagus of quartzite. On the 5th, Lacau sent his congratulations. But the same day, the government brought two complaints: that Carter had allowed a second representative of the *London Times* to enter the tomb without official permission; and that no Egyptian inspector had been present when the shrines were opened. Neither accusation was true, but Carter's troubles were not over.

When they discovered the tomb, Carnarvon and Carter fully expected to be awarded a share of the objects. From a tomb filled with thousands of spectacular artifacts, they could reasonably look forward to taking away with them many significant pieces. On January 10th, Lacau wrote a letter to Carter implying that the tomb and its entire contents were the property of Egypt (again, something that seems obvious now, but came as a great blow in 1924). The tone of this letter was so upsetting to Carter that he retained a lawyer, and war between the archaeologist and the Antiquities Service was unofficially declared.

In early February, Carter met with Lacau and Morcos Pasha Hanna, the new Minister of Public Works (under which the Antiquities Service lay), to work out arrangements for the official opening of the sarcophagus. The date set was February 12, 1924. On that day, Hanna sent a message to Carter outlining the program that was to be carried out at the tomb for the next few days. Carter was offended by both the tone and the terms of the letter, but the opening proceeded. At about 3 o'clock in the afternoon, the great lid was raised. Inside the sarcophagus, the team could see the outlines of a coffin covered with brittle linen shrouds. They were sure that Tutankhamun himself lay inside.

The plan was for the press to have a viewing, and then for the wives of Carter's collaborators to be permitted a special visit to the tomb. Late on February 12th, someone in the government decided that the visit of the wives should not be permitted. Carter was furious. At 12:30 in the afternoon, he put up the following notice:

"Owing to impossible restrictions and discourtesies on the part of the Public Works Department and its Antiquities Service, all my collaborators in protest have refused to work any further upon the scientific investigations of the discovery of the tomb of Tut.ankh.amen. I therefore am obliged to make known to the public that, immediately after the Press view of the tomb this morning, between 10 am and noon, the tomb will be closed, and no further work can be carried out."

The outermost coffin of Tutankhamun represents the king in an unusual version of the nemes headcloth. A uraeus and vulture, wrapped in a wreath by the funeral party, guard his brow.

This was a rash and ill-considered move. Among other things, Carter had left the sarcophagus lid suspended in a temporary fashion, having expected plenty of time to secure it properly. He complained that he had been forced to shut down the work. The Egyptian authorities retaliated by accusing Carter of negligence, and the situation rapidly disintegrated.

Carter began legal proceedings against the government, requesting apologies from the government and Lacau for the disrespect they had shown the wives of his colleagues. Hanna responded by canceling Lady Carnarvon's concession. He ordered Lacau to open Tutankhamun's tomb and the nearby tombs being used by the team and ensure the safety of the artifacts. Lacau invited Carter to help supervise, but Carter refused. On

Two life-size figures of the king, one in a nemes headcloth and the other in the khat headdress, were found flanking the entrance to the Burial Chamber. The partially dismantled blocking to the chamber can be seen here, with the outermost gilded shrine visible behind.

February 23rd, Lacau had his officials cut open Carter's padlocks and proceeded to carry out his minister's orders. Carter responded by bringing a second lawsuit.

In early March, the Minister offered terms for a new concession under the condition that Carter sign a waiver stating that he would never make any claim on the objects from the tomb. Both Carter and Lady Carnarvon agreed, and it seemed that matters might be resolved.

At the beginning of April, an inventory was taken of all the materials contained in the various storage and workshop areas. In the tomb of Ramses XI, the committee found a Fortnum and Mason box containing an exquisite painted head representing Tutankhamun as Nefertem rising from a lotus. Carter claimed that the piece had been found in the fill of the descending

corridor, but had not yet been fully registered. It is still unclear whether or not Carter was trying to steal this piece: It was not mentioned in the first volume of his publication, and he seems even to have forgotten it. Regardless of his motives or intentions, the result was that the government's suspicions were aroused.

A new administration came to power in 1924, and Carter was allowed back into the tomb. On January 7th, 1925, he agreed that the British team would repeat their renunciation of any claim on the tomb's contents; in return, the Egyptian government promised to be generous to Lady Carnarvon. On January 22, 1925, Carter saw the tomb for the first time since the debacle of the previous year. Things were a mess. The worst casualty was a huge gold-spangled linen pall that had been draped over the inner shrines, which he and Mace had painstakingly prepared for conservation. This had been left outside, and had been destroyed by the elements. Nonetheless the team cleaned things up, and worked until late March. In the next season, the winter of

1925-26, the coffins were opened. The young king was there, his mummy, for the time being, intact.

## The Curse of the Pharaohs

Clearance and conservation work continued with many interruptions until 1932. The most difficult season had been the winter of 1928–29. Mace had died, and Lucas and Burton were both taken seriously ill. These events reignited public speculation about "The Curse of the Pharaohs."

The demise of Lord Carnarvon less than six months after the opening of Tutankhamun's tomb caused some people to believe a curse was attached to the tomb. Newspapers reported that his death had been caused by mysterious forces unleashed from the mummy and its trappings; at least one even went so far as to mistranslate a text inscribed on a mud brick found before the Anubis shrine in the Treasury: *I will kill all of those who cross this threshold into the sacred precincts of the royal king who lives forever.* In reality, this text reads in part: *I am the one who prevents the sand from blocking the secret chamber.* (Translation by David Silverman)

Proponents of the Curse reported that the lights in Cairo went out at the precise moment of Carnarvon's death. His son added to the mystery by recounting that his father's dog, still at home in the family castle, let out a pitiful cry at the moment of its master's death, and then died also.

In fact, there were no real mysteries surrounding the death of Carnarvon. He died of blood poisoning and pneumonia triggered by an infected mosquito bite. The lights in Cairo may well have gone off when Carnarvon died, but the electrical system in Egypt was extremely unreliable in that era. There are no independent witnesses to the death of the dog.

But the Curse had been born, and soon acquired a life of its own. Newspaper reporters attributed every accident or death possible to it. Anyone who had visited the tomb and then died anytime soon was said to be a victim of the Curse. A radiologist on his way to the tomb died before he arrived; this was laid at the Curse's door. An Egyptian prince living in London, who had nothing to do with Tutankhamun and had never been to the tomb, murdered his wife; he was said to have been affected by the Curse. Even the early death at 42 in 1832 of Jean François Champollion, the decipherer of hieroglyphs, was retroactively put down to the Curse of the Pharaohs.

In reality, the mortality rate of the people most closely associated with the tomb was very low. For example, Carter himself lived until 1939 and died at the age of 65, and Lady Evelyn died in 1980 at the age of 79. Still, after 75 years, the phrase "Curse of the Pharaohs" still fascinates the public and Hollywood producers. Fortunately, there is no such thing.

## Carter's Legacy

The 1929–30 season was occupied by negotiations with the Egyptian government over the amount of compensation due Lady Carnarvon for her family's investment. In the early summer of 1930, the government paid the Carnarvons over £35,000 pounds sterling for their investment, of which Carter received about £8,500.

Finally, in February 1932, the last objects were sent to Cairo. Asked immediately afterward what his plans were for the future, Carter said that he would search for the tomb of Alexander! Unfortunately, although he would live for seven more years, Carter's health was poor, and he accomplished little else of note.

After his death, Carter's executors found a number of objects from the tomb in his possession. He or Carnarvon may have taken them early in the clearance, before they knew that there would be no division of the finds, or he may have stolen them later. It was decided immediately that these would be returned to Egypt. World War II interfered, but eventually the pieces were returned, becoming part of the Tutankhamun collection now housed at the Cairo Museum.

Carter gained a great deal of recognition through his discovery, but his relationship with the Egyptian government never recovered. At the Egyptian Museum, where there are monuments to famous archaeologists such as Mariette and Ahmed Pasha Kamal, a tribute to Carter has never been erected. However, with all his mistakes, he made a spectacular discovery and did an excellent job of clearing the tomb and conserving the artifacts. The Supreme Council of Antiquities is planning to honor him by making his house at el-Qurn, Castle Carter, into a museum dedicated to his memory.

STATUES OF TUTANKHAMUN AND ANKHSENAMUN AT LUXOR TEMPLE

# Tutankhamun, King of Egypt

*Tutankhamun, or Tutankhaten as he was then called, was born into luxury and privilege in about the tenth year of Akhenaten's reign. We know from a single fragmentary inscription that he was a king's son "of his body" (i.e. a prince), but his father is not named, and his parentage is still debated by scholars.*

His father was most likely either Amenhotep III or Akhenaten; Tiye, Kiya, Sitamun, and even Meritaten are mentioned as possible mothers. The young prince would have grown up with the royal family at Amarna. He was married either before gaining the throne or very early in his reign to the third of Nefertiti and Akhenaten's six daughters, Ankhsenpaaten. A number of objects from Tutankhamun's tomb bear the queen's name alongside the king's, and others are decorated with scenes of intimacy between husband and wife, similar in style and iconography to images from Amarna but otherwise novel in Egyptian royal art. Along with their ritual meanings, these scenes may provide evidence for real affection, even love, between the royal pair.

At the death of Akhenaten, the throne may have passed briefly to Smenkhkare. It is also possible, however, that Smenkhkare reigned only as a co-regent, and died before Akhenaten. The identity of this ephemeral king is another of the great mysteries of the Amarna period. Was he Akhenaten's brother, or his son? Was he Tutankhamun's elder brother, or even his father? Is the mummy in Tomb 55 the body of this king? Or was he a she, yet another incarnation of Nefertiti?

Sometime soon after Akhenaten's passing, Tutankhaten ascended the throne of Egypt. His coronation would have been a great affair, full of pomp and pageantry. Surrounded by courtiers and high officials, the young king would have been presented with a child-sized crook and flail, representing the power and responsibility of his new office. The priests presumably would have set on his head the crowns of Egypt, including the low red crown for Lower Egypt and the high white crown for Upper Egypt, the blue crown, the khat headdress, and the striped nemes headcloth. His brow would have been protected by the hooding cobra, Wadjet of the north, and by the vulture, Nekhbet of the south. Once the celebrations were complete, the boy was officially ruler of an empire that stretched across much of the known world.

Early in his reign, Tutankhaten began to move away from the Amarna religion, back to orthodox belief in Amun-Re and his pantheon. By his second year, the king and his queen had changed their names to Tutankhamun and Ankhsenamun, and the Amun temples at Thebes had been reopened. His artisans began to

The Golden Throne of Tutankhamun depicts the king and queen (perhaps originally Akhenaten and Nefertiti) under the rays of the Aten. The king's original birth name, Tutankhaten, was inlaid on this throne, and later changed to read Tutankhamun.

restore the name of the old god where it had been hacked out by Akhenaten's minions. Many statues and reliefs were carved for Amun's glory—with representations of the deity and his consort bearing the faces of the boy king and his young queen—and Amun's priests regained much of their former power.

Although they did not abandon Amarna completely, members of the royal family spent most of their time at the traditional administrative capital of Memphis, which had remained important even during the Amarna period. There are few remains from Tutankhamun's reign at Memphis, but a villa built for the young king has been excavated near the Great Sphinx at Giza, where the New Kingdom pharaohs traditionally hunted and did their military training. This residence would also have been used during religious festivals celebrated for the cult of the northern sun god. The king and queen went regularly to Thebes as well, where they performed key roles in the many religious festivals staged there.

## Head of the Government

Since he was still a child, Tutankhamun was particularly dependent on his advisors. The man closest to him seems to have been the "deputy of the king in the entire land," Horemheb ("Horus is in Festival"). This powerful man was also Commander in Chief of the army and Overseer of All Works. Another key figure was an elderly man named Aye, who was fanbearer on the right hand of the King and Commander of the Horses. Thought by some to have been Queen Tiye's brother, and perhaps also Nefertiti's father, he held the ambiguous title of God's Father, which is thought perhaps to refer to royal fathers-in-law. Aye and Horemheb most likely took principal responsibility for major decisions during Tutankhamun's minority; both later became pharaohs themselves.

Tutankhamun's treasurer was Maya, who was buried in the Memphite necropolis at Saqqara. Carter suggested that he was responsible both for readying Tutankhamun's tomb for the burial and for restoring it after thieves violated its sanctity. Maya donated two funerary figures to his king's equipment. Another official, Nakhtmin, gave the king five beautiful wooden

shabtis. Possibly Aye's son, Nakhtmin was a military commander under the young king.

The highest officials in the royal administration were the viziers. There were two of these, one each for the north and south: Under Tutankhamun, these were Usermont and Pentu. The king's Viceroy of Kush, Amenhotep-Huy, was responsible for the province of Nubia and thus for the flow of gold from the south into the royal coffers. These men, along with many others, performed the tasks that ensured the effective day-to-day running of the empire.

## Head of the Army

Tutankhamun was the last of a line founded by warrior pharaohs. The empire built by the early Tuthmosids had enjoyed stability and relative peace under Tuthmosis IV and at least part of the reign of Amenhotep III, but during the reign of Akhenaten the situation in the Near East changed dramatically. The Amarna Letters are full of references to chaos and turmoil, and reflect changing balances of power. In them, brother kings beg for alliances and gold, and vassal kings plead with the Egyptian pharaoh for protection from their neighbors.

On the northern edges of the Egyptian empire, the Hittite kingdom had risen to challenge the might of the Mitanni, once Egypt's enemy but now tied to it firmly through the bonds of diplomatic marriage. Sometime during the reign of Akhenaten, the Hittites took over the Mitanni's holdings in northern Syria, and then exploited the resulting local unrest to usurp the northernmost of Egypt's territories. Either Akhenaten or Smenkhkare seems to have attempted to retake this area, but was evidently defeated, as reflected in the words of Tutankhamun himself: "If an army [was] sent to Djahy (in western Asia) to broaden the boundaries of Egypt, they had no success…"

Wall scenes in the tomb of General Horemheb at Saqqara hint at military conflict during the reign of Tutankhamun with the three principal enemies of the Egyptians: the Nubians, the Hittites, and the Libyans. These reliefs show military encampments as well as prisoners of war, in some cases along with women and children, being presented to the tomb owner. Although in some ways these are very specific (for example, the

Tutankhamun, in a chariot, singlehandedly defeats an army of Nubians in a scene from a large painted chest found in the Antechamber of his tomb.

captured leaders have very distinctive features), they may simply be magical images representing the eternal victory of the Egyptians over their foes. Traditionally the pharaoh would have led the army himself, but most scholars are undecided (if the events are even real) about whether Tutankhamun marched himself or if Horemheb went in his stead. However, fragmentary battle scenes from Thebes, currently being studied by W. Raymond Johnson, suggest that the young king did in fact fight at least one major battle and led the Egyptian troops into battle himself.

Whether or not he actually went into battle, Tutankhamun was trained from youth to be a warrior. Six chariots were found in his tomb, at least one of which was a lightweight training or hunting vehicle. He would have been accompanied in most situations by a charioteer, but would also have been taught to drive his own horses. The New Kingdom pharaoh's weapon of choice was the bow, and Tutankhamun was buried with almost 50 of various types and sizes, many of them showing signs of use. Several were child-sized. There were also arrows of various sorts, some of the type used for war, and others for training or hunting. Included with Tutankhamun's equipment were two linen slingshots, over thirty boomerangs and throwsticks (used for both hunting and battle), thirteen clubs, two swords, and two daggers. In addition to an exquisite ceremonial corselet of flexible gold scales inlaid with glass and semiprecious stones, the king had a leather cuirass and eight shields, four ceremonial and four functional.

Although his tomb equipment certainly indicates that military prowess was one of his major concerns, we can never know how strong Tutankhamun was, or how skilled in the arts of war. Some scholars have suggested that he was not physically strong. He was buried with 130 sticks and staffs of various sorts, some ritual and some clearly used, and he is shown sitting in many

This mockup of
Tutankhamun's tomb in
the Valley of the Kings
shows model views of the
king's sarcophagus, three
nested coffins, and four
nested shrines above.

Scribes record prisoners of war in a scene from the tomb of Horemheb at Saqqara.

contexts, such as hunting birds, where he should normally be standing. Regardless of the reality, the message, echoed time and time again on the objects in the tomb, was that the king was victorious over all enemies. This was an essential part of the royal dogma: By defeating those who threatened Egypt and its divinely ordained role as ruler of the known world, the pharaoh was taking on the role of the god Horus, mythical defender of the cosmic order. Horus in turn functioned as a delegate of the creator god, ensuring that the universe would be eternally created and the cycle of life would continue forever.

## Head of the Church

As king of Egypt, lord of the Two Lands, Tutankhamun was also high priest of all the gods. At the outset of his reign he worshipped the Aten, but he soon turned back to the traditional gods. A stela from Amarna on which the king still bears the name Tutankhaten shows him with Amun and Mut; soon after this was carved, he changed his name and began the return to Thebes. We cannot know what prompted his return to orthodoxy—true belief, fear of the power of the Amun priesthood, the desire of his advisors, or simply convenience.

Tutankhamun's own rhetoric, perhaps composed by Aye or Horemheb (and eventually usurped by the latter), is preserved on a monument from Karnak. In this

"Restoration Stela," he claims: "The temples of the gods and goddesses from Elephantine to the Delta were destroyed, their sanctuaries allowed to decay. They had become rubbish heaps, overgrown with weeds.... The land was in sickness, the gods had turned their backs...." He goes on to describe how he "rose upon the throne of his father" and immediately determined to do something about the situation.

He fashioned images of Amun, Ptah, and the other gods out of electrum and semiprecious stones, rebuilt and endowed their temples, and made offerings, paying for it all out of the royal treasury. The great burst of building activity described here is borne out at least in part by the archaeological evidence: Although much of his work was usurped or built over by later kings, monuments from his reign have been found at Karnak and Luxor, at Memphis and its necropolis, Saqqara, and in Nubia. A significant number of stone statues with the face of the young king—both as himself and in the guise of various deities—have survived the millennia, most from Thebes.

Tutankhamun and his queen must have spent much of their time in religious celebrations, traveling to Thebes, Abydos, and other major cult sites, where they would have stayed in the royal palaces associated with state temples. Officiating at the many festivals in the Egyptian calendar would have occupied much of their time.

The objects from Tutankhamun's tomb illuminate his life and inform us about his various roles as head of state, commander in chief of the army, and high priest of the gods. Although certain pieces were made specifically for the Afterlife, others belonged to the king during his lifetime and were placed in the tomb to serve him in his eternal existence. Most fascinating and poignant of these are child-sized artifacts clearly used by the king before he reached adulthood. Many other pieces were originally made for one or more other kings and then usurped for use in Tutankhamun's burial.

A figure of Tutankhamun in the red crown (cat. 65), along with two statues showing him on a papyrus skiff, raising his harpoon to strike, stands in front of the shrine that contained it. Arranged in the Treasury were 22 of these resin-coated wooden shrines, each containing one or more figures of the king or his gods.

Found in the Treasury, these two sculptures were packed inside statue shrines along with other ritual figures of the king and gods. Both were wrapped in linen shawls with fringes on the ends, leaving only the faces and feet uncovered. Although the two figures were not found in the same shrine, they complement one another. Each stands on a wooden base, left leg forward in the traditional male striding pose. Each holds a flail, symbol of royal power, in the right hand, and a curved staff, emblem of the king as shepherd of the people, in the left. (This staff is often seen in its abbreviated form, as in cat. 70.). A broad collar covers neck and shoulders, a pleated kilt folded into a sporran in front hangs low over the hips, and sandals of bronze covered with gold adorn the feet. Both figures have inlaid eyes and eyebrows of colored glass, and both are inscribed: "The good god, Nebkheprure, true of voice."

The major difference between the statues lies in their crowns. The figure on the left wears the so-called "white crown" of Upper Egypt, a tall conical cap symbolizing rule over the southern Nile Valley. It is interesting to note that an alloy of copper and gold has been used to gild this crown, giving it a reddish tint. The second figure wears the "red crown," low flat headgear that identifies the king as ruler of the Delta. Each crown is adorned with a bronze uraeus.

Stylistically, neither face is thought to be Tutankhamun's. The bodies bear the hallmarks of the Amarna Period, with visible breasts, narrow waists, and slightly bulging bellies. It is generally believed that these originally belonged to another king. Some scholars have suggested that they were made for Akhenaten early in his reign, then put aside at the time of his changes in religious dogma and move to Amarna; others believe that they were made for Nefertiti, or, if he was a separate king, for Smenkhkare.

According to the Egyptians' own view of history, their country was once two lands: the Delta, or Lower Egypt, and the Nile Valley, or Upper Egypt. A king called Men (Greek Menes) is credited with unifying these two lands and creating the Egyptian nation. This king is a historical figure, and has been convincingly identified as Aha, first king of the 1st dynasty. Although the archaeological record tells a somewhat different story, demonstrating that the unification was both more gradual and more complex, even the earliest Egyptian kings proclaimed this myth of unity from duality, and many paired symbols, such as the red and white crowns, expressed this concept. Other examples are the cobra of Lower Egypt (the goddess Wadjet) matched with the vulture of Upper Egypt (Nekhbet), and the papyrus of the Delta paired with the lotus or lily of the Nile Valley.

---

65  Tutankhamun as the King of Upper Egypt
Gilded wood
Height 62 cm; width 13.5 cm
Dynasty 18, reign of Tutankhamun
Thebes, Valley of the Kings, tomb of Tutankhamun (KV 62)
Carter 296b

66  Tutankhamun as the King of Lower Egypt
Gilded wood
Height 63 cm; width 13 cm
Dynasty 18, reign of Tutankhamun
Thebes, Valley of the Kings, tomb of Tutankhamun (KV 62)
Carter 275b

This jewel-like shrine, found in the Antechamber (above), is made of wood covered with gold foil inside and gold leaf outside. It sits on a silver-plated sledge. The door was closed with two bolts. Inside is a foil-lined back pillar engraved with prayers wishing Tutankhamun a long life and an ebony base carved with two small footprints. A precious-metal statue may once have stood here; alternatively, the footprints themselves may have magically represented some aspect of the king's being.

The shrine is decorated on all sides with names, titles, and images of Tutankhamun and his queen, Ankhsenamun, engraved in repoussé. The inscriptions identify the king and queen as beloved of a number of gods. Prototypes for many of the scenes had been in the repertoire of tomb decoration since the Old Kingdom; others seem to be based on scenes found more commonly in temples. The king, who most often wears a low-slung kilt with pleated front panel, is depicted in a number of different crowns and a wide assortment of regalia. The queen is always dressed in a transparent robe and a sash, but otherwise wears a variety of wigs and crowns. In many of the scenes, the focus is on the interaction between king and queen: for example, the seated king receives a lotus from his wife, or pours water into her hand as she kneels at his feet. On one side, the king is active, shown fowling in the marshes or shooting ducks with a bow and arrow. In these scenes, his queen accompanies and assists him.

Most of these scenes have sexual overtones that link them with regeneration, resurrection, and the desire for eternal life. The king shooting his bow or pouring liquid can both be seen as metaphors for ejaculation, as the verbs for shooting, pouring, and ejaculating share a common stem. In another play on words, the verb for "throw," as the king is doing in the fowling scene, is the same as the word for "beget." Ducks are potent sexual symbols, as are lotuses, oils, and necklaces. By symbolically impregnating his wife, who stands in for the great goddess, the king thus insures his own perpetual rebirth as her son.

### 67  Golden Shrine of a Statue

Wood and gold foil

Height 50.5 cm; width 26.5 cm; depth 32 cm

Dynasty 18, reign of Tutankhamun

Thebes, Valley of the Kings, tomb of Tutankhamun (KV 62)

Carter 108

### Statue Base and Back Pillar

Wood and gold foil

Height: 24.8 cm; width: 5 cm; depth: 11.2 cm

Dynasty 18, reign of Tutankhamun

Thebes, Valley of the Kings, tomb of Tutankhamun (KV 62)

Carter 108a

Six chairs were found in Tutankhamun's tomb. This one, discovered in a pile of other furniture and boxes in the Antechamber, is small and apparently made for a child. In shape, it resembles the famous Golden Throne and the chair on which the king sits in a number of representations (such as on the Golden Shrine, cat. 67), with a slightly rounded and tilted back, bowed armrests, and a deep, doubly curved seat.

The back is decorated in an attractive geometric pattern with strips of ebony and ivory, and is reinforced with three vertical slats that have been attached to the top rail and seat. Each armrest is inset with gold foil: The insides are embossed with naturalistic scenes of vegetation, and the outsides portray a recumbent

caprid turning its head back to taste a plant. Patterns of running spirals or vertical lines border these panels. This decoration has been borrowed from the Syrian and Aegean repertoires, attesting to the cosmopolitan nature of art in the 18th dynasty.

The seat is formed of five slats and set on legs ending in leonine paws on high trapezoidal tenons plated with metal. The front claws of these paws are inlaid with naturally colored ivory; the ivory of the dewclaws has been stained red. Ivory papyrus umbels cap the struts between the legs. The various parts of the chair are held together with bronze rivets covered with gold.

There were ten footrests in the tomb, some associated with specific chairs and the others, including this one, loose. This simple example is made of a reddish wood inlaid with darker wood and ivory. It is constructed in a number of pieces held together with plugs. The decoration set into the top consists of two square panels rimmed with double frames of ivory and dark wood, each containing 11 horizontal stripes of alternating dark and light wood.

## 68 Child's Chair with Footrest

Chair
Ebony and ivory
Height 71.5 cm; width 40.6 cm; depth 39.1 cm
Dynasty 18, reign of Tutankhamun
Thebes, Valley of the Kings, tomb of Tutankhamun (KV62)
Carter 39

Footrest
Wood and ivory
Height 5.8 cm; width 37.4 cm; depth 21.7 cm
Dynasty 18, reign of Tutankhamun
Thebes, Valley of the Kings, tomb of Tutankhamun (KV62)
Carter 92

Egyptian kings are often shown in both two- and three-dimensional art with their arms crossed on their chests, holding a short crook in one hand and a flail in the other. These fundamental items of royal regalia are also held by Osiris, primordial king of Egypt and ruler of the dead. The king carried the crook and flail at his coronation and again on the occasions when he renewed his power, such as the yearly Opet Festival and the Sed Festival.

The abbreviated and wrapped form of the crook, originally a shepherd's tool, became a hieroglyph for "ruler." The flail, tentatively identified as a flywhisk, appears as a royal symbol early in Egyptian history, although it is also seen in the hands of private people, presumably in contexts where they were identified with the king or Osiris. Together, they could be interpreted as representing power and responsibility: the coercive might of the flail and the gentle guidance of the crook. They were a standard part of royal funerary equipment from at least the Middle Kingdom on.

Three crooks and two flails were found with Tutankhamun, the only examples of such royal regalia ever discovered. Both of the objects here were discovered in the Treasury, inside a cartouche-shaped box inlaid with the king's name (cat. 97). They are constructed of rods of copper alloy around which cylinders of dark blue glass and gold have been mounted; the beads of the flail are made of gilded wood, carnelian, and glass. Disks capping the lower ends of these pieces display the cartouches of Tutankhamun.

An additional crook and flail were found inside the cartouche-shaped box, and a third crook was discovered in a box in the Antechamber. The other flail and the crook from the Antechamber are significantly smaller than this set, measuring 13.2 inches (33.5 cm) in length. The caps of this smaller set are inscribed with the young king's original birth name, Tutankhaten. These were likely used for the coronation; their smaller size can be taken as evidence that the king was not fully grown when he ascended the throne.

ABOVE: The crook and flail, along with other objects, as found inside the cartouche-shaped box.

70  Royal Flail
Gold; copper alloy; glass; wood; carnelian
Length 42.9 cm; diameter 2.1 cm
Dynasty 18, reign of Tutankhamun
Thebes, Valley of the Kings, tomb of Tutankhamun (KV62)
Carter 269e

69  Royal Crook
Gold; copper alloy; glass; wood; carnelian
Length 43.3 cm; width 10.2 cm
Dynasty 18, reign of Tutankhamun
Thebes, Valley of the Kings, tomb of Tutankhamun (KV62)
Carter 269h

73 Ceremonial mace
Gilded wood
Length 81.6 cm; diameter of head 12.2 cm; diameter of shaft 3.5 cm
Dynasty 18, reign of Tutankhamun
Thebes, Valley of the Kings, tomb of Tutankhamun (KV 62)
Carter 233

Among the ceremonial weapons, fans, and staffs that filled the Burial Chamber were two decorated wooden maces. The head of this example (left) is engraved with a scale pattern. At the top of the shaft, five parallel lines imitate the ties with which a real mace head would have been held to the staff.

Maces were important weapons and symbols of kingship, first appearing in the archaeological record in the Predynastic era in elite tombs. The mace was an important icon in early royal art, held by the king as he triumphs over his enemies. The image of the king smiting his enemies remained in the royal repertoire until the end of the pharaonic period. After the mace passed out of use as a real weapon, it continued to be seen in ritual contexts. Part of the royal regalia, it was presented to the mummy or statue at the end of the Opening of the Mouth ceremony. Tutankhamun holds a mace in a scene on the northern wall of his tomb. Two life-size statues found flanking the entrance to the Burial Chamber also hold maces, perhaps identifying them as protectors of the dead. Both staff and mace symbolized the dominion of the king over foreign peoples and thus identify him as the guarantor of order in the cosmos.

This staff (right), one of 130 sticks found in the tomb, was found lying on a bed in the Antechamber, tied to three similar examples. Primarily of gilded wood, its body is engraved with alternating patterns of rosettes, feathers, and herringbones. The handle is in the shape of a captive Nubian enemy. This prisoner—his head, arms, and feet carved separately in ebony—is shown with his elbows tied uncomfortably behind his back in the traditional pose of the defeated enemy. He has large, deep-set eyes, a broad, flat nose, and thick lips. His hair is arranged in rows of short curls, and his large ears sport hoop earrings. Pleats and folds have been indicated on his short-sleeved tunic and calf-length skirt. To add to the indignity endured eternally by this foreign prince, his position on the crook of the staff meant that he would always be upside down. The base or ferrule of the staff is a papyrus flower of faience marked with the cartouche of Tutankhamun.

71 Staff with a Handle in the Shape of a Nubian Captive
Gilded wood and ebony; faience
Length 115 cm
Dynasty 18, reign of Tutankhamun
Thebes, Valley of the Kings, tomb of Tutankhamun (KV 62)
Carter 48c

72 Staff Bearing a Figure of the King
Silver, wood
Length 130.4 cm; height 8.4 cm; diameter of staff 0.95 cm
Dynasty 18, reign of Tutankhamun
Thebes, Valley of the Kings, tomb of Tutankhamun (KV 62)
Carter 235b

This is one of two matching staffs topped by small sculptures of the king wearing a knee-length kilt and the blue crown. This example is cast in silver and its counterpart is of gold. The two figures are quite similar in many aspects, but their facial features differ significantly: The golden figure seems to be that of a child wearing a placid expression, with a round, smooth-cheeked face, large eyes, long eyebrows, a snub nose, and full lips. In contrast, the silver figure is thought to represent an aged ruler, his face drawn, his eyes smaller and underscored by bags, his nose wider at the base, and his lips thinner and slightly turned down at the corners. The bodies are typically Amarna-style in their contours: plump, with a high waist and rounded belly. The crowns are more or less identical, and the kilts are similar, with small differences in detail, most significantly in that the golden king wears a sash on which his throne name, Nebkheprure, has been inscribed inside a cartouche. Both figures stand left leg forward, hands at their sides with the palms facing backwards in attitudes of prayer. This pose is more usually seen with figures wearing the kilt with starched trapezoidal front panel (cat. 86).

This staff and its golden mate were found between the walls of the outermost and second shrines in the Burial Chamber. Bundled together and wrapped with a length of linen, these two elegant and valuable items of uncertain function traveled to the Netherworld in close proximity to their owner. They have been compared to standards carried in ritual processions, but such standards are usually longer than these examples and are generally topped with sacred birds and animals or mummiform figures. It has also been suggested that the staffs are wands of some sort, or that they were used to mark out geographic locations during some type of ritual. Perhaps the young king carried them during his coronation, or perhaps priests used them during his funeral ceremonies. In any case, the figures display symbolism that connects them to the realm of the divine. The young king is golden, the color of the sun, and thus represents the sun god during his daily journey through the sky; the old king is silver, the color of the moon, and thus is connected with the deceased sun god as he travels through the Netherworld.

74  Silver Trumpet with Wooden Core
Trumpet: Beaten silver; gold
Length 58.2 cm; width 8.2 cm; thickness 2.5 cm
Core: Painted wood
Length 58.7 cm; diameter 8.2 cm
Dynasty 18, reign of Tutankhamun
Thebes, Valley of the Kings, tomb of Tutankhamun (KV 62)
CG 69850; Carter 175

Tutankhamun was buried with two trumpets, two *sistra,* and a pair of clappers in the shape of human arms inscribed with the names of Meritaten and Tiye. This trumpet, with its wooden core stored inside, was found in the Burial Chamber. The second trumpet, of copper alloy, was discovered in the Antechamber.

Tutankhamun's trumpets are the only such instruments to have survived from ancient Egypt. This one is of fine, thinly beaten sheet silver with a gold mouthpiece. The gently flaring bell, adorned with a narrow band of gold leaf at the end, has been engraved to resemble a stylized lotus blossom, with the king's cartouches placed so that they are right side up when the trumpet rests on its end. A trapezoidal panel, inserted later, has a vignette showing Amun-Re between Ptah and Re-Horakhti, historically three of the most important state gods of Egypt. In the wake of the Amarna heresy they became a trinity: Amun was the hidden spirit, Ptah was the visible body, and Re was the tangible being. The wooden core, which helped the delicate instrument keep its shape when not in use, echoes the decoration of the trumpet, with the petals of a lotus blossom in alternating blue, red, and green on its bell.

When he discovered this trumpet, Carter ". . . managed to get a good blast out of it which broke the silence of the Valley." A British trumpeter damaged it when he inserted a modern mouthpiece and played it on a live BBC broadcast in 1939; it has since been repaired but no longer sounds properly. It had a limited range of pitches in any case, with its only truly clear note the C above middle C. Trumpets were used in both military and religious processions, most likely to sound out rhythmic patterns.

Two sistra (cultic rattles) of gilded wood were found together on top of the cow-headed ritual couches in the Antechamber. Their slightly tapering handles each have eight facets; the tops are loops of gilded copper set atop square capitals. Three thin copper wires in the form of uraeus serpents, each hung with three diamond-shaped pieces of thin copper, have been threaded through each loop. When shaken, these rattles would have made a pleasant jingling sound. Wear on the bronze shakers indicates that they were used.

Sistra were used mainly by women and priestesses in cultic rites, and are most often associated with the goddess Hathor. For example, during her Beautiful Feast of the Valley, they were shaken to reanimate the ka of the deceased. Sistra were traditionally ornamented with Hathor heads, a practice temporarily abandoned during the Amarna period and then revived during Tutankhamun's reign. These sistra, then, may have been made during the reign of Akhenaten and then used during the young king's funeral ceremonies.

75  Sistrum
Gilded wood and bronze
Length 51.5 cm; width 7 cm; height 3.8 to 4.3 cm
Dynasty 18, reign of Tutankhamun
Thebes, Valley of the Kings, tomb of Tutankhamun (KV 62)
CG 69317a; Carter 76;

76 Dummy Folding Stool
Wood; ivory; gold
Height 37.5 cm; width 46.3 cm; depth 31.7 cm
Dynasty 18; reign of Tutankhamun
Thebes, Valley of the Kings, tomb of Tutankhamun (KV 62)
Carter 83

Twelve stools of six different types were among the many items of furniture in Tutankhamun's tomb. This is classified as a folding stool, although it cannot actually be collapsed. It was found in the Antechamber, set in front of the row of ritual couches.

Carved of wood painted dark brown to imitate ebony, and inlaid with ivory, the stool has a double-curved seat decorated to look as if it is made of cow or goat hide, with legs indicated at each corner and a tail hanging from one of the short sides. An ivory inlay engraved with wavy lines represents the tuft of hair at the end of the tail. The animal's "backbone" is inlaid in lighter wood down the center of the seat. The stool's crossed legs curve out slightly and end in goose heads, their mouths open to bite the horizontal bars, capped with gold, that form the base. The tongues of the geese are made of red-tinted ivory. The points at which the legs cross are also covered with gold, as are the ends of the nails that hold them together.

Real folding stools had seats of leather or animal skin, as is imitated here. Two functional examples were found in Tutankhamun's tomb; they are similar to this one in that they have legs that end in goose heads. Each had a leather seat and could be folded in half.

BELOW: **The two real folding stools found in Tutankhaumn's tomb**

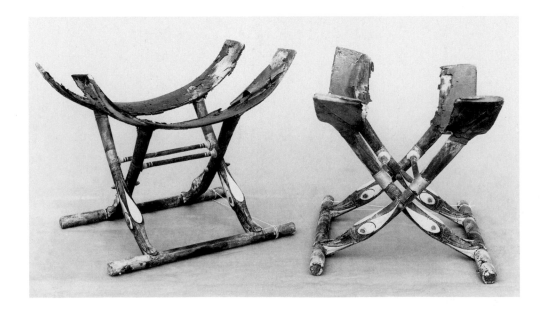

LEFT: Another fan from the tomb, discovered with its plumes intact

There were eight fans buried with the young king: one hand-held example and seven on staffs to be wielded by an attendant. All but one, which originally belonged to Akhenaten, bore the names of Tutankhamun. This unique example was discovered in the Burial Chamber between two of the gilded shrines. It consists of a long staff with a circular disk at the lower end and a support in the shape of a papyrus blossom, a petal drooping on either side, at the upper end, with a semicircular plate above. Both staff and plate are made of wood covered with beaten gold of a reddish hue; the plate is decorated in repoussé with engraved details.

On the front of the plate is the king in his chariot, pulled by two stallions shown in the flying gallop pose adopted from Aegean art, a hunting dog running beneath them. Behind the king is the anthropomorphized figure of an ankh holding a similarly shaped fan, cooling and shading the king as well as symbolically providing him with the breath of life. The king wears a short Nubian wig with uraeus, a broad collar, a corselet (an actual example of which was found in the Antechamber), a bracelet on one wrist and a wristguard on the other, and a pleated kilt that falls to his knees. The horses' reins are wrapped around his waist so he can steer the chariot. He aims his bow at two young ostriches in front of the horses' hooves: One of these has fallen; the other is still standing, but has been hit by two arrows. An inscription above the scene reads, "the good god, Nebkheprure, given life like Re forever"; before the king's face is written, "Lord of might."

The scene on the opposite side shows the successful outcome of the hunt. The king is still in his chariot, but his horses now proceed at a stately pace. Two attendants march in front of him, carrying the dead ostriches over their shoulders. A lengthy inscription, its vertical columns woven into the scene, praises his prowess at the hunt.

A text on the shaft claims that the fan commemorates a real event, a hunt in the desert east of Heliopolis (near modern Cairo) at which the young king killed the two ostriches that provided the fan's feathers. The fan was in fact discovered with ostrich plumes, alternately white and brown (originally 15 of each), attached to several of the holes that ring the upper surface of the plate. These had been badly gnawed by insects, and did not long survive the opening of the tomb. The ancient Egyptians valued ostriches for both their plumes and their eggs, which could feed up to eight people. Seen in the early periods of pharaonic history primarily in desert hunt and tribute scenes, they are known to have been domesticated by the Ptolemaic period.

Fans had practical uses, since the climate of Egypt is very hot and frequently airless, as well as symbolic meaning: To breathe was to live, and thus ankhs are often depicted fanning kings and courtiers and giving them the "breath of life." Fans were also used to shade their users from the burning sun.

## 77  Fan Depicting an Ostrich Hunt

Gilded wood
Height of shaft 105.9 cm; height of fan 10.5 cm; width of fan 18.8; depth 1.4 cm
Dynasty 18, reign of Tutankhamun
Thebes, Valley of the Kings, tomb of Tutankhamun (KV 62)
Carter 242

Eight shields were found in the Annexe of Tutankhamun's tomb. Four were relatively small and were functional, made of solid wood covered with antelope or cheetah skin and adorned with a central panel of gilded gesso bearing the names of Tutankhamun. The other four were larger and of open designs that would not be effective in battle, and thus are classified as ceremonial.

This shield, an example of the ceremonial type, depicts the king as a winged sphinx wearing a nemes headdress topped by the double crown (the headgear of Upper and Lower Egypt joined together). His body is bedecked with feathers, his folded wings are visible against his back, and a broad collar lies around his neck. His chin bears the false beard of royalty. His four paws rest on the prostrate figures of two Nubian enemies wearing gilded kilts. Behind the sphinx is an ostrich feather fan, on which a falcon, most likely to be interpreted as Montu, the Theban god of war, alights. On the upper arc of the shield is a winged sun disk, symbol of Horus of Idfu, protector of the king. A line of

rolling hills, the hieroglyph for foreign or desert lands, decorates the shield's lower edge.

An inscription before the sphinx-king reads, "The good god, who tramples the foreign lands, who smites the great ones of all the foreign lands; lord of might like the son of Nut, ferocious like Montu, who dwells in Thebes; King of Upper and Lower Egypt, Lord of the Two Lands, Nebkheprure, given life, son of Re whom he loves, Tutankhamun, like Re."

The king was, in theory, the leader of the Egyptian army. It was crucial that he be seen, at least symbolically, defeating his enemies. This served to protect Egypt magically from hostile neighbors, and thus secure the borders. The king also stood in as a delegate of the gods. As a winged sphinx, he was an incarnation of the sun god, and his headgear may associate him with the great creator god of Heliopolis, Atum. He is also linked with Montu, who is represented as a sphinx as well as a falcon. By vanquishing his enemies, symbols of chaos, the king was helping to maintain the proper order of the cosmos.

78  Ceremonial Shield
Gilded wood
Height 89 cm; width 54 cm
Dynasty 18, reign of Tutankhamun
Thebes, Valley of the Kings, tomb of Tutankhamun (KV 62)

reads, "I give to you life, dominion, and all health, Lord of Maat."

The lioness-headed goddess Sekhmet, consort of Ptah and goddess of war, sits behind Tutankhamun. Her face, arms, and feet are turquoise. She wears a long, tight-fitting net dress of archaic design, a broad collar, and a long, dark blue wig; a sun disk of carnelian rests upon her head. With her left hand, she touches the king on his shoulder; with her right, she holds a notched palm rib symbolizing millions of years. The caption before her reads, "Sekhmet, mistress of the sky, I am giving to you years of kingship for eternity."

The god Heh kneels behind Ptah, holding in each hand a notched palm rib. Above his head is a crypto-graphic writing of Tutankhamun's name. The space behind Sekhmet is filled by a figure of the king's ka, his spiritual double, holding an ostrich plume signifying maat in its right hand, and carrying a *serekh* (a niched façade often used to enclose royal names) surmounted by the Horus falcon wearing the white crown on its head.

The inlaid decoration of the wide bands that held this pectoral consists of paired cartouches of the king alternating with various symbols, including the god Heh holding two notched palm ribs, an ankh flanked by was scepters atop a basket, the hieroglyphs for "King of Upper and Lower Egypt," and a winged cobra.

The counterweight (left) is smaller than the pectoral, but equally elaborate. The king, still wearing the war helmet with attached ribbon, is dressed in a pleated kilt, broad collar, armlets, and wristlets. Seated on a low-backed throne, he holds a crook in his right hand. With his left, he reaches forward to grasp an ankh held out to him by a winged figure of the goddess Maat. Goddess and king are within a shrine formed by two lotus-shaped columns of green. From the lower edge of the counterweight hang strings of blue glass and gold beads, tiny golden fishes dangling from the ends.

This intricate pectoral of openwork gold and semiprecious inlay (right) was found within a box inscribed, "Gold jewelry for the funeral made for the bed-chamber of Nebkheprure"; the associated bands and counterweight were inside a cartouche-shaped chest (cat. 97). Clearly used for ceremonial occasions, this piece is adorned with intricately wrought figures inlaid with vibrant colors, creating the effect of a tapestry. Each carefully chosen element has symbolic meaning linked to both the king's coronation and his ceremony of rejuvenation, the Sed Festival.

In the center of the pectoral the king, clad in a knee-length golden corselet, armbands, and ribboned war helmet, holds the crook and flail. Although his arms and legs are the traditional reddish yellow of male skin, Tut-ankhamun's face is black, a color associated with fertility.

The standing king faces a seated figure of Ptah. The god's face and hands are turquoise, also a color associated with fertility and rejuvenation; his mummiform body is the silver of divinity. An inscription before the god, whose throne is set upon the hieroglyph for maat,

## 80   Inlaid Pectoral and Counterweight

Gold; silver; glass; semiprecious stones
Pectoral: Height 11.5 cm; width 14.1 cm
Dynasty 18, reign of Tutankhamun
Thebes, Valley of the Kings, tomb of Tutankhamun (KV62)
Carter 267q (Pectoral); Carter 269ij (Counterweight and bands)

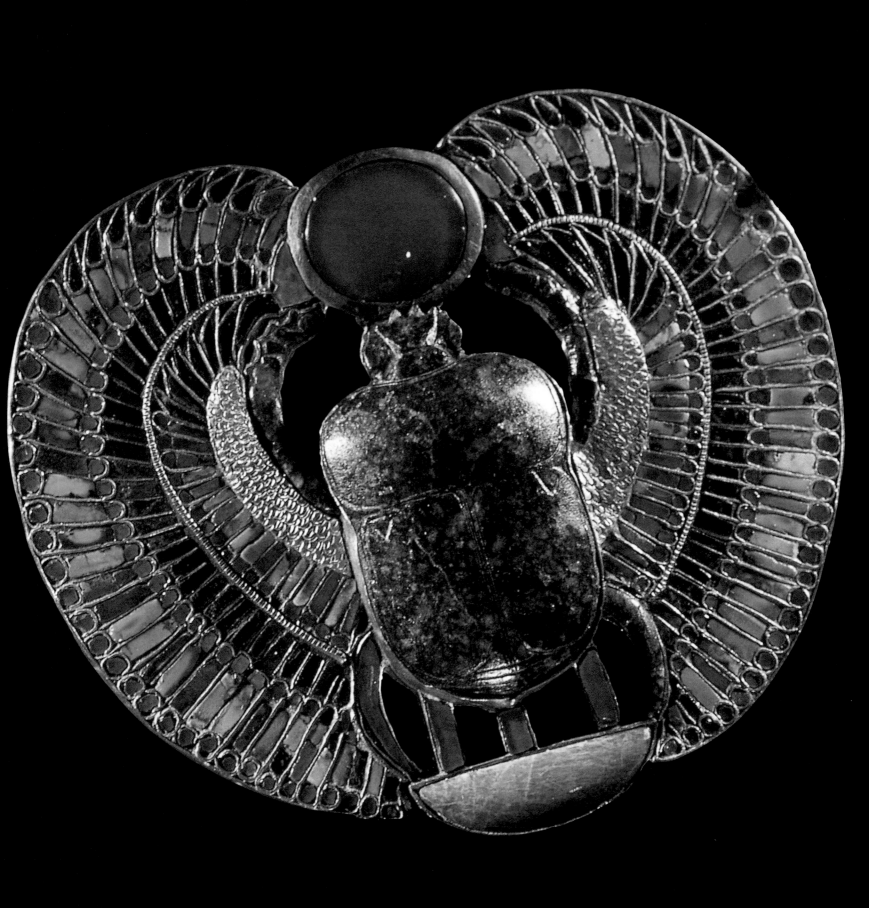

This vibrant jewel is a rebus for the throne name of Tutankhamun—Nebkheprure—which can be translated as "Re is the lord of manifestations." It was found, along with a number of other pectorals (jewels to be worn over the breast) within a chest in the Treasury. The framework and backing are of gold, with inlays of various semiprecious stones. At the bottom is a basket, the hieroglyph for "all" made of turquoise. Above this is a lapis lazuli scarab beetle meaning "creation" or "manifestation," with three vertical lines below to make it plural. A carnelian sun disk, symbol of the sun god Re, is pushed up and forward by the beetle's front legs. The scarab has beautifully detailed wings of carnelian, lapis, and turquoise, with the inner feathers in gold. They sweep up to the sun disk and down to the basket, giving the composition both movement and unity.

The back of the jewel is also beautifully wrought, engraved with details such as feathers. Attached to the center of the sun disk in back is a hollow tube, through which a chain would have been passed to hang the jewel around the king's neck.

The scarab was the symbol of the god Khepri, identified as the sun at dawn. As real beetles push balls of dung containing the eggs of their young across the ground, so Khepri was imagined both to be the sun and to push its disk across the sky. Perhaps due to the fact that young scarabs hatch from these balls of dung, seeming to create themselves, the scarab was also connected with regeneration and resurrection.

ABOVE: This object was found along with other jewels within an ebony and ivory casket in the Treasury.

81 Inlaid Pectoral Spelling out the Name of the King
Gold; semiprecious stones
Height 9 cm; width 10.5 cm
Dynasty 18, reign of Tutankhamun
Thebes, Valley of the Kings, tomb of Tutankhamun (KV62)
Carter 267a

Both of these gilded wooden ritual figures were discovered within shrines in the Treasury. The falcon-headed statue is identified on its base as the god Herwer (right), "the Great Horus," a sky god linked with the ascension of the king to the stars. When found, its mummiform body was wrapped in a linen shawl, a wreath (thought to be of sprouting barley) around its neck. Herwer's body has wide hips and sturdy legs. His tight-fitting costume is plain; at his chest he wears a broad collar and on his head a long, tripartite wig. His beak has been painted black and his eyes are inlaid with black glass. Around his eyes are cosmetic lines inlaid with blue and red glass; these mimic the markings of a real falcon and also form wedjat eyes, the sacred eyes of Horus.

The second figure is clearly identifiable as Ptah by its mummy wrappings and tight-fitting skullcap. It too was wrapped in a linen cloth, a wreath of pomegranate leaves around its neck. The cloth bore an inscription dating to Year 3 of the reign of the Aten, and thus was most likely leftover material brought from Amarna. The base is shaped like a throne platform, a hieroglyphic abbreviation for maat; on this base are the cartouches of Tutankhamun and the name of Ptah, described here as "Lord of maat."

The gilding on the god's narrow-chested, wide-hipped body has a high copper content, making it appear red; the gold of the face is more yellow. A broad collar hangs around his neck, and his costume has been engraved with feathers in a pattern now known by the Arabic term rishi. The god holds a was scepter, for dominion, along with an ankh for life and a djed pillar for stability. In temple scenes, gods are often shown offering these insignia to the king. Both these symbols and the god's divine beard are worked in a copper alloy. His eyes are inlaid with limestone and obsidian,

**79  Statue of Herwer (Horus the Elder)**
Gilded wood
Height 58 cm; width 14.5 cm
Dynasty 18, reign of Tutankhamun
Thebes, Valley of the Kings, tomb of Tutankhamun (KV62)
Carter 293a

his eyebrows and cosmetic lines are of blue glass, and his skullcap is of faience glazed in a rich cobalt blue.

Ptah, the tutelary god of Memphis and patron of artisans, was one of the most ancient gods in the Egyptian pantheon. Originally an earth god, he features as the creator god in the Memphite version of the Egyptian cosmology. With Amun and Re, Ptah was one of the chief gods of the Egyptian state, and was also important in mortuary religion. One spell from the Afterworld Texts, recited during the Opening of the Mouth ceremony, helped the deceased to become Ptah

**82  Statue of Ptah**
Gilded wood; faience; glass
Height 52.8 cm; width 11.6 cm
Dynasty 18, reign of Tutankhamun
Thebes, Valley of the Kings, tomb of Tutankhamun (KV 62)
Carter 291a

AYE PERFORMS THE OPENING OF THE MOUTH ON TUTANKHAMUN;
FROM THE NORTH WALL OF TUTANKHAMUN'S TOMB.

# The Glint of Gold Everywhere

*Suddenly, just as he was reaching young manhood, Tutankhamun*
*died. He most likely had recently taken the reins of the monarchy*
*into his own hands after years in the shadow of his advisors.*
*After almost ten years of an eventful reign, during which Egypt*
*underwent many crucial changes, the golden boy was dead.*

The king passed away without an heir. Two fetuses—one miscarried at about five months gestation and the other probably stillborn—were carefully buried with him in his tomb. These have been identified as female; most scholars believe that they were his daughters with Ankhsenamun. The royal couple had no living children.

The events immediately following Tutankhamun's premature death are shrouded in mystery. Egypt was almost certainly thrown into a state of turmoil. Some scholars believe that, as the most powerful figure in Egypt, General Horemheb should have succeeded Tutankhamun, but he did not: The next king was instead the elderly Aye. There are many possible reasons for this: Perhaps Horemheb was in the north defending Egyptian territory against the onslaught of the Hittites, and Aye took the opportunity to seize the throne. Perhaps Ankhsenamun preferred Aye to the younger general. Perhaps the two men had conspired to kill the young king, and Aye was rewarded with the throne. Or perhaps Aye was in fact the brother of Queen Tiye, and thus was considered the heir by blood.

Isis protects Tutankhamun in a scene from one of the gilded wooden shrines that surrounded his sarcophagus.

A fascinating glimpse into this moment in time has been preserved in the archives of the Hittites, found at their capital, Hattusas (in modern-day Turkey). These tell of a queen of Egypt, convincingly identified as Ankhsenamun, who wrote in great distress to the Hittite king Suppiluliuma. In her letter, she announces that her husband has died and asks Suppiluliuma to send her a son to marry: "My husband has died and I have no son. They say that you have many sons. You might give me one of your sons and he might become my husband. I would not want to take one of my servants. I am loath to make him my husband." The queen offers peace between Hatti (the land of the Hittites) and Egypt, saying that the two kingdoms could become one country.

Suppiluliuma was immediately suspicious. No Egyptian princess, much less a queen, had ever wed a foreigner, although Egyptian kings had for several generations been marrying the sisters and daughters of their allies. So he sent an envoy to Egypt to investigate the situation first-hand.

The envoy returned, along with a high-level Egyptian diplomat and a second letter from the queen, begging again for a prince. "I have not written to any other country, I have written only to you.... He will be my husband and king in the country of Egypt." What prompted the queen to take such an unprecedented step? Hatred of Horemheb or Aye? The knowledge that her husband had been murdered by one or both of them? Some combination of fear of the Hittites and common sense, coupled with a desire to create a lasting peace and an invincible empire? Whatever Ankhsenamun's motives, Suppululiuma was convinced and sent his son Zananza on the long journey south to Egypt. But before he reached Memphis, Zananza died, perhaps assassinated by forces hostile to the young queen.

Suppululiuma was furious. Back in Egypt, Ankhsenamun was apparently forced to marry Aye, as suggested by two faience rings that bear their names next to one another within cartouches. By the spring (late March, to judge from the fruits and flowers used in his funeral garlands), Tutankhamun had been laid to rest, and Aye had become pharaoh. After an exchange of letters in which the Hittite king accused the Egyptians of killing his son and attacking his country, Suppululiuma went on the offensive. Sending his army against Egypt, he won a great battle and carried prisoners back to Hattusas—bringing with them the Black Plague.

## The Burial of Tutankhamun

The Zananza episode must have taken place while Tutankhamun's body was being prepared for burial. Although it is generally assumed that the king died in January or even later, the chronology of the events described in the Hittite archives argues that he passed away in late summer. The traditional period for mummification and preparation of the body was 70 days, but Tutankhamun may well have spent several extra months in the mummification tent, the *per-nefer,* with the embalmers while the succession was under dispute.

The king's body would have taken about 40 days to desiccate and prepare for wrapping. It would have been laid on an embalming table and the viscera removed through an incision running from his navel to his left hipbone. Each organ was mummified separately and placed in a miniature coffin. The brain, which would hasten the process of decay if left in the body, was removed through the nose and resin was poured into the skull cavity. Natron packed around the body drew moisture from the remaining tissues, preventing it from decomposing.

The body was then carefully wrapped. Plugs of resin-soaked linen were placed in the eyes and nostrils. The head was shaved, coated with some sort of fatty material, then covered by a beaded cap (the cartouches on which contain the names of the Aten). The arms were bent and folded across the abdomen, left above right. Each finger and toe was wrapped individually and capped with a golden stall, and golden sandals were placed on the feet. Layered sheets of linen were bound to the front of the body as far as the knees. The penis was held to the body as if erect.

Within the linen sheets and bandages that enveloped the mummy were about 150 objects, most of gold. They included necklaces and bracelets of gleaming metal and semiprecious stone; pectorals; protective amulets of various sorts; bracelets; and two daggers, one of gold and the other of iron. Many of these objects were carefully placed according to the principles set out in the Netherworld texts, and were designed to ensure the magical transformation of the king.

Golden bands inlaid with glass and semiprecious stones were wrapped around the body and a human-headed bird (symbol of the king's ba, or spirit) placed above the royal abdomen. On the king's chest hung a scarab of black resin; flanking this were hands of gold, one clasping a crook and the other a flail. Necklaces were placed around the king's neck, and the royal diadem was placed on his head.

While the body was being prepared, Aye was readying the royal tomb. It is possible that Tutankhamun began a tomb in the Royal Wadi while still at Amarna: One partial cutting there has been tentatively assigned to him. When he went to Thebes, a tomb was started for him in the West Valley, near that of Amenhotep III. But he was not buried there—instead, Aye finished this large and clearly royal tomb during his short reign as pharaoh and used it for his own burial. Tutankhamun was interred in a small tomb in the royal valley. Of the type used for important private citizens like Yuya and Tjuya, this was rapidly transformed for the royal burial.

A reconstructed, cutaway view of the Burial Chamber of Tutankhamun shows the Antechamber to the left and the Treasury below right.

# The Tomb of Tutankhamun

The plan of Tutankhamun's tomb is simple. A stairway of sixteen steps leads to a doorway, from which a long corridor descends west into the bedrock of the Valley of the Kings. Beyond a second doorway lies the rectangular Antechamber, oriented north-south. From the southwest corner of this room an opening leads to a smaller chamber, dubbed the Annexe by Carter. In the north wall of the Antechamber is an entrance to the Burial Chamber. From the north end of the Burial Chamber's east wall, another door leads to the Treasury.

Like most other royal tombs of the 18th dynasty, only the Burial Chamber was decorated. The walls were prepared with a thick layer of plaster, then painted golden yellow, the color of the sun god. On the south wall, interrupted by the doorway, is an image of the king in the khat headdress. He is flanked by Hathor and Anubis, tutelary deities of the Theban necropolis. Hathor stands before him and offers an ankh to his nose, so that he can inhale the breath of life through his nostrils. Anubis stands behind him and places a hand on his shoulder. Behind Anubis (to the east of the doorway, and now in fragments) is Isis, welcoming the king to the Netherworld with pure water. Three minor gods of the underworld sit behind Isis. Above Tutankhamun, an inscription asks that he be given life "eternally and forever."

On the eastern wall is a scene illustrating the king's funeral. It shows a shrine draped with garlands and decorated with two friezes of hooding cobras, within which lies the king's mummy on a lion-shaped bed. The shrine is on top of a boat in which small images of Isis and Nephthys stand, their arms raised to mourn the king. This equipage in turn rests atop a sledge pulled by twelve men, labeled as the great nobles of the royal house; two of these, with shaved heads, are the king's viziers. As they drag the sledge, the pallbearers speak: "The Osiris, king, Lord of the Two Lands, Nebkheprure, to the West. They say in one voice, Nebkheprure, come in peace, O god, protector of the earth." Above the mummy is again the prayer for eternal life.

Three scenes occupy the north wall. First from the east is an unusual vignette depicting Aye, dressed in the leopard skin of a funerary priest and the blue crown that identifies him as heir to the throne, performing the ritual of the Opening of the Mouth on Tutankhamun. The king has taken the form of Osiris: He is wrapped like a mummy, holds the crook and flail, and wears the high white crown flanked by the feathers of maat. On his chest, his winged heart scarab is visible. According to Egyptian mythology, Horus took charge of the burial of his father, Osiris, and by doing so, secured his right to the throne of Egypt. Each crown prince was responsible for burying his father, and thereby presented himself to the country as the next Horus. By burying Tutankhamun, Aye proclaimed himself the legitimate heir and new king. The inscriptions above this scene reinforce this theme, with the two kings—deceased and living—identified with parallel titles and epithets.

In the center of the wall, the king is shown after his transformation into an effective spirit. He wears a short wig with diadem (cat. 112) and holds a straight staff, a mace, and an ankh as he faces the goddess Nut, who welcomes him with pure water. In the third vignette, the king. followed by his divine ka—his double—embraces Osiris, who reaches his hands out of his bandages to touch the king.

The west wall was decorated with images from the *Imy-Duat (What is in the Underworld)*. Below a single band of text is a register containing five gods, including Maat and Horus, leading the solar bark. Inside the bark, the sun god takes the form of the scarab beetle, symbol of rebirth. Male figures labeled as Osiris kneel on either side of the beetle, raising their arms to praise and protect him. The remainder of the wall is divided into twelve boxes, each of which contains a baboon. Known for their habit of facing the rising and setting sun, these creatures were identified by the Egyptians as minor deities who were active in the first hour of the night.

Taken together, these scenes served the same purpose as the decoration of the 18th-dynasty royal tombs before Akhenaten: to help guide the king on his successful journey to the afterlife and guarantee his eternal survival and perpetual rebirth. Stylistically, the images show the influence of the Amarna period, with sagging bellies and large almond-shaped eyes.

## The Burial

Once the tomb had been prepared and the body readied, the time had come for the funeral itself. This must have been an elaborate event, attended by the highest officials in the land as well as the royal family. Care would have been taken also to maintain some secrecy, in order to protect the enormous wealth buried with the king. One can imagine the procession—the mummy on its sledge followed by the canopic shrine and a long line of bearers with furniture, models, food, and the other equipment to be buried with the king— winding its way into the hidden folds of the Theban hills, the royal necropolis guards barring the way to profane eyes.

Although robbers later disturbed the contents of the tomb, and the necropolis guards made only a cursory attempt to put things back together, the way in which the tomb was discovered gives us some idea of how the ancient funeral party and priests originally left it.

We can guess that the Treasury, as the innermost room, was the first to be filled. Against the east wall, still on its gilded sledge, was the square canopic shrine of gilded wood, its sides protected by beautiful free-standing images of Isis, Nephthys, Neith, and Selket. Rows of ivory and wooden boxes filled with jewels and regalia, as well as resin-blackened shrines holding gilded statues of the king and various gods, filled the rest of the room. Model boats rested atop these boxes and shrines, and two chariots lay jumbled in a corner. Carefully mummified and placed in their own coffins were the two children of the king and his young queen. In front of the canopic shrine, as if to protect it, was a gilded head of the Celestial Cow, a linen shawl draped around its neck. Finally, a life-size figure of Anubis in the form of a super-jackal, resting atop a portable shrine, remained in the doorway to guard the room's contents.

The doorway from the Antechamber into the Burial Chamber was guarded by two life-size statues of the king, one wearing the bag wig (khat) and the other the nemes headdress. Neither statue was set square on its base: One was twisted slightly to the left and the other to the right, so that when the bases were against the wall, the figures would turn toward the viewer. Like the other ritual figures in the tomb, these statues of resin-coated and gilded wood were shrouded in linen shawls. The figure in the bag wig is labeled specifically as the ka of the king.

Photographs taken at the time of discovery show a basket and a pile of rushes in front of this doorway; it has been suggested that these were placed by Carter and Carnarvon to hide the evidence of their unofficial reconnaissance of the rooms beyond. Through the sealed doorway, filling the Burial Chamber, was the nest of shrines and coffins that protected the mummy of the king. At the time of the funeral, the huge quartzite sarcophagus in the center of the chamber would already have been in place. A low bed of solid wood, with the feet and head of a lioness, was placed inside this sarcophagus.

Some time after the extensive rituals of the Opening of the Mouth, the mummy was put to rest. Unguents were ladled with a generous hand over the body of the king. The head was also anointed and then covered with the magnificent mask of solid gold, inlaid with lapis lazuli, carnelian, quartz, obsidian, turquoise, and glass. The golden face of the king on this mask wears the nemes headdress and is protected by the cobra of Wadjet and the vulture of Nekhbet. On his chin is a braided and curled beard of divinity and around his neck is a broad collar. An inscription on the back of the mask asks for protection from various gods.

The body was set inside a solid-gold coffin weighing 245 lb (111.04 kg) and inlaid with semiprecious stones. This coffin was created as an image of Tutankhamun in the nemes headdress and divine beard. He wears a string of beads around his neck and a broad collar over his shoulders and chest, and holds a crook and flail. Wadjet and Nekhbet in the form of birds with outstretched wings embrace and protect the body. A collar of flowers, leaves, berries, fruits, and blue glass beads, all sewn onto a papyrus backing, was placed over the breast. The funeral party covered this coffin with a red linen pall.

The inner coffin was placed inside a second coffin of gilded and inlaid wood, also an image of Tutankhamun in the nemes headdress grasping the crook and flail. Laid over this coffin were another linen shroud and the remains of flower garlands. The outermost coffin was also made of wood, in this case cypress, overlaid with gold sheeting. Here the king is enfolded by the wings of Isis and Nephthys and holds the crook and flail in his

Tutankhamun embraces and is embraced by Osiris, ruler of the underworld, in a scene from the north wall of the Burial Chamber.

crossed arms. On his chin is the divine beard. The head-dress on the outermost coffin seems to be an unusual version of the khat, with a bag wig over the head and the ends of a long wig falling over the chest in front. This coffin was slightly too large for the sarcophagus, and its foot end had to be adzed so that the lid would close.

The sarcophagus itself was carved from a single block of golden yellow quartzite, a stone with strong solar overtones. It is rectangular, with a high cavetto cornice. The four tutelary goddesses of the dead (Isis, Nephthys, Selket, and Neith) are carved in high relief on the corners, their winged arms outstretched to surround the body of the king. Above a dado of alternating tjet amulets and djed pillars, symbols of Isis and Osiris respectively, are vertical columns of text, primarily spells chanted by the goddesses to protect the king, surmounted by a horizontal line containing more spells. A

recent study has demonstrated that the original decoration of this sarcophagus was quite different, and was completely reworked by Tutankhamun's artists. The lid, sloping and curved at one end to give the sarcophagus the shape of a shrine, is red granite painted yellow to match the base. This replacement lid was at one time cracked across the middle and repaired with gypsum.

The burial assemblage of Tutankhamun represents an enormous concentration of wealth. Not every piece was originally created for Tutankhamun himself: The second coffin and the mummy bands, like some other objects in the tomb, were taken from the burial equipment of the mysterious Ankheprure and perhaps also from materials originally made for Akhenaten.

Once the body had been placed in its nest of coffins and the lids lowered into place, four shrines of gilded wood were erected around the sarcophagus. These had been stacked in the Burial Chamber in sections to be assembled after the funeral. Each part was marked carefully with its proper orientation, but a decision was made at some point to reverse everything, so that the doors, supposed to be to the west, were instead to the east, near the entrance to the Treasury.

The innermost shrine was in the shape of the *Per-nu,* the prehistoric shrine of Lower Egypt. The outer walls are decorated with figures of the major mortuary gods and the ceiling adorned with the goddess Nut, incarnation of the sky; a spell from the Book of the Dead graces the inner walls. The next two shrines, like the sarcophagus itself, are in the form of the *Per-wer,* the shrine of Upper Egypt. The second is covered with vignettes, extracts from Egyptian religious texts, and processions of gods in sunk relief. On the third shrine from the inside is a portrait of the king before Osiris and Re-Horakhty as well as vignettes from the Book of the Dead. Between the outermost two shrines was a wooden frame over which had been draped a pall of coarsely woven dark brown linen. Sewn to this at regular intervals were large marguerites, flowers of gilded bronze, giving the whole, in the words of Carter, the appearance of a "night sky spangled with stars."

The outermost shrine filled the Burial Chamber to within two feet of its walls. The roof slopes up to each end and has been compared to the roof of the Sed festival pavilions. The shrine's sides and back panels are alternating *tjet* knots and djed pillars of gilded wood against a backdrop of intensely blue faience. On the doors are rectangular panels decorated with enigmatic figures in sunk relief. The interior is inscribed with excerpts from the Netherworld texts.

The shrines were closed with ebony bolts that slid inside large copper hoops coated with silver. Once the bolts were shot, they were wrapped with cord and coated with mud, then stamped with an official seal. Carter found only the seals of the middle two shrines intact.

The burial party left a number of objects in the narrow spaces between the shrine and the walls of the Burial Chamber, as well as between the walls of the nested shrines. These included 11 magical oars, a model Anubis fetish (thought to represent an animal skin filled with embalming solution), boxes and wine jars, weapons, several fans, and some elaborate alabaster vessels. A funerary bouquet remained in one corner.

Magical bricks were placed inside niches cut into the four walls of the Burial Chamber. Once these were in place, the niches were hastily plastered over and painted to match the surrounding scenes. In the south wall was a djed pillar; to the east an Osiris figure; to the north a reed torch; and in the west wall an Anubis figure. These bricks helped to protect both the tomb and the body, and were also connected with rebirth.

The Antechamber was filled with furniture and boxes, including four huge ritual couches, chairs and stools, boxes, alabaster vessels, dismantled chariots, and many containers full of mummified meat. Most of these were stacked against the south and west walls, with other objects scattered about— a total of 600 to 700 objects in all. Tutankhamun's bust (cat. 1) was found here, hidden behind a stack of furniture. Another important piece, discovered on the floor near one of the guardian statues, was a large painted box holding clothing evidently worn by Tutankhamun as a child. This has been nicknamed the "Hunting Box" because of the scenes painted on its sides and vaulted lid, which show the king in his chariot, hunting desert game and in symbolic battle against the Syrians and Nubians. Many items found in this chamber bore the names of other kings, including Akhenaten, Tuthmosis III, Smenkhkare, and Amenhotep III.

Over 2,000 objects were jammed together in the Annexe, the smallest of the chambers. To judge from its state when found, not only had thieves made a mess of the room, but the necropolis guards had cleaned up by jamming everything together haphazardly. The room held about 40 wine jars, almost as many alabaster vessels for oils and unguents, and basket upon basket of foodstuffs. On top of these were beds, chairs, stools, chests, and boxes. Most of the king's shabtis were here.

Although the tomb is significantly smaller than the usual royal sepulchre of this period, it contained 5,398 items, many of them made of or covered with gold. They cover all of the king's needs: his clothes, sandals, much of his jewelry (what was not taken by the thieves), jar after jar of unguent and oil, weapons and armor, his chariots, food, and all of the ritual figures and implements needed to guide him to the next world. His loved ones made sure that the young king would be fully equipped both for his journey to the Afterlife and for his eternal existence once he arrived.

## 83  Statue of Duamutef

Gilded wood

Height 52.5 cm; width 14 cm; depth 11.1 cm

18th Dynasty, reign of Tutankhamun

Valley of the Kings, tomb of Tutankhamun (KV62)

Carter302a

LEFT: Two ritual figures, both with human heads, were found inside their shrines.

This statue was found in the Treasury tomb. Like most of the other ritual figures, it was found wrapped in linen with only its face exposed. Identified by an inscription on its rectangular base as "Duamutef, living god," this deity was one of the four sons of Horus responsible for protecting the body and viscera. In typical Amarna fashion, this figure has ample hips and thighs and narrow shoulders. His hands are held together at the level of his sternum within a skin-tight garment (meant to represent mummy wrappings). He wears a broad collar and tri-partite wig with no part, and his ears, adorned with ear-rings, are visible in front of his wig. His face is a wide oval with a strong nose, full lips turned down slightly at the outer corners, and long-lobed ears pierced for ear-rings. Black-painted copper has been used as inlay for his eyes and eyebrows, and a beard of the same mate-rial has been attached to the god's chin.

A second statue of Duamutef, in this case with the head of a jackal, was discovered in a shrine that also contained a falcon-headed Qebehsenuef; these two figures were unusual in that they were not wrapped in linen shawls. Neither was inscribed. There were also inscribed figures of Imsety and Hapy, both with human heads.

In addition to their protective roles, these four sons of Horus aided the king in his transformation into an eternal god. Specifically, they helped the deceased monarch rise to the sky where he joined with the circumpolar stars, the heavenly bodies that never set. The ascension of the king to these stars was an ancient concept, dating back to the earliest religious spells that have survived from Egypt, the Pyramid Texts.

The presence of these and many other gods in Tut-ankhamun's tomb heralds the return to orthodox religion that took place during the rule of the boy king. The four sons of Horus, along with their protec-tive goddesses, had been proscribed during the later reign of Akhenaten. Here, they have returned to their original roles.

Gold, carnelian, obsidian, rock crystal, glass
Length 39.5 cm; width 11 cm; height 10 cm
Dynasty 18, reign of Tutankhamun
Thebes, Valley of the Kings, tomb of Tutankhamun (KV 62)
Carter 266g

Tutankhamun's canopic chest was divided into four hollowed-out sections. Inside each was a small coffinette representing a king in the form of a mummy; these, like the real mummy, were wrapped in linen and covered with resin. The miniature coffins are of beaten gold, exquisitely modeled and decorated with a feather pattern made with cloisonné inlays of colored glass and carnelian. The king, his eyes inlaid with obsidian and rock crystal, wears the nemes headdress protected by the vulture and cobra. On his chin is the divine beard (curled at the end), around his chest is a broad collar, and in his hands are a separately worked crook and flail. Two birds, one with a vulture's head and one with a cobra's head, embrace the king from the sides, their wings overlapping in front and back.

The coffinettes open horizontally from a seam running along the side. An image of one of the protective goddesses (in this case, Isis) decorates the inside of each lid. The trough displays spells designed to protect the viscera, including the first spell from the Book of the Dead. Within each coffin was a linen-wrapped bundle of dried viscera: liver, lungs, stomach, or intestines.

A line of inscription on the front of each coffinette records a spell spoken by the protective goddess, including the name of the son of Horus responsible for the contents. The inscription here reads: "Words spoken by Isis, I embrace with my two arms that which is therein, in order to protect Imsety, who is within, Imsety, the Osiris, king Nebkheprure, true of voice before the great god." The invocation of Imsety means that this coffinette contained the liver.

Like many of the objects in the tomb, the coffinettes appear to have been manufactured for another king. The face, although similar to Tutankhamun's, is slightly different, with fuller cheeks, a smaller chin, larger eyes, and a finer nose. They originally bore the name Ankhkheprure, Akhenaten's co-regent. This could have been either Ankhkheprure Neferneferuaten, perhaps to be identified with the great queen Nefertiti, or Ankhkheprure Smenkhkare, either yet another incarnation of Nefertiti or a male successor of Akhenaten.

BELOW: The tops of the coffinettes are visible inside the calcite canopic chest.

Against the east wall of the Treasury, facing west and reaching almost to the ceiling, was a nest of gilded shrines on a sledge. The outermost shrine was protected by free-standing figures of Selket, Isis, Nephthys, and Neith, traditional protectors of the body. (On Akhenaten's sarcophagus, Nefertiti had replaced these goddesses; their reappearance here is a mark of the return to orthodoxy.) A second shrine lay inside the first, and within this was a beautiful box carved of a single slab of Egyptian alabaster on a smaller sledge of wood covered with silver. When discovered, the box was draped with a linen pall. The four goddesses, carved in high relief on the corners, protected this chest. Inscriptions on the four sides of the chest repeat magical spells recited by the goddesses to protect the deceased king.

The interior of the chest was divided into four sections. A deep circular hollow, topped with a stopper in the form of the king's head, was carved into each one. All of these figures wear a nemes headdress defended by the vulture and cobra. Eyes, eyebrows, nostrils, lips, and ears have been painted delicately in black and red, and traces of paint also remain on the headdress,

especially on the protective deities at the brow. Although little color has been used, these details bring the royal face to life. On the shoulder of each stopper is a label indicating to which compartment it belongs.

There are subtle differences between the faces on these canopic stoppers (which are not completely identical, but which clearly represent one person) and the visage of Tutankhamun as seen, for example, on his mask and inner coffin. The eyes, although almond-shaped, are larger, the nose is slightly narrower, the face is wider and more square, and the chin less prominent. The face on these stoppers is probably that of Ankhkheprure, for whom a number of objects in the tomb were produced. How these pieces found their way into Tutankhamun's tomb is still a mystery. One explanation is that, for some reason, these pieces were kept in storage and never used for their original owner, perhaps because he/she died before Akhenaten and was buried with Atenist equipment: This and the other pieces are traditional, perhaps made toward the end of Akhenaten's reign when there may have been a partial return to orthodoxy. Alternatively, the pieces might have been made after the death of Akhenaten, but not used by their designated recipient because he or she had fallen into some sort of disgrace. Yet another theory holds that these objects were used in an Amarna burial, and then usurped by Tutankhamun when he moved its mummy to Tomb 55.

## 85 Canopic Stopper of Tutankhamun

Painted calcite

Height 24 cm; width 18.5 cm

Dynasty 18, reign of Tutankhamun

Thebes, Valley of the Kings, tomb of Tutankhamun (KV 62)

Carter 266e

ABOVE: The calcite canopic chest with all four stoppers in place.

This life-size statue of King Tutankhamun was discovered, along with a second, almost identical image (JE 38244, CG 42092), in the Karnak Cachette (p. 38). The two sculptures may have stood flanking a door or gateway in the great temple of Amun. Carved of gray granite, both depict the young king in the nemes headdress surmounted by a uraeus, wearing a knee-length kilt with a starched trapezoidal front panel. Tutankhamun strides forward, his sandaled feet set squarely on top of nine bows representing the enemies of Egypt, his hands resting in a gesture of worship on the front panel of his reconstructed kilt. The divine bull's tail, symbol of the king's virility and strength, is visible between his legs.

Cartouches on the back pillar identify the king as Tutankhamun. The face is clearly the young king's, with his regular features, full lips, and firm chin. His ears are pierced, a royal fashion associated with the Amarna period. The carving of the body, with a small waist and slightly sagging belly, also reflects the influence of the Amarna style. His legs are sturdy, with thick ankles. A screen between the legs supports the figure.

There are three inscriptions on the statue, two of which have been usurped by Horemheb. A formulaic text on the base asks for long life and calls the king (originally Tutankhamun and now Horemheb) beloved of Amun-Re; Horemheb's cartouche (again a usurpation) appears on the belt; and on the back pillar, which stops at the level of the king's shoulders, a text praising Amun-Re reads: "The perfect god, who founded Thebes, who passed perfect laws, and who upholds maat; Lord of the Two Lands, Nebkheprure, Son of Re, Lord of Appearances, Tutankhamun, beloved of Amun-Re, king of the gods." The laudatory text and the presence of this statue and its mate at Amun-Re's principal cult center are tangible evidence for the young king's return to Thebes and his dedication to the worship of the old gods.

86  Granite Statue of Tutankhamun

Gray granite

Height 155.5 cm; width 29.5 cm; depth 53.5 cm

Dynasty 18, reign of Tutankhamun

Karnak, Temple of Amun, Court of the Cachette

This one-third life-size statue of graywacke was found in the Karnak Cachette. The god, clearly identified by his costume as Amun, stands on a square base that is slightly rounded in front. He wears a low flat crown, a tight-fitting, knee-length kilt with an "Isis knot" amulet (perhaps a ritual girdle tie) hanging from its belt, a broad collar, armbands, and a corselet. Both arms are broken off below the elbow, but traces on the kilt show that they originally hung down by the god's sides. Also missing are the two tall feathers that would once have stood above the crown, as well as part of the divine beard (narrow and curled slightly at the end), which was once attached with a tenon.

The statue clearly dates to the Amarna aftermath. Two distinct artistic styles can be traced to this period, perhaps representing two different workshops. One style is more "Amarna" like, the male bodies featuring breasts and sagging bellies, the faces soft, with high cheekbones and full lips. The second, of which this is an excellent example, is more like the pre-Amarna style, with more muscular chests and flatter stomachs. The legs here are solidly muscled, with extremely thick ankles. Since so many pieces from Tutankhamun's reign were usurped by his successors, it can sometimes be difficult to assign pieces to a particular king. However, the god's features are thought to be modeled on Tutankhamun's: The almond-shaped eyes, wide nose, and full lips are characteristic of the young king, while the round face has a childlike aspect and the ears are large and protrude slightly.

87　Statue of Amun with the Features of Tutankhamun

Graywacke

Height 58 cm; width 14.5 cm

Dynasty 18, reign of Tutankhamun

Karnak, Temple of Amun, Court of the Cachette

JE 38049

This lovely ivory casket was found in the Antechamber inside a larger box of ebony. It is constructed of ten separate pieces, with hinges and foot caps of gold. The knobs on top and front are gilded; around these are wrapped the remains of the string that once held the box closed. A beautifully carved inscription within a rectangular field on the front of the box reads: "The Horus, Mighty Bull, Tutmesut (another of the king's names), the King of Upper and Lower Egypt, Nebkheprure, son of Re, Tutankhamun, ruler of the Southern Heliopolis, given life like Re forever." On the back, in high relief, is a column with a lily capital. Tutankhamun's throne and birth names appear again on the top, this time with different epithets: "King of Upper and Lower Egypt, Lord of the Two Lands, Lord of Appearances, Nebkheprure, son of Re of his body, Tutankhamun, living forever."

Carter found a number of miscellaneous pieces inside this box, including an ivory mirror handle, seven small shells, a winged scarab, and a damaged pendant. However, a hieratic (cursive) inscription on the top of the box reads: "Gold rings for the funeral procession." Although the box held no rings, eight gold rings were found wrapped in a knotted cloth inside one of the other boxes in the Antechamber. Perhaps the rings were originally inside this ivory box and were taken by the thieves who violated the tomb. When these robbers were caught, the necropolis guards put the stolen goods back in some semblance of order, but, as these rings suggest, were not careful to return objects to their original places.

ABOVE: These rings, perhaps originally placed inside this chest, were found elsewhere in the tomb.

88 Chest for Jewelry

Ivory

Height 13.1 cm; width 15.7 cm; depth 12.6 cm

Dynasty 18, reign of Tutankhamun

Thebes, Valley of the Kings, tomb of Tutankhamun (KV 62)

Carter 54ddd

101  Attached Pair of Vessels
Calcite
Height 28.8 cm; width 22.8 cm
Dynasty 18, reign of Tutankhamun
Thebes, Valley of the Kings, tomb of Tutankhamun (KV 62)
Carter 417

highly. Any contents from this flask might have been taken by the robbers, who typically emptied vessels of their precious oils and unguents. These were valuable commodities, as they were portable and could not be traced to their original source; because they quickly went bad, they were only worthwhile if taken soon after the tomb was closed.

The double vessel (left), found in the Annexe, was carved from a single solid block of calcite in the form of two amphorae set side by side. The two bases were carved and attached separately. Inside, only one cavity spans both vessels. On both rims are traces of the mud used to seal them, indicating that the vessel was filled before being placed into the tomb. The amphora was a shape introduced to Egypt from abroad, but the concept of the double jar was an Egyptian one, dating back to Predynastic times. Almost all of the stone vessels in the tomb had once been closed with stoppers or lids. Robbers removed them so that they could take the valuable oils and unguents. When the necropolis officials put the tomb back into a semblance of order after the robberies, they threw various small objects into some of these vessels.

The elegant shape and decoration of this large vase (right), discovered in the Annexe of the tomb, is similar to that of pottery wine jars of the 18th dynasty, especially of the Amarna period. Carved in one piece, it has an ovoid body tapering into a long elegant neck. It is inlaid with three bands of lotus petals hanging down from a narrow register of alternating black and white squares. The top and bottom bands are of dark turquoise faience and calcite; the middle band is of calcite and dark green faience. This and an almost identical bottle show signs of use, and may have been part of the furnishings of Tutankhamun's palace.

This vessel was empty when found, but may originally have held some sort of fat or oil. Such materials were an essential part of the funerary equipment, as they were in everyday life. Oil spoils very rapidly, so stone, which keeps out the heat, was a favored material for its storage. Oils and fats, from both animal and vegetable sources, were used for many purposes, from simple cooking to embalming. They were also used in the unguents and perfumes that the Egyptians prized so

89  Oil Vessel with Inlaid Decoration
Calcite
Height 65.8 cm; diameter 19 cm
Dynasty 18, reign of Tutankhamun
Thebes, Valley of the Kings, tomb of Tutankhamun (KV 62)
Carter 344

## 90 Cosmetic Container in the Shape of a Duck or Goose

Ivory

Length 9.8 cm

Dynasty 18, reign of Tutankhamun

Thebes, Valley of the Kings, tomb of Tutankhamun (KV 62)

Carter 54s

This ivory cosmetic dish, discovered in a box full of ritual vessels, is in the shape of a trussed duck or goose with its neck bent back in a graceful curve. The head, neck, and the lower part of the legs are stained black. The lid swivels open to reveal the hollowed-out space within; some sort of unguent or other cosmetic was presumably kept inside.

Quite a few cosmetic items were found in Tutankhamun's tomb, including several containers for kohl (eye paint), along with the sticks for applying it. There were also lumps of galena (lead sulphide), used to make black eye paint, malachite (hydrated copper carbonate) for green eye paint, and a gold ointment container for ritual use. The tomb also held many jars, mostly of calcite, that once contained oils and unguents. Cosmetics were important to the ancient Egyptians, who used them for practical, aesthetic, and religious reasons. Kohl, for example, helped to protect its wearer from sun and flies, and also enhanced the size and brilliance of the eyes.

Carter had a number of cosmetic containers in his possession when he died. They included one box in the form of a grasshopper, with movable wings for lids, an ointment spoon, and a pomegranate-shaped bowl with a swivel lid. In addition, he had two duck-shaped boxes identical to this one; these are not recorded in his notes, but he may have taken them from the tomb.

## 92 Unguent Vessel in the Shape of the God Bes

Faience
Height 9 cm, width 3.6 cm, depth 6 cm
Dynasty 18, reign of Akhenaten/Tutankhamun
Thebes, Valley of the Kings (KV 55)
JE 39660

The two figures are cleverly designed and appealing in their simplicity. The servant girl bends to one side to compensate for the weight of the large vessel she carries on one shoulder. Her face is attractive and placid, with no sign of strain. The figure of Bes is nicely balanced, with the god facing forward and offering a round bowl known as an omphalos. This deity was a composite creature with a stunted body, a lion's tail, and a grotesque face: he has flat features, a wide mouth from which his tongue protrudes, lion's ears, and a mane. Bes's primary function was to keep evil spirits

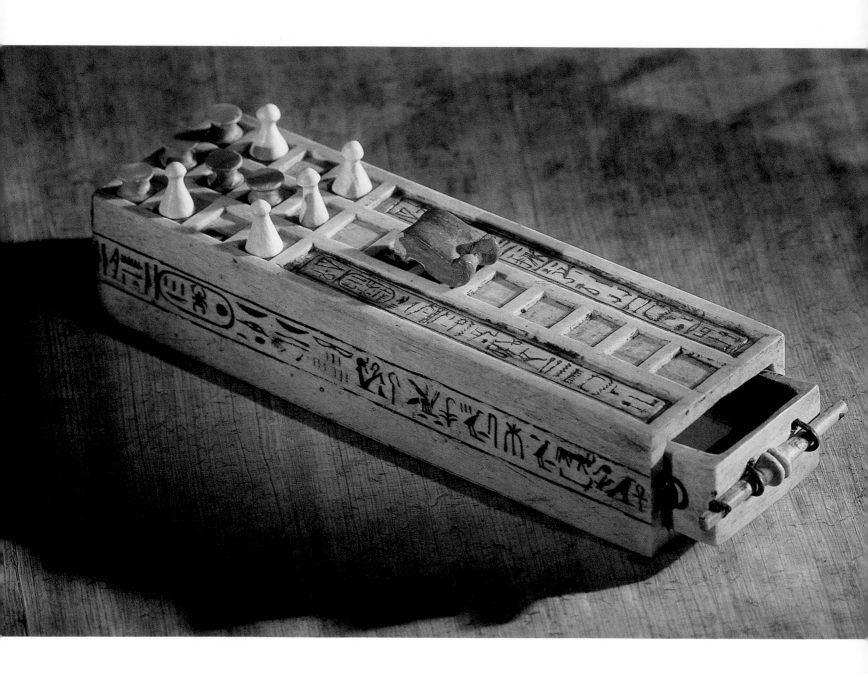

Tutankhamun took at least five, and possibly six, game boards with him into the afterlife; four of these were discovered intact. All of the complete examples, including this one, came from the Annexe. Six sets of knucklebones (the ancient Egyptian version of dice), two sets of casting sticks, and fifty-six gaming pieces were also found in the tomb.

This example (left) is carved from a single block of ivory. Three rows of playing spaces are carved about 0.04 in (1 mm) deep into the surface. Most of the spaces are oblong, except for one exact square at the end of the middle row. Nine playing pieces (out of an original ten) and one of the two knucklebones were found scattered around the Annexe and Antechamber. They would have been stored in an ivory drawer at one end of the board, directly under its central row. This was closed with an ivory bolt thrust through two staples of impure gold. There are four inscriptions on the box, each filled with blue pigment.

The earliest preserved Egyptian game boards date from the Predynastic periods, attesting to the enduring popularity and importance of such pastimes. In the New Kingdom, the most popular of these games had 20 or 30 squares. The 30-square game was known as Senet. Two players, each with differently shaped and colored pieces, threw knucklebones or casting sticks to count their moves. The pieces moved in an S-shaped path around the board, which was mined with good-luck and bad-luck squares that influenced the play. To win the game, one player had to remove all of his or her pieces before the opponent did. This game functioned at one level as a metaphor for the journey of the sun god and the deceased through the dangerous realm of the Netherworld—thus, winning the game stood magically for rebirth and resurrection. Although the details of the game are not understood, Twenty Squares seems to have lacked the religious connotations borne by the game of Senet. Each player had five pieces, which he or she had to move into the central line of squares.

ABOVE: Ebony senet board from the tomb of Tutankhamun.

93  Inscribed Game Board with Twenty Squares
Ivory
Length 13.5 cm; width 4.1 cm; height 2.7 cm
Dynasty 18, reign of Tutankhamun
Thebes, Valley of the Kings, tomb of Tutankhamun (KV 62)
Carter 393

94  Glass Headrest
Blue glass
Height 19.5 cm; width 27 cm
Dynasty 18, reign of Tutankhamun
From the collection of King Farouk
TR 2.3.60.1

Tutankhamun's tomb contained three large ritual couches and six examples of everyday beds. Associated with these couches and beds were eight headrests, low pillars with curved tops on which the head was laid. Headrests were used both in mortuary context, to support the mummy's head, and in everyday context as pillows. To render them more comfortable, they were often wrapped with strips of cloth. Sometimes spells were inscribed on headrests to help protect their users from the many dangerous demons that threatened both the dead and the living. Egyptians even produced amulets in the form of headrests that could be inscribed with protective spells; one of these, made of iron, was found wrapped in the bandages around Tutankhamun's head.

Six of the headrests that Carter found were of the typical New Kingdom form, with an oblong or rectangular base, a waisted pillar, and an oval top that curves upward at the sides. This simple and elegant example is made of a single piece of blue glass and edged with gilding, with a faceted central support. It bears a single vertical line of inscription on the front, incised and then inlaid with white paste, which reads, "Live the good god, Lord of the Two Lands, Lord of ritual, Nebkheprure, given life like Re forever."

This particular headrest is not mentioned in Carter's inventory or in his publications. It came to the Egyptian Museum in 1960 from the collection of King Farouk, to whom it was apparently given by the archaeologist.

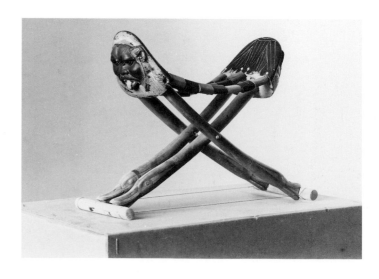

RIGHT: Folding headrest decorated with heads of the protective god Bes.

Discovered in the Antechamber beneath one of the ritual couches, this traveling chest is made of cedar or some other coniferous wood. It belongs to a type known from tomb scenes as early as the Old Kingdom, but this is the only example found to date. Almost a meter long, it is rectangular, with a high gabled lid and four short legs to support it when set down. Four poles protruding from the short ends are attached to the underside with copper clamps; the poles would have been used by the two porters who carried the chest.

The sides of the chest are framed by bands of paste-filled hieroglyphs. The texts here are spells, some associated with the Opening of the Mouth ceremony, spoken by various gods to protect the king and aid him in his journey to the afterlife. On one end is a depiction of the king making offerings to Osiris. These details make it clear that the chest was designed solely for funerary use.

The chest contained a number of vases and cups of alabaster, limestone, serpentine, and glass, as well as several stone knives, lumps of resin and incense, small dried fruits and garlic bulbs, and several broken ostrich feathers. Most of these objects were used in the Opening of the Mouth ceremony; this, coupled with the inscriptions and images on the piece, suggest that the portable chest was used to carry the implements for this important ritual.

ABOVE. View of the interior of the chest, as discovered.

95  Portable Chest with Carrying Poles
Wood, ebony, ivory, gold leaf, copper alloy, paste
Length 83 cm; width 60.5 cm; height 63.5 cm
Dynasty 18, reign of Tutankhamun
Thebes, Valley of the Kings, tomb of Tutankhamun (KV 62)
Carter 32

96 Cosmetic Jar with a Recumbent Lion on the Lid
Calcite, ivory, gold
Height 26.7 cm; width 22.0 cm
Dynasty 18, reign of Tutankhamun
Thebes, Valley of the Kings, tomb of Tutankhamun (KV 62)
Carter 211

Ornately carved and decorated, this unguent jar was discovered in the Burial Chamber between the walls of the first and second shrines. It still held traces of its original contents, a mixture of animal fat and vegetable resins that together formed a cosmetic material. The receptacle is a cylinder, incised with figures of lions and dogs attacking prey. As is common with desert hunt scenes from the earliest times forward, the figures in the scene are not bound to the ground line, but seem to float in the air; desert plants are scattered randomly among the groups of animals. The background has been roughened and painted a bluish black. Below is a band of narrow vertical rectangles (the so-called palace façade) and above are pendant triangular shapes representing lotus petals against a background of red, white, and black stripes of varying widths, bordered top and bottom with wavy lines.

Flanking the receptacle are two lotus pillars topped with heads of Bes, a protective household deity. Their shafts are inscribed with the king's cartouches and titles. Details of Bes's features have been enhanced with paint, and a tongue of pink-tinted ivory hangs from his mouth. The petals of the lotus bud capitals have been painted green, and a band of gilding has been added between columns and capitals. A crest on top of each head forms an abacus for the columns.

Four stone heads of defeated enemies protrude from the base of the jar, their chins thrust forward as if their bodies continued beneath the vessel. Two are clearly Nubian, carved of black stone with Negroid features

and "gold" rings (actually ivory) in the ears; the other two are bearded Asiatics, carved of red stone.

The lid of the jar is round, with square protrusions to each side that cover the tops of the Bes columns. One square is topped by a rounded button, the other by a round knob. Below this knob, in the center of one of the faces of Bes, is a second knob; a string wound around these knobs would have sealed the container. The button and the two knobs are made of pinkish ivory. The jar's lid swivels open around a pin under the button.

On top of the lid, carved from the same block of calcite, is the figure of a lion. It lies comfortably, curled into a semicircle, with its crossed paws and head facing forward and its tail also curved to the front. The eyes, lines of the brow, ears, nose, and tip of the tail have been painted dark blue, and a long tongue of pinkish ivory hangs from its panting mouth. Across its shoulders is written, "The good god, Nebkheprure." Its visible toenails are also painted blue. Gilding has been used to enhance some features.

Like many of the objects in the tomb, this piece symbolizes the king in his guise as defender of the creator god, maintaining order over chaos. As indicated by the cartouche in its body, the lion on the lid is an embodiment of the power and virility of the king himself. The lion is seen again in the hunt scene, helped by his hunting dogs, acting as the enemy of the denizens of the desert, themselves symbols of the forces of chaos. The entire piece rests on defeated enemies, also related to the powers that threatened the cosmos and had to be subdued.

## 97 Box in the Shape of a Cartouche

Wood, ebony, and ivory
Length 64 cm; width 30.7 cm; height 33.2 cm
Dynasty 18, reign of Tutankhamun
Thebes, Valley of the Kings, tomb of Tutankhamun (KV62)
Carter 269

LEFT: Interior of the box, with objects, including
the ankh-shaped mirror box, still inside.

To the Egyptians, a person's name was one of his or her most important aspects. If the name survived, the person could live forever and be recognized in the Afterlife. An object decorated with a person's name would belong to that person for eternity.

Like all New Kingdom pharaohs, Tutankhamun had five names. Most important were his birth name—originally Tutankhaten but later changed to Tutankhamun—and his throne name, Nebkheprure, given to him at his coronation. These two names are the ones most often found inscribed on his monuments and artifacts. The other names, which appear less frequently, were often inscribed inside *serekhs,* rectangles bordered at the bottom with a series of niches and surmounted by the Horus falcon. Tutankhamun's Horus name, "Strong Bull, fitting of created forms," associated him with the great falcon-headed sky and sun god. His Golden Horus name and his "Nebty" name, which gave him the protection of the tutelary goddesses of Upper and Lower Egypt, varied over the course of his short reign.

This large chest is in the shape of a cartouche, symbolizing the circuit of the sun and thus representing the known world over which the king, at least theoretically, had dominion. On the upper surface, inlaid in large, clearly recognizable hieroglyphs, is the king's modified birth name, Tutankhamun, followed by the epithet "Ruler of Upper Egyptian Heliopolis." The original town of Heliopolis, located near modern Cairo, was the cult center of the sun god, Re; "Upper Egyptian Heliopolis" was Thebes, the domain of the king of the gods, Amun-Re.

Inside the band of the cartouche around Tutankhamun's birth name are more of his names, titles, and epithets. Three of the royal names also appear on the flat end of the base, and names, titles, and epithets also run in three horizontal registers around the curved part of the base.

The fastening system, like that for so many of the containers, consists of two knobs: one on the lid, and the other on the body of the box. A string would have been wound around these knobs and then secured with a glob of clay imprinted with a seal. This system is still used in Egypt today, only with wire and melted lead instead of string and mud.

One of over fifty boxes (four of which were cartouche-shaped) buried with the king, this was found in the Treasury. Inside were many items of jewelry, some royal regalia (cats. 69, 70), and a gilded mirror case (cat. 109). It is possible that this box was originally used for regalia pertaining to Tutankhamun's coronation or rituals connected with his role as ruling king.

This elegant chest, discovered in the Antechamber, had been opened and rifled by tomb robbers, who left only four headrests and an unidentified piece of clothing inside. It is made of wood painted a reddish brown to imitate expensive coniferous wood, with details of the decoration in black paint and gilding.

Relatively simple in design, the chest is almost square, and stands upon four long, black-painted legs. Framing each side is a band of hieroglyphs engraved and inlaid with colored paste; hieroglyphs also frame the lid, with an additional band running down the center. A wide band of alternating ankh and was signs, symbols of life and dominion, run around the lower part of the chest above the baskets that stand for "all." These hieroglyphs have been executed in open-work cutouts.

The lid opens upward from a hinge of copper alloy along the back edge. Two knobs, one on the top and one on the front, served as fasteners, around which a string would have been wrapped. Gold foil engraved with the names of the king covers the knobs (throne name on one and birth name on the other). The inscriptions on the chest, like many of the texts in the tomb, provide the names, titles, and epithets of the king. Some of these epithets refer to the pious acts carried out by the king when he opened temples that had been closed during the Amarna heresy.

ABOVE: View of the antechamber, with furniture piled high along its walls

98 Chest with Long Legs and Decorative Fretwork
Painted wood, partially gessoed and gilded, colored paste
Height 70 cm; width 43.7; depth 40 cm
Thebes, Valley of the Kings, tomb of Tutankhamun (KV 62)
Carter 403

Thirty-five boats were discovered among Tutankhamun's burial equipment. Eighteen were in the Treasury, most perched on top of the chests along the south wall, and all with their prows facing west. The remaining seventeen, including the two shown here, were in the Annexe, where they had been thrown carelessly.

This papyrus skiff (bottom left), painted to look like a bundle of papyrus reeds tied together at intervals and flattened at prow and stern, is one of two such simple craft from the tomb. Most likely the earliest type of boat manufactured in Egypt, these archaic vessels were used in later times for swamp-hunting rituals that symbolized the maintenance of order over chaos. In Egyptian art, such boats are shown carrying kings and nobles, accompanied by their families, into the papyrus swamps, where they hunted the wild animals and birds that symbolized the forces of disorder that constantly threatened the created world. Such scenes, although they may have had a basis in real hunts, are most likely depictions of ritual events in which the actors represented Horus and his family, reenacting the moment of creation and thus symbolically ensuring that the world would continue. Two ritual figures of the king found in the Treasury show him standing on such skiffs, ready to throw a harpoon. According to the Book of the Dead, the deceased also traveled the rush fields of the Afterlife in such skiffs (Spell 110).

Other ceremonial vessels included with Tutankhamun's equipment were two "night barks" and four "day barks," in which the king would have accompanied the sun god on his daily trips through the sky and Netherworld.

Tutankhamun's 27 river-going craft have been divided into a number of different categories, such as simple fishing boats, river barges, and more elaborate vessels with cabins. This example (top left) of a more complex vessel is of average size, with a single steering oar, a simple cabin, and a mast. It is decorated in geometric and feather patterns of red, blue, and green, with the tip of the oar painted black. The cabin boat was probably intended primarily for transport in the Afterlife.

99  Model Ship for River Travel
Painted wood
Length 116 cm; width 19 cm; height 9 cm; height with mast 104 cm
Dynasty 18, reign of Tutankhamun
Thebes, Valley of the Kings, tomb of Tutankhamun (KV 62)
Carter 437

100  Model Papyrus Skiff for River Travel
Painted wood
Length 124.3 cm; width 22.5 cm; height 10.5 cm
Dynasty 18, reign of Tutankhamun
Thebes, Valley of the Kings, tomb of Tutankhamun (KV 62)
Carter 464

Calcite
Height 18.3 cm; width 28.3 cm; diameter 16.8 cm
Dynasty 18, reign of Tutankhamun
Thebes, Valley of the Kings, tomb of Tutankhamun (KV62)
Carter 14

LEFT: Many elaborate calcite vessels were
found in Tutankhamun's tomb.

Carved of translucent alabaster, this goblet takes the form of an open lotus blossom, flanked by other blossoms and buds. Details of the petals and sepals are engraved on the outer surface of the vessel; the rounded tops of these petals indicate that this is a white lotus. Atop the blossoms to either side are figures of Heh, god of infinity, on a basket, holding the notched palm ribs that symbolize millions of years, along with an ankh sign. The palm ribs stand on tadpoles, the hieroglyph that means one hundred thousand. Taken together, these hieroglyph groupings symbolize long life.

The names and titles of Tutankhamun and the epithet "beloved of Amun-Re, lord of the thrones of the two lands, lord of the sky" are painted inside a square field outlined with blue in the center of the cup. Around the rim of the cup are two horizontal inscriptions, each beginning with an ankh sign at the center and moving to one side. In one direction are more of the names and titles of the young king; the other inscription reads, "May your ka live, and may you pass (live) one million years, one who loves Thebes and dwells in it, your face toward the northern wind: may your eyes see the good place."

As a potent symbol of rebirth and regeneration, the lotus blossom was used in many different contexts to guarantee eternal life. Here the lotus is offering long life and happiness to the king; consequently, this piece is often called a "wishing cup." The king would likely have drunk some liquid, perhaps water or wine, out of it.

Over 80 vessels altogether were found in the tomb, including 25 inscribed jars, vases, and cups of calcite. The oldest of these had belonged to Tuthmosis III, four generations before Tutankhamun. Another had once been inscribed for Amenhotep III and Tiye, the probable grandparents of the young king, and another, according to Carter, had once born the names of Amenhotep III and Akhenaten, side by side.

A full quota of shabti figures was found in Tutankhamun's tomb: 365 workmen, one for each day of the year, and 48 overseers—36 to supervise the 10-day weeks and 12 to take charge of the months—making a total of 413. Carter also discovered almost 2,000 tiny agricultural tools, many still held by the shabtis for whom they had been made. Almost all of the funerary figures were found in the Treasury and Annexe inside a number of shabti boxes. Some of the more elaborate examples bear inscriptions stating that they were donated to the burial by high officials such as General Nakhtmin and Maya, a royal treasurer.

The shabtis vary enormously in size, material, and iconography. Some of the most elaborate were made of wood, while others were faience, limestone, Egyptian alabaster, granite, or quartzite. There are nine different types of wig styles and headdresses represented, each type seen both with and without the protective cobra or vulture. To complicate matters further, not all of the shabtis were manufactured originally for Tutankhamun, as indicated by variations in their facial features. Some even have the low slung hips characteristic of the female body in the Amarna period, and thus seem to have been made for a woman.

This beautiful wooden figure is one of the largest and most exquisite of the shabtis. The king wears a short Nubian wig (originally worn by soldiers and adopted by the Amarna royal family), elaborately carved and painted black, with a protective cobra and vulture of bronze attached separately to a gilded band. The eyes and eyebrows are painted, and the face is carved with the distinctive features of the king. His broad collar is of gold foil, as are the bracelets that adorn his wrists. Now empty, his crossed hands may have once held a crook and flail. Four lines of hieroglyphs carved onto the body bear a version of Spell 6 from the Book of the Dead, promising that the shabti will work on behalf of the king in the afterlife.

103  Wooden Shabti of Tutankhamun

Gilded and painted wood

Height 54 cm; width 15.5 cm; depth 8.5 cm

Dynasty 18, reign of Tutankhamun

Thebes, Valley of the Kings, tomb of Tutankhamun (KV 62)

Carter 326a

## 105 Limestone Shabti of Tutankhamun

Painted limestone

Height 27.2 cm; width 8.7 cm; depth 6.4 cm

Dynasty 18, reign of Tutankhamun

Thebes, Valley of the Kings, tomb of Tutankhamun (KV 62)

Carter 330m

## 104 Faience Shabti of Tutankhamun

Faience

Height 30.1 cm; width 8.7 cm; depth 5.6 cm

Dynasty 18, reign of Tutankhamun

Thebes, Valley of the Kings, tomb of Tutankhamun (KV 62)

Carter 326e

This elegant limestone statuette (near right) was found with 14 other shabtis of various materials and 75 model tools in a chest bearing the hieratic (cursive) inscription: "What is in it: smooth gold and mry-wood shabtis." The figure wears a tripartite wig with uraeus, in front of which its pierced ears are visible, and a divine beard. In its crossed hands it holds a crook and flail. Many of the details are outlined or filled in with black, and the lips are painted a pale red. A vertical column of text, carved and filled with black paint, runs down the front of the mummiform body.

This reads: "The good god, Lord of the Two Lands, Nebkheprure, beloved of Osiris, the great god."

The faience shabti (far right) is beardless and wears a Nubian wig. It was found in a shabti chest in the Annexe along with 15 other figurines. Details such as eyes and eyebrows, neck folds, broad collar, and the folded cloth and flail that identify this as an overseer were picked out in black paint. A vertical line of text reads: "The good god, Lord of the Two Lands, Nebkheprure, son of Re, Lord of Appearances, Tutankhamun, Ruler of Upper Egyptian Heliopolis, given life like Re forever."

## 107  Ritual Vessel (Nemset Vase)

Faience

Vessel: Height 10.2 cm; diameter 10.9 cm

Lid: Height 6 cm; diameter 7 cm

Dynasty 18, reign of Tutankhamun

Thebes, Valley of the Kings, tomb of Tutankhamun (KV 62)

Carter 54bbb

## 106  Ritual Vessel (Heset Vase)

Faience

Vessel: Height 16.8 cm; diameter 6.1 cm;

Lid: Height 3.2 cm; diameter 5.5 cm

Dynasty 18, reign of Tutankhamun

Thebes, Valley of the Kings, tomb of Tutankhamun (KV 62)

Carter 46lr

Sixty-seven ritual vessels were found in the tomb, distributed originally between one box in the Antechamber and another in the Annexe. Box 54, in which the nemset (teapot-shaped) vase was found, was in the Antechamber, and bore a docket listing the contents as "17 blue faience nemset-ewers." Sixteen of these were still present, along with all seventeen lids and many other miscellaneous pieces. It is possible that this box was used as a general receptacle when partial order was restored after an episode of robbery, as there were scraps of cloth and some gold sequins, a bronze snake, a woven robe, a gold corselet, a scarab, a small wooden model tool, and two throwsticks laid above the ewers, probably dumped there by the priests. The short, squat nemset vase is a deep cobalt blue, with a lid in the form of an upside-down lotus blossom and a curved spout. Opposite the spout, engraved and filled with a white paste, are the throne and birth names of the king, along with the wish that he live forever, all set within a rectangle.

The tall, slender heset vase was discovered in the box in the Annexe, along with seven more heset vases and a number of other pieces. This shape is seen frequently in Egyptian art, and was so closely associated with ritual that it was used as the hieroglyph for "to praise." The ovoid body tapers at the bottom and then flares out again at the foot. Its spout is short and curved and the lid, set atop a short narrow neck and a disklike lip, is a hemisphere. Such vessels were used for rituals of purification and for libations to the gods and the blessed dead, including the ceremonies of the Opening of the Mouth.

RIGHT: **The interior of Box 54
contained many nemset vessels.**

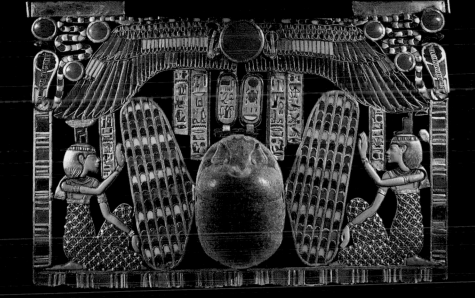

Set into the center of this pectoral of gold inlaid with semiprecious stones and glass is a scarab of green feldspar. This is Tutankhamun's heart scarab: Inscribed on its reverse is the "heart spell" from the Book of the Dead (30B). In this spell, the king's heart is asked to act as his witness before the divine tribunal, speaking aloud the "negative confession" assuring the gods that Tutankhamun has done no evil in his lifetime. This spell also specifies that the scarab should be made of green stone. It should have been placed within the mummy wrappings, close to the heart of the deceased (which was, in contrast to the viscera, left inside the body), but instead, it was found inside the Anubis shrine that guarded the entrance to the Treasury. The rest of the pectoral was found inside the cartouche-shaped chest (cat. 97). The embalmers may have forgotten to hang it around the king's neck. The fact that the two parts were in separate places suggests that it was taken by thieves and recovered by the guards, but had come apart in the process.

The scarab is flanked by oddly shaped wings, filled with a feather pattern in red, dark blue, and light blue. On either side kneel the protective goddesses Isis and Nephthys, their arms outstretched to embrace the wings. Both wear tight-fitting net dresses and bag wigs with ribbons down their backs; their skin is blue, indicating their divinity. Atop their heads are the hieroglyphs that spell their names. Directly above the scarab are Tutankhamun's cartouches, flanked by captions repeating transformation spells spoken by the goddesses. Before each goddess is another text asking protection for the king. The scene is protected by a winged sun disk, and everything is set within a rectangular border filled with squares and bands of alternating colors. Cobras bearing sun disks on their heads occupy the upper corners. The design can be seen as a representation of the king as the sun at dawn, carried to the heavens on the wings of Horus.

## 108 Inlaid Pectoral with a Winged Scarab

Gold, rock crystal, carnelian, feldspar, glass

Height 16.5 cm; width 24.4 cm

Dynasty 18, reign of Tutankhamun

Thebes, Valley of the Kings, tomb of Tutankhamun (KV 62)

Carter 261m (pectoral) and 269a(4) (scarab)

## 109 Mirror Case in the Shape of an Ankh

Wood, gold and silver leaf
Height 27 cm; width 13.2 cm; depth 4 cm
Dynasty 18, reign of Tutankhamun
Thebes, Valley of the Kings, tomb of Tutankhamun (KV 62)
Carter 269b

LEFT: Another mirror case from the tomb
took the form of the god Heh.

This mirror-case, one of two examples from the tomb, was found in the Treasury within a large oval chest bearing Tutankhamun's cartouche (cat. 97). When opened by the excavators, the case was empty—the mirror, cast most likely of precious metal, evidently had been stolen. Made of wood covered with sheet gold, coated inside with a thin sheet of silver, this box is in the shape of the hieroglyph for "life" (ankh), which is also a word for "mirror" as well as "floral bouquet," explaining the decoration of the case. It has been suggested that the ankh shape represents a sandal strap, seen from above, but more plausibly it should be interpreted as a ceremonial girdle knot or the symbols for male and female combined. A text on the case's handle reads, "The good god, lord of the Two Lands, Lord of Ritual, King of Upper and Lower Egypt, Nebkheprure, son of Re, Tutankhamun, Ruler of Southern Heliopolis (Thebes)." Additional inscriptions run around the loop; silver knobs were used to hold the lid to the case.

Within the loop is the king's throne name, Nebkheprure, in inlaid hieroglyphs of dark blue and light blue glass, imitating lapis lazuli and turquoise. The scarab that forms the *kheper* sign (the beetle) was carved of steatite and the circle representing the sun disk, Re, is an inlay of carnelian. Flanking the name are two uraeus serpents atop shen signs (tied ropes representing the circuit of the sun) with sun disks on their heads, and at the bottom of the field is inlaid an opened lotus blossom. Thus the throne name of the king emerges from the open lotus, as the sun god, in his guise as the child Nefertem, emerged from this blossom each morning.

This type of mirror case is first seen in the New Kingdom. Both men and women used mirrors for practical purposes such as the application of eye paint or the arranging of hair. These objects were also imbued with symbolism, functioning as icons of rebirth and regeneration; many early tomb stelae show mirrors beneath the chair of the deceased.

PAINTED GODS AND PHARAOHS LOOK ON AS THE FIRST
ALL-EGYPTIAN RESEARCH TEAM REMOVES THE COFFIN
OF THE WORLD'S MOST FAMOUS MUMMY.

# The Mummy of Tutankhamun

*The gilded shrines that surrounded Tutankhamun's mummy had been opened and the lid taken off his huge sarcophagus of quartzite in the early months of 1924, then the tomb had been shut for almost a year while Carter and the Egyptian government worked out their differences.*

In January 1925, the team came back to Luxor, and spent the next few months cleaning up and getting ready for the next great phase of work. On October 12th, Carter returned to the Valley after a summer abroad, and found the tomb in good condition.

On October 13th, the lid of the outermost coffin was lifted, and a second coffin was revealed. The linen shroud that covered its gilded surface showed damage from humidity, giving the team their first clue that the mummy might not be in perfect condition. Fit snugly inside the first coffin was a second. When the lid of this was removed, a reddish linen drape and floral garlands covering yet another anthropoid container were revealed. After the shroud was stripped away, the astonished team realized that the third and final coffin was of solid gold.

The shell of the second coffin was moved into the Antechamber. The team found that some sort of black resin or unguent had been poured generously over the masterpiece inside. This had solidified and glued everything together in a great mass. On November 10, 1925, the lid of the inner coffin was raised with great

Three-dimensional reconstruction of the skull of Tutankhamun, from the 2005 CT scan, shows skull sutures.

difficulty, and the mummy of Tutankhamun saw the light of day again, more than three thousand years after loving hands had anointed him with libations, draped him with garlands, and said the prayers for the dead. The young king's head was hidden by a magnificent golden mask, the single most famous artifact to emerge from ancient Egypt.

Unveiling the king was an elaborate process, more difficult than anyone had imagined. The unguents had been poured liberally over the royal body, and the mummy was stuck to the inside of the coffin, the head of the king held fast inside its golden helmet. Carter took the coffin out of the tomb and set it in the hot desert sun for several hours, hoping that the unguent would soften (a move that no archaeologist today would even contemplate). However, the resin was impervious to the heat, and Carter decided that the mummy would have to be examined within its golden coffin. Everything was moved to a nearby tomb, and preparations were made for the big day.

On November 11th, Carter and his staff, accompanied by officials of the Antiquities Service, began to carry out the first examination of the mummy. The forensic specialists were Douglas Derry, an anthropologist teaching in Egypt, and Saleh Bey Hamdi, a professor on the Faculty of Medicine in Alexandria. Paraffin

A hush descends as members of the Egyptian Mummy Project
unveil the mummy of Tutankhamun (above). The young king's
scarred face (opposite) gazes across centuries.

wax was poured over the linen shroud that was stuck
fast to the mummy. After it hardened, Derry took a
knife and cut through the delicate material. The
decayed outer wrappings came away in large pieces;
the inner wrappings had been reduced to the consis-
tency of soot which Lucas, the team's chemist, attributed to some kind of spontaneous combustion.

Carter and Pierre Lacau worked together to unravel
the delicate bandages. The job took four days, as each
of the objects wrapped inside was recorded. Finally,
Carter and his team removed the mummy in pieces
from the trough of the coffin: They cut the head off at
the neck, used hot knives to extract the skull from the
mask, separated the pelvis from the trunk, detached the
arms and legs, and did other assorted damage to the
body. They reconstructed the dismembered body in a

sand tray, arranging it carefully so that it looked intact,
and even rejoined the hands and feet to their respective
limbs with resin.

Derry and Saleh examined the mummy, which was
of a young man about 5′6″ tall in life. Their report concluded, based on the degree of fusion of the epiphyses
(the ends of the long bones, separated from their main
bones by layers of cartilage that gradually ossify) and
the partial eruption of the wisdom teeth, that he had
died between the ages of 18 and 22. (In order to see the
teeth, Derry may have made an incision along the jaw
and looked in with a mirror, then covered his tracks
with some resin.) It was not clear whether or not the king
had been circumcised. In October 1926, Carter rewrapped
the body and laid it, in its tray of sand, back within the
outermost coffin, which was still inside the sarcophagus.
A plate glass lid was laid on top to protect the coffin.

The mummy of Tutankhamun was examined for
the second time in 1968 by a team from the University
of Liverpool, led by professor of anatomy R.G. Harrison.

The plate glass was removed and the coffin opened. Resin or unguent still adhered to much of the body, and gave off a sweet smell. The new team, whose primary purpose was to X-ray the body, discovered that it was in pieces (a fact that Carter had not mentioned in his publication). The body was quite fragile. The rewrapping was very sloppy and, to their great surprise, the penis was now missing, as was one thumb.

Harrison's examination of the body revealed a number of interesting details. As Derry had noted, the skull is almost exactly the same size and shape as the skull from Tomb 55; but Tutankhamun's face was slightly narrower than Smenkhkare/Akhenaten's. Both young men were about the same height as well, and similarly proportioned. The 1968 team also managed, with some difficulty, to X-ray the skull. They found that it was empty except for two thick deposits of opaque material, evidently solidified material that had collected during the mummification process (one mass while the king was flat on his back, and the other when his head was tipped back off the edge of the embalming table), and a fragment of bone. Their X-rays also seem to show a thickened or fuzzy area on the back of the skull. Several theories have been put forth suggesting that one or the other of these skull anomalies constitute evidence that Tutankhamun was murdered by a blow to the head. However, the X-rays are not very clear, and the bone fragment may well be postmortem—as more than one person has noted, if it were antemortem, it would most likely have gotten stuck in the embalming material that was poured into the head and would not be floating around loose. Based on their examination of the bones and teeth, Harrison's team agreed with an age range of 18-22, more likely earlier than later.

The 1968 X-rays also revealed that the sternum and some of the king's frontal ribs are missing. One scholar has suggested that the king was injured in a chariot accident that crushed the front of his rib cage. Another theory holds that Tutankhamun was "pigeon-chested," and that this represents a birth defect. Harrison's team also noted that the spine shows signs of scoliosis, supporting the idea that the young king was physically frail.

The body was interred a second time, and left undisturbed for ten years. In 1978, the sarcophagus was reopened by an American team led by University of Michigan professor of orthodontics James E. Harris, who X-rayed the head again. These findings were never published, but photographs taken at this time reveal still more damage to the battered body of the king. Harris's team has suggested, without detailing their rationale, that the king was between 23 and 27 when he died; most Egyptologists disagree with this on both archaeological and physiological grounds.

The other test that was carried out on Tutankhamun's remains was a blood analysis, done on a sample of bone. This concluded that his blood types were A2 and

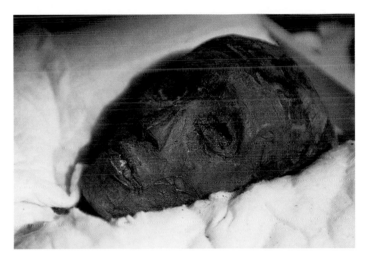

MN (based on two different systems, the ABO and the MN, which measure different antigens in the blood). These are identical to the results of the blood typing done on the Tomb 55 body, reinforcing the theory that the two were closely related. Serological studies were also carried out on the mummies of Amenhotep III, Yuya, and Tjuya. Amenhotep III was A2M, and both Yuya and Tjuya were A2N. Thus both Sitamun and Akhenaten would have been A2MN. Possible parents for Tutankhamun and the Tomb 55 mummy thus still include Amenhotep III, Akhenaten, Sitamun, and Tiye.

## Scanning Tutankhamun

I am currently the head of the Egyptian Mummy Project, designed to inventory and analyze all of the known mummies, both royal and nonroyal, in Egypt. For this project, National Geographic Society and Siemens, Ltd., have donated to the Supreme Council of Antiquities (SCA) a state-of-the-art CT scanning machine, along with its own trailer and funds for maintenance over a five-year

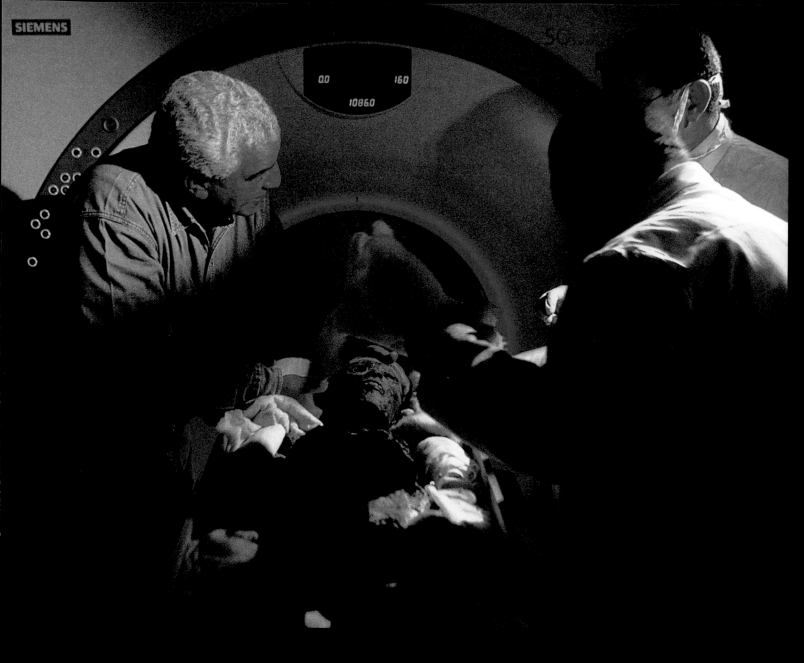

0.0        160

10860

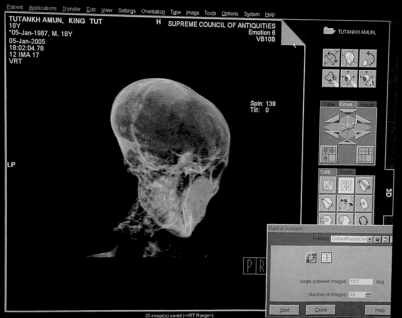

Patient  Applications  Transfer  Edit  View  Settings  Orientation  Type  Image  Tools  Options  System  Help

TUTANKH AMUN, KING TUT          H    SUPREME COUNCIL OF ANTIQUITIES
18Y                                                    Emotion 6
*05-Jan-1987, M, 18Y                                   VB10B
05-Jan-2005
18:02:04.78
12 IMA 17
VRT

                                        TUTANKH AMUN,

                                    Spin: 139
                                    Tilt: 0

LP

                                    Type  Orien  Image

                                    Settl  Topo

                                                        3D

                            Radial Ranges
                            Presets  DefaultRadialSet

                            Angle between images  19.5    deg
                            Number of images   19

                            P R

                        Start      Close           Help

20 image(s) saved (<VRT Range>)

Dr. Zahi Hawass (above, left) helps prepare the mummy for its historic CT scan. Original views, like the one shown left, reveal an intact skull with no signs of trauma, debunking the theory that Tutankhamun was murdered by a blow to the head. In a composite image, opposite, a white shadow indicates the loose fragment of bone discovered in the 1968 X-rays. Because the fragment is loose on the surface of the embalming resin, and has moved since 1968, it must have been dislodged long after Tutankhamun's entombing—most likely by Howard Carter in the 1920s.

period. CT scanning represents a significant advance from X-rays. Instead of producing one image at a time, the CT scanner takes hundreds of "slices," images of individual sections of the body, without having to move it. These slices can be taken at multiple angles, and then put all together into a complete, three-dimensional image of the body. One of the goals of the project will be to CT scan as many mummies as possible, in order to gain more information about life expectancy, injuries, diseases, and general health of the ancient population.

As part of this project, the Permanent Committee of the SCA approved the scanning of Tutankhamun. The mummy is in such delicate condition that it was decided not to move it, but to do the examination in the Valley of the Kings. The CT scanner arrived in Cairo and was set up in the courtyard west of the Egyptian Museum. After the machine was calibrated, the team began to scan a series of nonroyal mummies. In early January, the machine was driven to the Valley of the King.

We chose January 5, 2005 as the day for the scan. I went to Luxor one day before the scan was scheduled. With me was my all-Egyptian team, including Sabri Abdel Aziz, head of pharaonic monuments; Ahmed Soeib, head of conservation; Abdel Hamied Kotb, SCA architect; and the local team from Luxor. Operating the machine was Dr. Hani Abdel Rahman, an Egyptian expert. We arrived at the Valley of the Kings at 4 PM, as the tourists were leaving for the day. At 5:30 PM we entered the tomb of Tutankhamun and began to prepare to move the mummy out of the tomb. Although an Egyptian anatomy professor led the first examination of the mummy, this was to be the first investigation carried out solely by Egyptians.

We took the glass cover off of the stone sarcophagus carefully and placed it to one side. The lid of the outermost coffin was exposed, and we could see that its gilding was cracked in many places. This was not surprising, as this coffin had never undergone conservation and had lain in the uncontrolled climate of the Burial Chamber since 1925. The team tied this lid securely, and then took a half hour to pull it out of the sarcophagus. When the team had put the lid down on the west side of the chamber, I looked inside, and saw that the mummy was covered with a cotton blanket and some linen. I reached down gingerly and took the

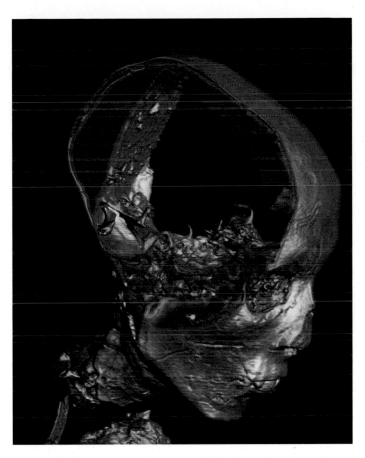

cover off the head so that I could look at the face. My first impression was that he looked older than I had expected. Then I saw a card on his chest, on which someone had written the names of the members of previous expeditions.

The team moved the mummy, still in its tray of sand, slowly out of the coffin and sarcophagus. I could see clearly that it was in pieces, some of which lay in the sand like isolated stones. The only well-preserved parts of the mummy were the face, the feet, the legs, and the hands. We continued out of the tomb, to the trailer containing the CT machine, and put it inside.

On the way from my hotel to the Valley of the Kings, my driver came frighteningly close to hitting a young child of about nine. I couldn't help mentioning the Curse of the Pharaohs. We continued to the valley, and shortly before we arrived, my sister called me to tell me that her husband had died. A few minutes after I got to the valley, it was hit by a huge rainstorm. The people around me began to talk about the curse of Tutankhamun.

For an hour after we put the mummy inside the CT scanner, the machine refused to work. This is one of the best machines of its type in the world, made by the

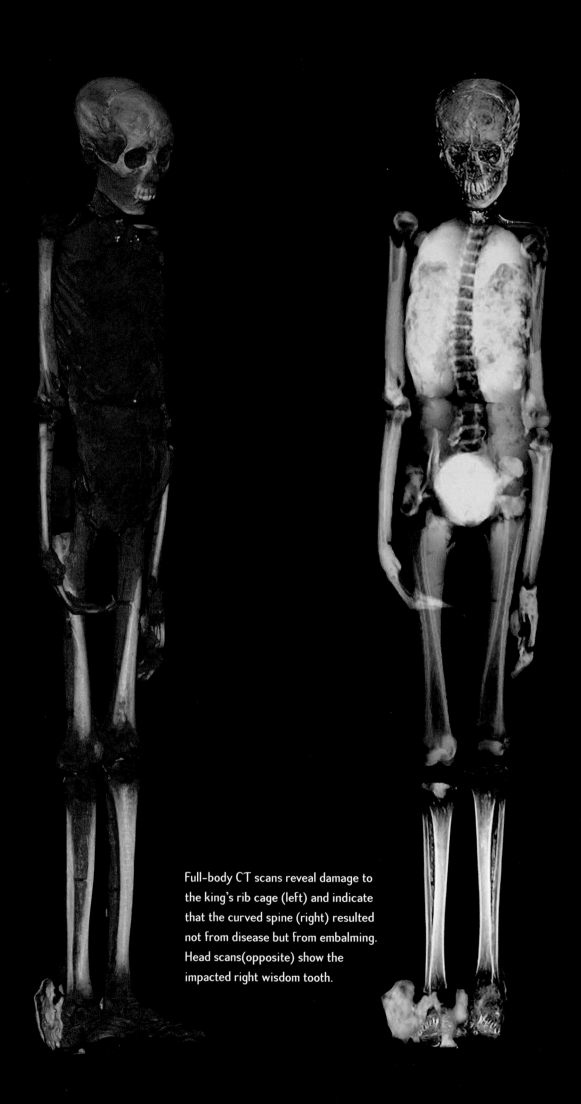

Full-body CT scans reveal damage to the king's rib cage (left) and indicate that the curved spine (right) resulted not from disease but from embalming. Head scans(opposite) show the impacted right wisdom tooth.

top company in the field, so at first we could not understand what was happening. I was afraid that we would wait all night, and end up having to put the king back into the tomb without doing the scan. Finally the problem was diagnosed as the cooling system. White plastic fans were brought and placed next to the machine, and the scanner worked perfectly for the rest of the night. When we left the Valley of the Kings, we took with us 1,700 images, stored on the scanner's computer.

## The Results

An Egyptian team, under the auspices of the Cairo University Faculty of Medicine, spent January and February analyzing the images. The team members are Dr. Mervat Shafik, Dr. Essam el-Sheikh, and Dr. Ashraf Selim, all professors of radiology; Dr. Sherief Abdel Fatah, a lecturer in the same field; Dr. Fawzi Gaballa, professor of anatomy; and Dr. Aly Gamal Eldin, professor of forensic medicine. A team of foreign consultants, consisting of Dr. Edward Egarter, a forensic pathologist from the Archaeological Museum of South Tyrol, Italy; Dr. Paul Gostner, a radiologist from the General Hospital of Bolzano, Italy; and Dr. Frank J. Rühli, an anatomist and paleopathologist from the University of Zurich, joined the Egyptians to give their opinions. On almost every point, the scientists were unanimous.

The results of this analysis serve to confirm or clarify many of the conclusions reached by the earlier investigators, and also add some fascinating new details. Using modern developmental milestones as their guide, the team has fixed the king's age at death at about 19. This is based primarily on examination of the epiphyses, with confirmation from the incompletely erupted wisdom teeth. The overall health of the king was good, at least to judge from his bones. He was moderately tall, perhaps about 170 cm (five feet and a half), and slightly built. He shows no signs of childhood malnutrition or chronic disease, and seems to have been well fed and cared for. His teeth are in excellent condition, although his upper left wisdom tooth was impacted. This was not life-threatening, but caused a slight thinning of the sinus cavity above, suggesting he might have been in some pain. Sharing the overbite of his Tuthmosid ancestors, he had large front incisors

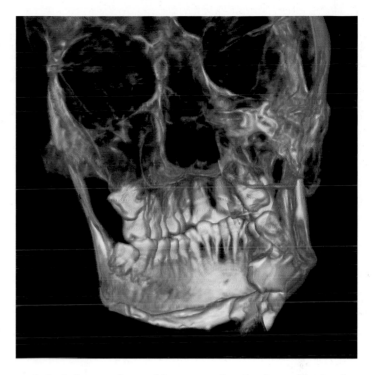

and slightly misaligned lower teeth. The king also had a slight cleft in his palette. The team believes, however, that this was not severe enough to have produced an external expression such as a harelip.

The young king does have an extremely elongated skull, something that has been seen before but is particularly evident in the CT scan. His cranial sutures have not prematurely fused, however, allowing the team to rule out a pathological cause for this feature. Instead, they categorize this as a normal anthropological variation, one clearly depicted in Amarna art. He did not, however, have scoliosis. The bend in the spine noted by Harrison is not associated with any rotation or deformed vertebra, and thus is most likely due to the way the embalmers placed the body.

Tutankhamun was not murdered by a blow to the skull. There is no evidence for a partially healed injury to the back of the head, and the current team reiterates that the loose pieces of bone in the skull could not have come from an antemortem injury. In fact, they were able to match these bone fragments to their original sources: One is part of the topmost vertebra, and the other comes from the foramen magnum (the large opening at the base of the skull). A majority of the team sees evidence in this area for a second route through which embalming material was introduced to the brain. The pools of solidified liquid at the top of the cranial cavity noted in the X-rays were poured in through the nose. But there is more material, of a different density, toward the back of the cranial cavity and in the neck, which can be traced to the back of the neck. Although this part of the team believes it possible that these bones were broken by Carter's team, they think it equally plausible that the embalmers broke them while preparing the route for this material.

The sternum and much of the front rib cage is certainly missing. The CT scan reveals that the ends of the ribs were cut with a sharp instrument. Much of the chest wall is also gone, and a pectoral and string of beads visible in Burton's photographs of the unwrapped body are now missing. The scientific team thinks it possible that this area was removed by the ancient embalmers, but insists it cannot be evidence for a massive chest injury, as there is no associated trauma visible. While they do not rule out a smaller chest injury, they prefer the theory that this area was removed by Carter's team, after the last photographs were taken, in order to retrieve the pectoral and beads. Although Carter's notes state that these were left in situ, covered with wax, they are certainly gone now. It is also hard to imagine that Derry and Saleh, whose notes are detailed and thorough, would not have noticed that such an extensive part of the body was missing entirely. As an Egyptologist, I also believe that if the embalmers had removed the ribs, they would have wrapped them carefully and buried them with the king.

One of the most interesting theories to emerge from the analysis is that the king might have suffered an accident in which he broke his leg shortly before he died. He has a fracture of the lower left femur, at the level of the epiphyseal plate. There are many other fractures of the limbs, but most were probably caused by Carter's team. However, Derry notes this fracture himself, and is unlikely to have caused it, for several reasons: This fracture is different because it has ragged rather than sharp edges, and because two thin layers of embalming fluid have entered the fracture. The majority of the team believes that this fracture must have occurred either during the embalming or during the king's life, and more likely the latter.

The scientists note that this type of fracture is seen in young men in their late teens. If the leg was broken

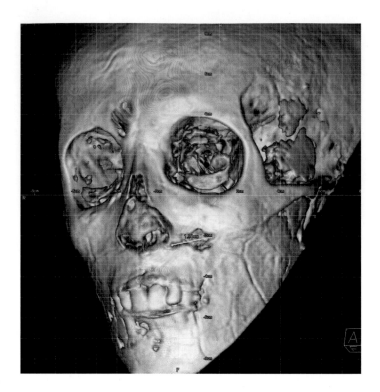

during life, it would have occurred a few days at the most before the king's death, as there is no evidence of extensive healing, and the associated skin wound cannot have had time to mend. Derry had also noted that the left kneecap was loose (it has now been wrapped with the left hand), which the current team sees as possible evidence for further damage to this area of the body. Although the theorized break would not itself have been life-threatening, infection might have set in.

Another advantage to the CT scan is that it was able to see through the sand surrounding the body. There are many fragments hiding there, including a thumb, parts of other fingers, small pieces of ribs and vertebrae, and one bundle that looks like it may well be the missing penis.

The body of the king was not prepared hurriedly or sloppily, as has sometimes been suggested. There were several different types of embalming fluid used, and efforts were clearly made to give the young king the best possible care. This is in accordance with the wealth of treasure with which he was surrounded and laid to rest.

Miracle of forensics: This latex model based on Tutankhumun's skull brings an ancient king to life (opposite). The cheek scar cuts through layers of skin on the skull itself (above).

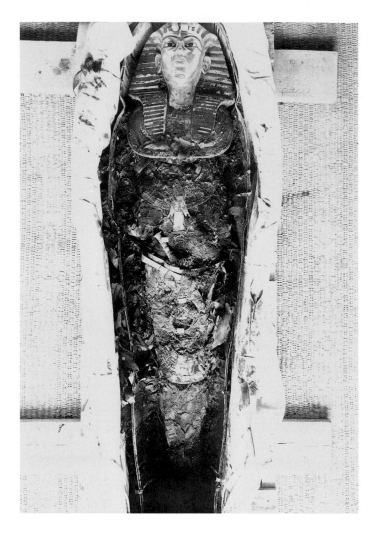

## 110  Ceremonial Dagger and Sheath

Gold, cloisonné

Dagger: Height 31.8 cm; width 3.4 cm

Sheath Height 20.6 cm; width 4.3 cm

18th Dynasty; reign of Tutankhamun

Thebes, Valley of the Kings, tomb of Tutankhamun (KV 62)

Carter 256dd

running spiral at the base) were derived from foreign models. The blade, of a more reddish gold than the handle, is ribbed, and engraved on both sides with a floral motif and a band of diamonds. The elaborate sheath is worked on one side in inlay and granulation with a pattern of scales, bordered at the top with stylized lilies and at the bottom by the head of a canine (perhaps a jackal). The other side, worked in repoussée, bears a stylized hunting scene, with ten animals, including ungulates attacked by dogs and lions, arranged in groups of hunter and hunted. At the top, above a band of running spirals, is an inscription that reads, "the good god, lord of might, Nebkheperure, given life."

The second dagger wrapped with the mummy had a blade of iron. It has been noted that this dagger resembles the description of several mentioned in the Amarna Letters as having been sent to Amenhotep III by the king of the Mitanni. Iron was rare in Egypt at this time, and was not worked locally before the 6th century B.C. Iron artifacts dating back to the Old Kingdom have been found, but these were probably made from meteoric iron.

The objects wrapped with Tutankhamun were likely his most essential jewels and amulets, necessary to help him on his journey to the afterlife and for his use once he arrived safely. This dagger and its companion must have been special to the young king, perhaps given to him as special gifts. In addition to any personal meaning they might have had, they were important for his protection in the Netherworld.

Among the objects in Tutankhamun's tombs were many weapons, including bows and arrows, slings, throwsticks, boomerangs, clubs, swords and daggers, a leather cuirass that served as body armor, and eight shields. These range in size from suitable for a child to the appropriate size for an adult, suggesting that they were used by the king over the course of his lifetime.

Carter found two daggers, including the one illustrated here, within the wrappings of the body. This one was thrust through a girdle of sheet gold that had been wrapped around the king's waist with its hilt just to the right of his umbilicus and the point against his left thigh. Both blade and handle are of solid gold. The hilt is inlaid with granulation and cloisonné work of red and blue in elaborate geometric and floral patterns. Many of these patterns (for example, the Aegean-style

## 111 Decorated Uraeus from Royal Headdress

Gold; Glass; Obsidian; Carnelian

Length 19 cm.; maximum width 2.6 cm.

18th Dynasty; reign of Tutankhamun

Thebes, Valley of the Kings, tomb of Tutankhamun (KV 62)

Carter 256, 4,q

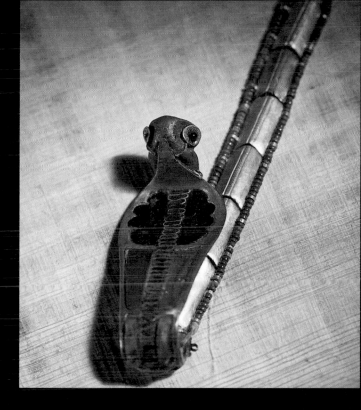

This elaborate royal diadem (left) was found on Tutankhamun's head. So that the outer golden mask could be fitted over it, the separately worked vulture and uraeus for the brow were placed along the thighs. Grooves on these elements, which fit into tongues on the diadem, suggest that they could have been used with other headdresses. The diadem consists of a gold fillet fastened at the back by a bow formed out of two stylized flowers flanking a circle to which two long streamers have been attached with hinges, which made it possible to wear the fillet with different wigs. Two additional flexible gold ribbons, again attached with hinges, hang down on either side of the bow. Along the edges of these run the golden bodies of uraei, their heads inlaid with color. The fillet and the streamers are decorated with circles of carnelian and gold. A pattern in alternating red, green, and blue runs vertically down the center of each hood, with the hieroglyph for the goddess Neith in the center of the largest area. The detachable uraeus and vulture for the brow are each small masterpieces, facing the world above the king's face and protecting him from harm. The cobra's long snakey body winds across the top of

## 112 Inlaid Diadem

Gold; Glass; Obsidian; Semiprecious Stones

Length 19.9 cm; width 17.5 cm

18th Dynasty; reign of Tutankhamun

Thebes, Valley of the Kings, tomb of Tutankhamun (KV 62)

Carter 256 4o, r, and s

the head, stretching to the back of the fillet and serving to stabilize the diadem.

On top of several layers of bandages on the head of the mummy itself were the decayed remains of a headdress (perhaps the khat) of fine linen, of which unfortunately only the pigtail survived. Sewn to its brow was this flexible uraeus (above) of gold inlaid with glass and semiprecious stones, with the body of the serpent arcing up and across the king's skull. The cobra's hood is made of gold inlaid with dark blue glass and carnelian. The head is of lighter blue glass, with eyes of obsidian. The golden body, framed by small beads of light blue glass, is divided into twelve segments formed of individual plates. All were carefully designed for maximum freedom of movement. Across the center of the skull, on top of the cobra's tail, was a vulture of sheet gold, its wings outstretched to embrace the king's head. Together, these protective icons served to keep Tutankhamun safe from harm on the dangerous journey into the Afterlife, and to mark him as the king.

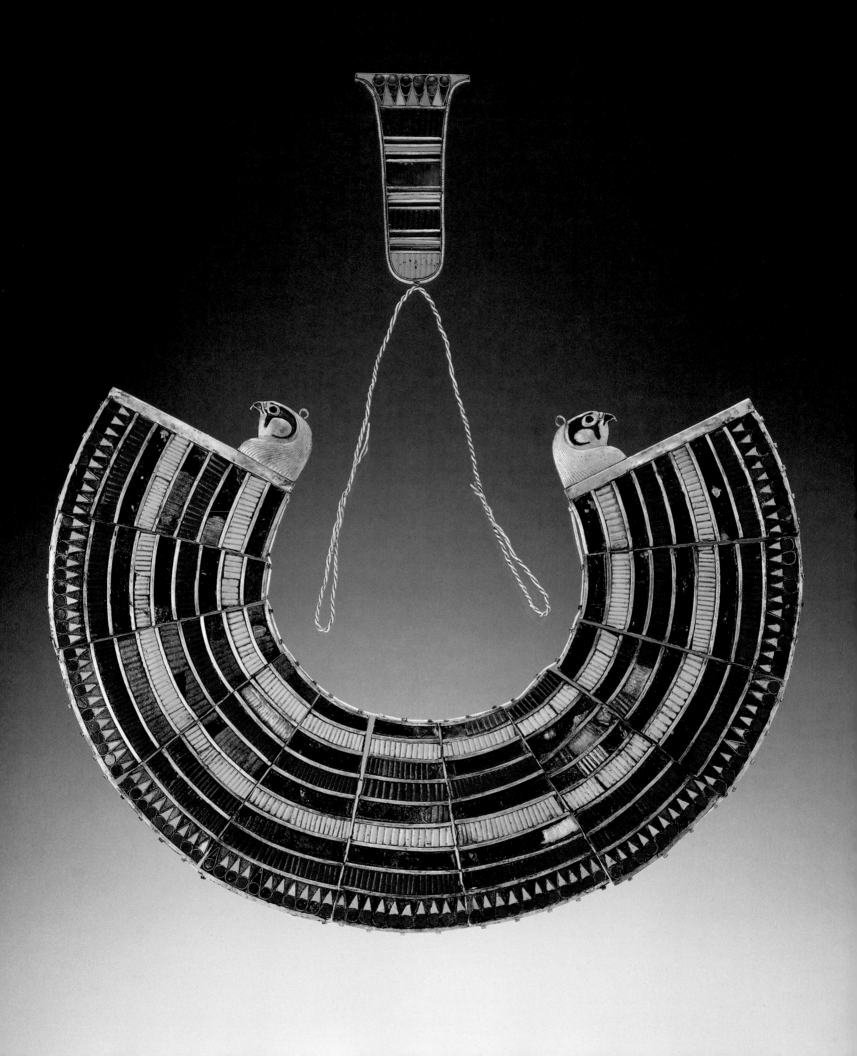

The jewelry buried with the king inside his innermost coffin included six broad collars. All of these had falcon heads adorning their ends. The broad collar (called by the Egyptians *wesekh,* meaning "wide") was an important item of jewelry. It was worn by royalty and nobility, both male and female, and is seen as early as the Old Kingdom. It was worn especially for ritual occasions.

This example was found draped across the front of the king's thighs, evidently placed there during the embalming rituals or funeral. It consists of eight rows of plaques, set into a backing and frame of gold. Alternating between dark blue glass (imitating lapis lazuli), light blue glass (for turquoise), and red (for carnelian), these plaques are incised at regular intervals to give the appearance of small tubular beads. The ninth, outermost row is filled with tear-shaped beads of light blue filled with red circles and alternating with dark blue triangles. These probably represent flowers. At each end of the necklace are golden falcon heads, their eyes and facial markings inlaid with glass. The chain of the counterweight was attached to small circles atop the heads of these falcons.

The counterweight is a striped pendant in the shape of an elongated lotus blossom, with three wide bands of light blue, dark blue, and red (in this case, real carnelian), alternating with narrower bands, all set into a gold frame. At the end, where the blossom flares, are inlays shaped like those in the outermost band of the collar, but with a different color scheme.

There were a number of jewel boxes found in Tutankhamun's tomb, many with dockets detailing their contents. Judging from these dockets, perhaps as much as 60% of the jewelry buried with the king was stolen by the thieves. However, there were still over 200 pieces left, including a number of broad collars. These jewels were of various materials, including pure and alloyed gold, electrum, silver, bronze, and iron, with inlays of semiprecious stones, faience, glass, resin, and shells. The techniques with which these pieces were worked range from the simple threading of beads to granulation, chasing, and repoussé. Although many of these pieces may have been made specifically for mortuary use, signs of wear on others show that they were most likely used during the king's life.

## 113  Inlaid Broad Collar and Counterweight

Gold, carnelian, and glass

Collar: Height 27.2 cm; width 35.5 cm

Counterweight: Height 11 cm; width 5.8 cm

18th Dynasty; reign of Tutankhamun

Thebes, Valley of the Kings, tomb of Tutankhamun (KV 62)

Carter 256aa(1)

## 114  Pectoral in the Shape of a Falcon

Sheet gold, gold wire
Collar: Height 16.5 cm; width 30.3 cm
Counterweight: Height 9.5 cm, width 4 cm
18th Dynasty; reign of Tutankhamun
Thebes, Valley of the Kings, tomb of Tutankhamun (KV 62)
Carter 256t

This collar represents a falcon, wings outstretched and curved upwards to wrap around the king's neck, head turned to one side. It is made of a thin sheet of gold, elaborately chased on both sides to indicate the feathers, the markings of the face, and the details of the stylized floral decoration of the counterweight. In his talons, the falcon holds a shen ring, symbolizing the circuit of the sun and eternity. The counterweight is attached to the falcon with thin gold wire.

Originally a sky and sun god, the falcon was an extremely important symbol to the ancient Egyptians, able to soar into the sky and reach the realm of the gods. In traditional Egyptian iconography, the falcon represented Horus, simultaneously protector and embodiment of the king. Other gods, most often Re, Re-Horakhti (a syncretized god combining Re and Horus), the war god Montu, and Qebehsenuef (one of the four sons of Horus), were depicted as falcon-headed; Horus and Montu are also shown as full-bodied falcons.

The icon of the falcon holding the shen ring is seen often in royal scenes, placed in pairs at the upper edges of the scene. In many cases, this bird is identified by inscriptions as Horus the Behedite (Horus of the town of Idfu), who offers eternal protection to the king. A number of falcon jewels were found draped around Tutankhamun's neck, guarding the king from any evil that might attack him. Along with these were many vulture necklaces and amulets, representing the goddesses Nekhbet (tutelary goddess of Upper Egypt) and Mut (consort of Amun and mother goddess), as well as cobra-shaped jewels (representing Wadjet, tutelary goddess of Lower Egypt, and other goddesses) and other objects meant to ward off injury. Altogether there were about 150 objects wrapped with the king, set in place according to instructions laid out in the Book of the Dead. All of these pieces served to protect the king on his journey to the Afterlife, making certain that he could successfully join the gods and work with them to help ensure the proper functioning of the cosmos.

# ACKNOWLEDGMENTS

I would like to thank the many people who helped in many ways to make this book. First of all, I would like to thank Mohamed Megahed and Nadja Tomoum from my office. My dear friend Ali Radwan offered valuable advice on this period of Egyptian history. I am very grateful to Ken Garrett, a great photographer and my good friend, for his images. I wish to thank also Dr. Wafaa El Saddik and the curators who helped put this exhibition together. From the National Geographic Society, I offer my appreciation to Lisa Lytton and Nina Hoffman for their hard work. A special thanks should be given to my dear friend Terry Garcia, Executive Vice President of National Geographic, and I am also grateful to Farida el-Reedy for her help and always sound advice.

My thanks also to my colleagues who read the text and gave valuable comments: Ed Brovarski, Betsy Bryan, and David O'Connor. Ray Johnson and Salima Ikram also offered their expertise on specific points, and were generous with their time. Any errors, however, are my own.

I am extremely grateful to the Egyptian team who examined the mummy of Tutankhamun while it was in the CT-scan machine in the Valley of the Kings, and offer my admiration to the excellent Egyptian radiologists, pathologists, and anatomists who worked so hard to investigate the cause of Tutankhamun's death. The foreign team who came to participate in this great event also did a wonderful job, and I thank them as well. Last but not least, I would like to thank my colleague Janice Kamrin for editing this book, and for her dedication and advice. It would never have happened without her.

# SOURCE BIBLIOGRAPHY

Abitz, Friedrich. *Statuetten in Schreinen als Grabbeigaben in den ägyptischen Königsgräbern der 18. und 19. Dynastie.* Weisbaden, 1979

Aldred, Cyril. *Akhenaten and Nefertiti.* New York, 1973.

———. *Jewels of the Pharaohs: Egyptian Jewellery of the Dynastic Period.* London, 1971.

Allen, S. J. "Tutankhamun's Embalming Cache Reconsidered." In Z. Hawass, ed., *Egyptology at the Dawn of the Twenty-first Century: Proceedings of the Eighth International Congress of Egyptology, Vol. I.* Cairo, 2003: 23–29.

Altenmüller, H. "Papyrusdickicht und Wüste. Überlegungen zu zwei Statuenensembles des Tutanchamun." *Mitteilungen des Deutschen Archäologischen Instituts Abteilung Kairo* 47 (1991): 11–19.

Andrews, Carol. *Ancient Egyptian Jewellery.* London, 1990.

Arnold, Dorothea. *The Royal Women of Amarna.* New York, 1996.

Beinlich, Horst. "Das Totenbuch bei Tutanchamun." *Göttinger Miszellen* 102 (1988): 7–18.

Beinlich, Horst, and Mohamed Saleh. *Corpus der Hieroglyphischen Inschriften aus dem Grab des Tutanchamun.* Oxford, 1989.

Bell, Martha. "An Armchair Excavation of KV 55." *Journal of the American Research Center in Egypt* 27 (1990): 97–127.

Borchardt, Ludwig. *Statuen und Statuetten von Konigen und Privatleuten im Museum von Kairo:* 1–1294. Three volumes. Berlin: 1930.

Bosse-Griffiths, K. "The Great Enchantress in the Little Golden Shrine of Tutankhamun." *Journal of Egyptian Archaeology* 59 (1973): 100–108.

Brier, Bob. *The Murder of Tutankhamen.* London, 1998.

Bryan, Betsy M. "Portrait Sculpture of Thutmose IV." *Journal of the American Research Center in Egypt* 24 (1987): 3–20.

———. *The Reign of Thutmose IV.* London and Baltimore, 1991.

Carter, Howard, and Arthur Mace. *The Tomb of Tut.ankh.Amen.* (3 volumes) London, 1923–33.

Cerny, Jaroslav. *Hieratic Inscriptions from the Tomb of Tutankhamun.* Oxford, 1965.

Chassinat, Émile. "Tomb inviolé de la XVIIIe Dynastie découvert aux environs de Médinet el-Gorab dans le Fayoûm." *Bulletin de l'Institut Français d'Archéologie Orientale* 1 (1901): 225–234.

Chevrier, Henri. "Rapport sur les travaux de Karnak (Mars-Mai 1926)." *Annales du Service des Antiquités de l'Égypte* 26 (1926): 119–130.

Daressy, Georges. *Fouilles de la vallée des rois.* Cairo, 1902. (1902a)

———. "Rapport sur la trouvaille de HAt-iAy." *Annales du Service des Antiquités de l'Égypte* 2 (1902): 1–13 (1902b)

Davis, Theodore M., et al. *The Tomb of Thoutmôsis IV.* London, 1904.

———. *The Tomb of Iouiya and Touiyou.* London, 1907.

———. *The Tomb of Queen Tîyi.* San Francisco, 1990.

Dodson, Aidan. *The Canopic Equipment of the Kings of Egypt.* London, 1994.

———. "The Canopic Coffinettes of Tutankhamun and the Identity of Ankhkheperure." In M. Eldamaty and M. Trad., eds., *Egyptian Museum Collections around the World: Studies for the Centennial of the Egyptian Museum, Cairo.* Cairo: SCA Press, 2002: 275–285

Eaton-Krauss, Marianne. "Die Throne Tutanchamuns." *Göttinger Miszellen* 76 (1984): 7–10.

———. "Walter Segal's Documentation of CG 51113, the Throne of Princess Sat-Amun." *Journal of Egyptian Archaeology* 75 (1989): 77–88.

Eaton-Krauss, Marianne, and Erhart Graefe. *The Small Golden Shrine from the Tomb of Tutankhamun.* Oxford, 1985.

Edwards, I.E.S. *Treasures of Tutankhamun.* New York, 1976.

El-Khouli, A. *Stone Vessels, Pottery and Sealings from the Tomb of Tutankhamun.* Oxford, 1993.

Englebach, Reginald. "A Hitherto Unknown Statue of King Tut'ankhamûn." *Annales du Service des Antiquités de l'Égypte* 38 (1938): 23–28.

———. "A Hitherto Unknown Statue of King Tut'ankhamûn—Further Remarks." *Annales du Service des Antiquités de l'Égypte* 39 (1939): 195.

Feucht-Putz, Erika. *Die Königliche Pektorale.* Bamberg, 1967.

Fisher, Clarence S. "The Eckley B. Coxe Jr. Egyptian Expedition." *The Museum Journal* 8, no. 4 (1917): 211–237.

Forbes, Dennis. "Ritual Figures in KV 62." *Amarna Letters* 3 (1994): 110–127.

Freed, Rita, ed. *Pharaohs of the Sun.* Boston, 1999.

Gabolde, Marc. *D'Akhenaton à Toutânkhamon, Collection de l'Institut d'Archéologie et d'Histoire de l'Antiquité* 3. Lyon, 1998.

Germer, Renate. *Flora des pharaonischen Agypten.* Cairo, 1991.

Graefe, Erhart. "The Royal Cache and the Tomb Robberies." In N. Strudwick and J.H. Taylor, eds. *The Theban Necropolis: Past, Present and Future.* London, 2003.

Habachi, Labib. *Tell Basta.* Cairo, 1957.

Hickmann, Hans. *Instruments de Musique.* Cairo, 1949.

Hornung, Eric, et al. *The Quest for Immortality: Treasures of Ancient Egypt.* Washington, 2002.

Ikram, Salima, and Aidan Dodson. *The Mummy in Ancient Egypt: Equipping the Dead for Eternity.* London, 1998.

James, T. G. H. *Tutankhamun: The Eternal Splendor of the Boy Pharaoh.* Vercelli, Italy, 2000.

———. *Howard Carter: The Path to Tutankhamun.* Cairo, 2001.

Johnson, W. Raymond and Peter Lacovara. "A Composite Statue of Amenhotep III in the Cairo Museum." In M. Eldamaty and M. Trad, eds., *Egyptian Museum Collections around the World: Studies for the Centennial of the Egyptian Museum, Cairo.* Cairo, 2002: 591–594

Johnson, W. Raymond, Peter Lacovara, and Nicholas Reeves. "A Composite Statue Element in the Museum of Fine Arts, Boston." *Revue d'Égyptologie* 47 (1996): 173–179.

Jones, Dilwyn *Model Boats from the Tomb of Tutankhamun,* Oxford, 1990.

de Jong, Aliel. "Feline Deities." In D. Redford, ed., *The Oxford Encyclopedia of Ancient Egypt,* Vol. I. Oxford, 2001.

Kamal, M. "Fouilles du Service des Antiquités à Tell el-Amarna en 1934." *Annales du Service des Antiquités de l'Égypte* 35 (1935): 193–196.

———. "Some Fragments from Shawabti-Figures of Akhenaten in the Egyptian Museum." *Annales du Service des Antiquités de l'Égypte* 39 (1939): 381–382.

Kessler, Dieter. "Zu den Jagdszenen auf dem kleinen goldenen Tutanchamunschrein." *Göttinger Miszellen* 90 (1986): 35–44.

Killen, Geoffrey. *Ancient Egyptian Furniture, vol. I: 4000–1300 BC.* Warminster, 1980.

———. *Ancient Egyptian Furniture, vol. II: Boxes, Chests and Footstools.* Warminster, 1994.

Kozloff, Ariel, and Betsy Bryan. *Egypt's Dazzling Sun: Amenhotep III and His World.* Cleveland, 1992.

Laboury, Dimitri. "Mise au point sur l'iconographie de Neferneferouaton, le predecesseur de Toutankhamon." In M. Eldamaty and M. Trad, eds., *Egyptian Museum Collections around the World: Studies for the Centennial of the Egyptian Museum, Cairo.* Cairo, 2002: 711–722.

Leek, F. Filce. *The Human Remains from the Tomb of Tutankhamun.* Oxford, 1972.

Legrain, Georges. "Rapport sur les travaux exécutés à Karnak du 31 octobre 1902 au 15 mai 1903." *Annales du Service des Antiquités de l'Égypte* 5 (1904): 1–43

———. *Statues et Statuettes de rois et de particuliers,* vol. I. Cairo, 1906.

———. *Répertoire généalogique et onomastique du Musée du Caire. Monuments de la XVIIe et de la XVIIIe dynastie.* Geneva, 1908.

Loret, Victor. "Le tombeau d'Amenophis II et la cachette royale de Biban el Molouk." *Bulletin de l'Institut d'Égypte* 9 (1899): 98–122.

Manniche, Lise. *Ancient Egyptian Musical Instruments.* Munich, 1975. (1975a)

———. *Musical Instruments from the Tomb of Tutankhamun.* Oxford, 1975. (1975b)

———. "The so-called scenes of daily life in the private tombs of the Eighteenth Dynasty: an overview." In N. Strudwick and J.H. Taylor, eds., *The Theban Necropolis: Past, Present and Future.* London, 2003: 42–45.

Mariette, Auguste. *Notice des Principaux Monuments exposés dans les galeries provisoires du Musée d'antiquités égyptiennes de S.A. Le Vice Roi á Boulaq.* Alexandria, 1868.

Martin, Geoffrey. *The Royal Tomb at el-Amarna: vol. I: The Objects.* London, 1974.

Müller, Hans-Wolfgang, et al. *Nofretete-Echnaton.* Mainz: Philipp von Zabern, 1976.

Müller, Maya. *Die Kunst Amenophis' III. und Echnatons.* Basel, 1988.

Murray, Helen, and Mary Nutall. *A Handlist to Howard Carter's Catalogue of Objects in Tutankhamun's Tomb.* Oxford, 1963.

Newberry, Percy. *Funerary Statues and Model Sarcophagi, Volume II and Volume III.* Cairo, 1930–1957.

*Nofret—Die Schöne: Die Frau im Alten Ägypten.* Munich, 1984

Nolte, Birgit. *Die Glasgefässe im alten Ägypten.* Munich, 1968.

Pendlebury, J.D.S. "Preliminary Report of the Excavations at Tell el Amarnah, 1932–33." *Journal of Egyptian Archaeology* 19 (1933): 113–118.

———. *Tell el-Amarna.* London, 1935.

———. *The City of Akhenaten, Part III: The Central City and the Official Quarters* 44. London, 1951.

Petrie, W.M.F. *Kahun, Gurob, and Hawara.* London, 1890.

———. *Tell el Amarna.* London, 1894.

———. *Researches in Sinai.* London, 1906.

Pusch, Edgar B. *Das Senet-Brettspiel im Alten Ägypten.* Munich, 1979.

Quibell, James. "A Tomb at Hawaret el Gurob." *Annales du Service des Antiquités de l'Égypte* 2 (1902): 141–143.

———. *Tomb of Yuaa and Thuiu, nos. 51001–51191.* Cairo, 1908.

Reeves, C.N. "On the Miniature Mask from the Tutankhamun Embalming Cache." *Bulletin de la Société d'Égyptologie, Genève* 8 (1983): 81–83.

Reeves, Nicholas, and Richard Wilkinson. *The Complete Tutankhamun.* London, 1990.

Reeves, Nicholas. *The Complete Valley of the Kings*. London, 1996.
———. *Ancient Egypt: The Great Discoveries. A Year-by-Year Chronicle*. London, 2000.

Roth, Ann Macy, and Catherine Roehrig. "Magical Bricks and the Bricks of Birth." *Journal of Egyptian Archaeology* 33 (2002): 120–139.

Saleh, M. and Hourig Sourouzian. *The Egyptian Museum Cairo: Official Catalogue*. Mainz, 1986.

Schneider, Hans D. *Shabtis: An Introduction to the History of Ancient Egyptian Funerary Statuettes with a Catalogue of the Collection of Shabtis in the National Museum of Antiquities at Leiden. Vols. I and II*. Leiden, 1977.

Schorsch, D. "Precious-Metal Polychromy in Egypt in the Time of Tutankhamun." *Journal of Egyptian Archaeology* 87 (2001): 63–71.

Silverman, D. "Cryptographic Writing in the Tomb of Tutankhamun." *Studien zur alatägyptischen Kultur* 8 (1980): 233–36.

Tait, W.J. *Game-Boxes and Accessories from the Tomb of Tutankhamun*. Oxford, 1982.

Thomas, Elizabeth. "The Four Niches and Amuletic Figures in Theban Royal Tombs." *Journal of the American Research Center in Egypt* 3 (1965): 71–78.

Tiradritti, Francesco. The *Treasures of the Egyptian Museum*. Vercelli, Italy, 1999.

Vandersleyen, Claude. "L'iconographie de Tutankhamon et les effigies provenant de sa tombe." *Bulletin de la Société d'Égyptologie, Genève* 9–10 (1984–85): 309–321.

Wallert, Ingrid. *Der verzierte Löffel. Seine Formgeschichte und Verwendung im alten Ägypten*. Cairo, 1967.

Westendorf. W. "Bemerkungen zur 'Kammer der Wiedergeburt' im Tutanchamungrab." *Zeitschrift für Ägyptische Sprache und Altertumskunde* 94 (1967): 139–150.

Wiese, André, and Andreas Brodbeck, eds. *Tutankhamun: The Golden Beyond*. Basel: Antikenmuseum Basel und Sammlung Ludwig, 2004.

Wildung, Dietrich, and Günther Grimm. *Götter-Pharaonen*. Mainz, 1978.

Wilkinson, Alix. *Ancient Egyptian Jewellery*. London, 1971.
———. "Jewelry for a Procession in the Bed-Chamber in the Tomb of Tutankhamun." *Bulletin de l'Institut Français d'Archéologie Orientale* 84 (1984): 335–345.

Winlock, H.E. *Materials Used at the Embalming of Tut-ankh-amun*. New York, 1941.

Zakbar, V. "Correlation of the Transformation Spells of the Book of the Dead and the Amulets of Tutankhamun's Mummy." *Mélanges Vercoutter*: 375–388.

Ziegler, Christiane, ed. *The Pharaohs*. Milan, 2002.

## OBJECT BIBLIOGRAPHY

This is a partial bibliography and not meant to be comprehensive. Howard Carter's original notes for all objects found in the tomb of Tutankhamun are available at www.asmol.ox.ac.uk/gri/carter/Carter#.html.

1 **Painted Wooden Torso of Tutankhamun** Wiese, no. 90; Reeves 1990, p. 155

2 **Statue of Thutmosis IV and his Mother** Wiese, no. 1; Bryan 1987, pp. 3–20; Bryan 1991, pp. 99f, fig. 8; Reeves 2000, pp. 118–120; Legrain 1906, pp. 46–47, pl. 49; Legrain 1904, pp. 35f, pl. 5

3 **Guardian Statue of Amenhotep II** Wiese, no. 2; Daressy 1902a, p. 155, pl. 31; Reeves and Wilkinson, pp. 102f; Ziegler, no. 258; Hornung, cf. pp. 111f, no. 28; Forbes, p. 113

4 **Face from a Royal Composite Statue** Wiese, no. 25; Legrain 1906, pp. 58–59, Pl. 64; Johnson and Lacovara; Johnson, Lacovara, and Reeves; *Nofret*, pp. 188f, no. 93

5 **Sculpted Head of a Princess from Amarna** Wiese, no. 46; Freed, p. 217, no. 45; Arnold, pp. 52–65; Saleh and Sourouzian, cf. no. 163

6 **Canopic Jar of Queen Kiya** Wiese, no. 48; Davis 1990, pp. 24–25, pls. 7–19, 120–122; Bell, pp. 102, 119; Dodson 1994, pp. 57–61; Hans-Wolfgang Müller, no. 51; Freed, cf. nos. 234, 235

7 **Votive Figure of Amenhotep III** Wiese, no. 23; Legrain 1906, pp. 48f., pl. 51; Legrain 1908, p. 140, no. 245a

8 **Head of a Figurine of Queen Tiye** Wiese, no. 24; Tiradritti, p. 180; Kozloff, cf. pp. 209–210; Petrie 1906, p. 126f, fig.133

9 **Face from a Composite Statue of Nefertiti** Wiese, no. 45; Fisher, pp. 211–237; Arnold, fig. 65; Freed, no. 41; Hans-Wolfgang Müller, no. 54

10 **Statue of Khaemwaset and his Wife Manana** Weise, no. 37; Habachi, pp. 104–107, pls. 39, 20 and pp. 95–97, pls. 28, 29–A, B

11 **Model of an Unrolled Papyrus** Wiese, no. 13; Ziegler, no. 250; Daressy 1902a, p. 138, pl. 30

12 **Model of a Throwstick** Wiese, no. 15; Reeves and Wilkinson, p. 107; Davis 1904, p. 110

13 **Model of a Pomegranate** Wiese, 16a; Daressy 1902a, p. 144; Germer, p. 42f

14 **Model of a Piece of Fruit** Wiese, no. 16b; Daressy 1902a, p. 145; Germer, p. 148f, pp. 169–171

15 **Model of a Lotus Bud** Wiese, no. 16c (mis-numbered); Daressy 1902a, p. 150; PL. 30;; Germer, p. 37–39

16 **Model of a Lotus Bud** Wiese, no. 16d (mis-numbered); Daressy 1902a, p. 147; Germer, p. 122

17 **Polychrome Perfume Bottle** Wiese, no. 20; Daressy 1902a, pp. 24f., pl.7; Reeves and Wilkinson, pp. 179–181; Nolte, pp. 51f., pls. 1, 9

18 **Decorated Drinking Bowl** Wiese, no. 21; Ziegler, no. 159; Daressy 1902a, p. 24, pl. 6; Reeves and Wilkinson, p. 181

19 **Decorated Collar for a Dog** Wiese, no. 22; Daressy 1902a, p. 34, pl 11; Reeves and Wilkinson, p. 181

20, 21, 22 **Imitation Stone Vessels** Weise, no. 36a, b, c; Quibell 1908, pp. 42, 44, 45, ps. 20f; Davis 1907, p. 32, pls. 27f.; Reeves and Wilkinson, p.174

23 **Elaborately Decorated Chest** Wiese, no. 34; Davis 1907, p. 47, pl. 39; Killen 1994, pp. 46–49, fig. 57; Quibell 1908, pp. 56f, pls. 46f.; Reeves and Wilkinson, p. 178

24 **Part of an Unguent Spoon with a Handle in the Shape of a Swimming Female** Weise no. 40; Wallert, pp. 16–23 and 95f, K14–K17; Mariette, p. 158, no. 33

25 **Unguent Vessel in the Shape of a Servant Bearing a Jar** Wiese, no. 41; Daressy 1902b, pp. 1–13, fig. 9

26 **Model Boat of Amenhotep II** Wiese, no. 8; Reeves and Wilkinson, p. 100–103, 199; Daressy 1902a, p. 241f, pl. 48; Loret 1899, p. 98–122; Landström, p. 107–112; Ziegler, no. 261

27 **Ankh Sign** Wiese, no. 12b; Reeves and Wilkinson, p.107; Davis 1904, p. 103

28 **Vessel in the Shape of an Ankh** Wiese, no. 12a; Reeves and Wilkinson, p. 100–103; Daressy 1902a, p. 122

29 **Model of a Ritual Vessel** Wiese, no. 11a; Ziegler, no. 245 (referred to here as CG 3870); Daressy 1902a, p. 222; pl. 46

30 **Model of a Roll of Cloth** Wiese, no. 14 (incorrect provenance and CG); Reeves and Wilkinson, pp. 117f; Ziegler, no. 249 (incorrect provenance); Bell, p. 103; Davis 1990, p. 30, no. 27; cf. Davis 1904, p. 115, pl. 25

31 **Model of A Ritual Vessel** Wiese, no. 11b; Davis 1904, p. 59, pl. 18; cf. Ziegler, no. 255

32 **Shabti of Ptahmosis** Weise, no. 38; Newberry, pp. 343–345 and pl. 27; Bryan 1991, p. 244

33 **Funerary Figurine of Resi** Wiese, no. 39; Borchardt III, pp. 108f, pl. 150; Petrie 1890, p. 38f, pl. 22,8; Quibell 1902, pp. 141–143, pls. 1–2; Chassinat, pp. 225–234, pls. 1–2

34 **Reused Triad of Thutmosis I, Queen Ahmosis, and the god Amun** Wiese, no. 53; Freed, no. 244; Legrain 1906, p. 31

35 **Statuette of a Leonine Goddess** Wiese, no. 6; de Jong, 512–513; Daressy 1902a, p. 160, pl. 33; Reeves and Wilkinson, p. 100; Forbes, 110–127

36 **Serpent Goddess** Wiese, no. 7; Daressy 1902a, pp. 162f. pl. 35; Abitz, pp. 55f, pp. 110–113; Forbes, 110–127

37 **Sculptor's Practice Model in Sunk Relief** Wiese, no. 44; Pendlebury 1933, p. 117, pl 15.2; Pendlebury 1935, p. 134, pl. 5.3; Freed, no 134; *Nofret*, no. 32

38 **Funerary Figurine of Akhenaten** Wiese, no. 47; Kamal 1935, p. 194, no. 2; Kamal 1939, pp. 381–2, pl. 57b; Martin, no. 210, pl. 43, pp. 65–66

39 **Balustrade Showing Akhenaten and Family under the Aten** Wiese, no. 43; Petrie 1894, pl. 12 (3,4), p. 10; Saleh and Sourouzian, no. 164; Freed, no. 72; Pendlebury 1951, p. 77, pl. 69,5; Aldred 1973, p. 56, fig. 33; Hans-Wolfgang Müller, no. 46

40 **Head of Colossal Statue of Amenhotep IV** Wiese, no. 42; Chevrier, pp. 119–127, pl. 2; Freed, cf. p. 208, no. 22

41 **Small Gilded Funerary Mask for a Fetus** Wiese, no. 49; Reeves 1983, p. 81–83; S.J. Allen, p. 23–29; Winlock

42 **Gilded Funerary Mask of Tjuya** Wiese, no. 26; Quibell 1908, pl. 13; Davis 1907, p. 22, pl. 15; Reeves and Wilkinson, p. 175

43 **Gilded Coffin of Tjuya** Wiese, no. 27; Quibell 1908, pl. 10, 11; Davis 1907, p. 19, pl. 13; Reeves and Wilkinson, pp. 174–178

44, 45 **Shabti Boxes** Wiese, no. 31a and b; Quibell 1908, pp. 39–40; Reeves and Wilkinson, p. 177; Hornung, cf. no. 38.

46, 47, 48 **Lid and Base of Canopic Jar and Small Mask for Bundled Viscera of Tjuya** Wiese, no. 29a and b; Davis 1907, p. 24f, pl. 17; Quibell 1908, pp. 34f, pl. 16; Reeves and Wilkinson, pp. 149f

49 **Four Dummy Vessels on a Stand** Wiese, no. 35; Quibell 1908, p. 48, pls. 24f; Davis 1907, pl. 29; Reeves and Wilkinson, p. 178

50 **Funerary Figurine on a Bed** Wiese, no. 32; Quibell 1908, p. 49, pl. 27; Hans-Wolfgang Müller, no. 34; Schneider, pp. 163f, p. 214; Freed, cf. no. 15

51 **Djed (Endurance) Symbol** Wiese, no. 9; Ziegler, no. 242; Reeves and Wilkinson, pp. 100–102; Daressy 1902a, p. 132f; Hornung, cf. 27

52 **Ankh (Life) Symbol** Wiese, no. 10a; Ziegler, no. 243; Reeves and Wilkinson, p. 102; Daressy 1902a, p. 118, pl. 28; Hornung, cf. no. 26, p. 110

53 *Was* (Prosperity) Symbol  Wiese, no. 10b; Daressy 1902a, p. 126f, pl. 29; Ziegler, no. 244; Reeves and Wilkinson p. 102

54 Canopic Chest of Tjuya  Wiese, no. 28; Davis 1907, pp. 23–25, pl. 16; Quibell 1908, pp. 32f, pls. 15f; Reeves and Wilkinson, pp. 149f

55 Chair of Princess Sitamun  Wiese, no. 33; Davis 1907, pp. 37–41, pls. 33f; Quibell 1908, pp. 53f, pls. 38–43; Eaton-Krauss 1989, pp. 77–88; Reeves and Wilkinson, p. 178

56 Head of a Cow  Wiese, no. 5; Forbes, p. 122; Daressy 1902a, p. 163; pl. 34

57 Panther Base for a Statuette of Amenhotep II  Wiese, no. 3; Daressy 1902a, pp. 160f, pl. 34; Reeves and Wilkinson, p. 102f; Ziegler, no. 259; Hornung, cf. no. 29; Altenmüller, 11–19; Forbes, 110–127; Abitz, pp. 34f

58 Head of a Bovine Goddess  Wiese, no. 4; Reeves and Wilkinson, pp. 100–102; Daressy 1902a, p. 163, p. 34; Abitz, p. 55, pp. 108–110, Forbes, pp. 122f

59 Shabti of Tjuya  Wiese, no. 30a; Quibell 1908, p. 39, pl. 17; Reeves and Wilkinson, pp. 177f; Davis 1907, p. 26, pl. 20; Hornung, cf. p. 119, no. 35

60 Shabti of Yuya  Weise, no. 30b; Quibell 1908, p. 37, pl. 17; Reeves and Wilkinson, pp. 177f; Davis 1907, p. 26, pl. 18

61 Shabti (on Stand) of Yuya  Wiese, no. 30c; Quibell 1908, p. 38, pl. 17; Reeves and Wilkinson, pp. 177f; Davis 1907, pl. 19

62 Shabti of Thutmosis IV  Wiese, no. 19; Reeves and Wilkinson, p. 107; Davis 1904, p. 46

63 Shabti of Amenhotep II  Wiese, no. 18; Tiradritti, cf. p. 290; Reeves and Wilkinson, pp. 100f; Daressy 1902a, p. 89

64 Magical Brick of Thutmosis IV  Wiese, no. 17; Reeves and Wilkinson, 106f; Davis 1904, p. 9, pl. 4; Thomas, p. 74; Roth and Roehrig, p. 123

65, 66 Tutankhamun as the King of Upper and Lower Egypt  Wiese, no. 57a and b; Reeves and Wilkinson, p. 130f; Beinlich and Saleh, p. 134; Forbes, pp. 110–113; Abitz, p. 33; Vandersleyen, pp. 309–321; Forbes, p. 116

67 Golden Shrine for a Statue  Wiese, no. 58; Manniche 2003, 42–45; Wiese, no. 58; Beinlich and Saleh, pp. 39–46; Eaton-Krauss and Graefe; Bosse-Griffiths, pp. 100–108; Kessler, pp. 35–43; Reeves 1990, p. 140; Westendorff, pp. 139–150; Edwards, pp. 116–119

68 Child's Chair with Footrest  Wiese, no. 89a and b; Reeves 1990, 184–187; Killen 1980, p. 61, pl. 99; Killen 1994, p. 90, fig. 86, pl. 72; Eaton-Krauss 1984, pp. 7–10; James 2000, p. 297

69 and 70 Royal Crook and Flail  Wiese, no. 69a; Reeves 1990, pp. 153f; James, pp. 184f (flail with incorrect no.); Edwards, p. 106; Wildung and Grimm, no. 39 (with incorrect register no.)

71 Staff with a Handle in the Shape of a Nubian Captive  Wiese, no. 81; Reeves 1990, pp. 178f; cf. James, pp. 270f

72 Staff Bearing a Figure of the King  Wiese, no. 56; p. 245; Reeves 1990, p. 178f

73 Ceremonial Mace  Wiese, no. 80; Reeves 1990, pp. 174–177; James 2000, p. 278

74 Silver Trumpet with Wooden Core  Wiese, no. 82a and b; Manniche 1975a, pp. 31–35; Manniche 1975b, p. 7, pls. 5–10; James 2000, p. 266

75 Sistrum  Wiese, no. 83; Hickman, pp. 81–2, pl. 53a–c; Manniche 1975b, pp. 5, pls. 2–4

76 Dummy Folding Stool  Wiese, no. 88; James, p. 296f; Killen 1980, pp. 42f, pl. 64; Reeves 1990, pp. 184–187; Edwards, pp. 112–114

77 Fan Depicting an Ostrich Hunt  Wiese, no. 78; Reeves 1990, p. 179; Edwards, pp. 126f; James 2000, pp. 186–87

78 Ceremonial Shield  Wiese, no. 79; Reeves 1990, pp. 176f; James 2000, pp. 276f

79 Statue of Herwer (Horus the Elder)  Wiese, no. 61; Reeves 1990, pp. 130–34; James, cf. p. 153 (image of this statue with wrong number and identification); Abitz; Beinlich and Saleh, p. 133; Wildung and Grimm, no. 40.

80 Inlaid Pectoral and Counterweight  Wiese, no. 71; Reeves 1990, pp. 150–152; Feucht-Putz, pp. 51–54; Schorsch, pp. 55–71; A. Wilkinson 1971, pp. 143f; A. Wilkinson 1984, pp. 339f; Andrews, pp. 132; Aldred 1971, pp. 220 pls. 99f.; James 2000, p. 281

81 Inlaid Pectoral Spelling out the Name of the King  Wiese, no. 72; Aldred 1971, no. 79; Andrews, pp. 135f; Feucht-Putz, pp. 89–99; Reeves 1990, pp. 150–152; A. Wilkinson 1971, pp. 138–141; James 2000, pp. 212–13; Wildung and Grimm, no. 36; Silverman, pp. 233–236

82 Statue of Ptah  Wiese, no. 59; Abitz, James, p. 145, p. 148; Beinlich and Saleh, p. 133; Reeves 1990, pp. 130–134; James, p. 148

83 Statue of Duamutef  Wiese, no. 60; Abitz; Reeves 1990, pp.130–134; Beinlich and Saleh, p. 134

84 Coffinette for the Viscera of Tutankhamun  Wiese, no. 55; Beinlich and Saleh, p. 106–108; Dodson 2002, pp. 275–285; Dodson 1994, pp. 61–63; Laboury, pp. 716–718; Reeves 1990, pp. 120–123; Vandersleyen, pp. 309–321, esp. 312f; James, pp. 108f; Edwards, cf. no. 45, pp. 156–157

85 Canopic Stopper of Tutankhamun  Wiese, no. 54; Dodson 1994, pp. 48–47, esp. 62–64; Ikram and Dodson, pp. 276 292, esp. 285, 287; Reeves 1990, p. 156; Vandersleyen, p. 311; Laboury, p. 716; James, pp. 104f

86 Granite Statue of Tutankhamun  Wiese, no. 51; Englebach 1938, pp. 23–28; Englebach 1939, p. 195; Legrain 1906, pp. 53f, pl. 57 and 58

87 Statue of Amun with the Features of Tutankhamun  Wiese, no. 52; Wildung and Grimm, no. 49; Saleh and Sourouzian, no. 199

88 Chest for Jewelry  Wiese, no. 75; Reeves 1990, p. 167; Killen 1994, p. 61, fig. 68, pl. 54; Beinlich and Saleh, pp. 29–30; James 2000, p. 196; Cerny, no. 49

89 Oil Vessel with Inlaid Decoration  Wiese, no. 92; Edwards, no. 47; Reeves 1990, pp. 198f; Wildung and Grimm, no. 45; El-Khouli, pl. 5a

90 Cosmetic Container in the Shape of a Duck or Goose  Wiese, no. 77; Reeves 1990, p. 158

91 Unguent Vessel in the Shape of a Female Servant  Weise, no. 50a; Davis 1990, p. 43, no. 40, pl. III2; Bell, no. 32, p. 105

92 Unguent Vessel in the Shape of the God Bes  Weise, no. 50b; Davis 1990, p. 45, no. 44, pl. III1; Bell, no. 37, p. 105

93 Inscribed Game Board with Twenty Squares  Weise, no. 84; Tait, pp. 15–17, pls. 8, 19; Pusch, pp. 225f, pls. 62c; Reeves 1990, pp. 161; Beinlich and Saleh, pp. 179; cf. Hornung, no. 70

94 Glass Headrest  Wiese, no. 76; Reeves 1990, pp. 181

95 Portable Chest with Carrying Poles  Wiese, no. 86; Beinlich and Saleh, pp. 11–15; Killen 1994, pp. 51–53, figs. 60–61; Reeves 1990, pp. 188–193; Edwards, pp. 108f

96 Cosmetic Jar with a Recumbent Lion on the Lid  Wiese, no. 94; Reeves 1990, pp. 198f, Beinlich and Saleh, p. 65; James 2000, pp. 314f

97 Box in the Shape of a Cartouche  Wiese, no. 85; Reeves 1990, pp. 188–193; Beinlich and Saleh, pp. 118–120; James 2000, p. 302; Killen 1994, p. 76, pl. 61; Edwards, p. 139; A. Wilkinson 1984, pp. 342f

98 Chest with Long Legs and Decorative Fretwork  Wiese, no. 86; Beinlich and Saleh, pp. 180–183; Reeves 1990, pp. 188–193; Killen 1994, pp. 60–62, fig 67

99 Model Ship for River Travel  Wiese, no. 63; Jones, pp. 26–28; Landström pp. 99–101, figs. 313, 315, 318, 320; Edwards, cf. no. 36; James 2000, cf. pp. 283f

100 Model Papyrus Skiff for River Travel  Wiese, no. 63; Jones p. 5, p. 43. nos. 29, 60–62, pls. 3, 11, 26, 27; Landström, pp. 94–97; Altenmüller, pp. 11–19; cf. James 2000, pp. 283f

101 Attached Pair of Vessels  Wiese, no. 93; Reeves 1990, pp. 198f; El-Khouli, p. 29, no. 56, pls. 24a, 5b

102 Drinking Cup in the Shape of a Lotus  Wiese, no. 91; Edwards, no. 2; Beinlich and Saleh, pp. 5f; Reeves 1990, pp. 198f; James 2000, p. 310–311

103, 104, 105 Wooden, Faience, and Limestone Shabtis of Tutankhamun  Wiese, no. 64a, b, and c; James, pp. 110–129; Reeves 1990, pp. 136–139; Cerny, pp. 12f, p. 27, §55, pl.8; James, pp. 110–129

106 Ritual Vessel (Heset Vase)  Wiese, no. 62a; Cerny, p. 9, § 48

107 Ritual Vessel (Nemset Vase)  Wiese, no. 62b; Reeves 1990, pp. 200 and pp. 95–97; Wildung and Grimm, no. 44

108 Inlaid Pectoral with a Winged Scarab  Wiese, no. 73; Aldred 1971, pp. 219f, pl. 98 (listed as 261n instead of m); Beinlich, pp. 7–18, Feucht Putz, pp. 103–107; Reeves 1990, pp. 151f.; A. Wilkinson 1971, pp. 139 144f.; James 2000, pp. 224–25.

109 Mirror Case in the Shape of an Ankh  Wiese, no. 74; Edwards, no. 30; Reeves 1990, pp. 158f, Beinlich and Saleh, pp. 121f.

110 Ceremonial Dagger and Sheath  Weise, no. 70; Edwards, no. 20, pp. 129f; Reeves 1990, pp. 112f, p. 177; James 2000, p. 280.

111 Decorated Uraeus from Royal Headdress  Wiese, no. 66; Aldred 1971, p. 230, pl. 123; Reeves 1990, pp. 150–154; A. Wilkinson 1971, pp. 118–120

112 Inlaid Diadem  Wiese, no. 65; Reeves 1990, p. 154; A. Wilkinson 1971, pp. 118–120, pls. 42f; Aldred 1971, p. 132, pl. 123; Andrews, p. 108; James 2000, p. 182

113 Inlaid Broad Collar and Counterweight  Wiese, no. 67; Reeves 1990, pp. 112f; James 2000, pp. 204f.; A. Wilkinson 1971, pp. 110–112

114 Pectoral in the Shape of a Falcon  Wiese, no. 68; Reeves 1990, p. 112f; A. Wilkinson 1971, pp. 110–113

## NOTE ABOUT SPELLINGS AND DATES

There is no consensus among scholars about exact dates in ancient Egyptian history, nor about the proper way in which to spell names that, in hieroglyphs or hieratic, were indicated only by consonants. In this book, personal names featured in the Tutankhamun exhibition are spelled according to that exhibition's style. Place-names, as well as all dates, follow National Geographic style.

# INDEX

Page references in **bold** refer to illustrations.

**Illustration Credits:**

# TUTANKHAMUN
## AND THE GOLDEN AGE OF THE PHAROAHS

Zahi Hawass

Photographs by Kenneth Garrett

**Published by the National Geographic Society**

John M. Fahey, Jr., *President and Chief Executive Officer*
Gilbert M. Grosvenor, *Chairman of the Board*
Nina D. Hoffman, *Executive Vice President*

**Prepared by the Book Division**

Kevin Mulroy, *Vice President and Editor-in-Chief*
Marianne R. Koszorus, *Design Director*
Kris Hanneman, *Illustrations Director*

**Staff for this Book**

Lisa Lytton, *Editor*
Janice Kamrin, *Writer*
Patricia Daniels, *Text Editor*
Laura Lindgren, *Art Director*
Jane Menyawi, *Illustrations Editor*
Meredith Wilcox, *Illustrations Assistant*
Carl Mehler, *Director of Maps*
Joseph F. Ochlak, *Map Research and Edit*
Nicholas P. Rosenbach, *Map Research and Edit*
Gregory Ugiansky, *Map Production*
Tibor G. Tóth, *Map Relief*
Gary Colbert, *Production Director*
Lewis Bassford, *Production Project Manager*

**Manufacturing and Quality Control**

Christopher A. Liedel, *Chief Financial Officer*
Phillip L. Schlosser, *Managing Director*
John T. Dunn, *Technical Director*

**With special thanks to** NATIONAL GEOGRAPHIC **staff:**
Chris Johns, Editor; Chris Sloan, Senior Editor, Art;
Chris Klein, Art Director; John Echave, Senior Editor, Research
Grant Projects; Laura Lakeway, Illustrations Specialist, and
Elizabeth Snodgrass, Researcher.

And last, but not least, a special thank you to Dr. David Silverman,
curator of "Tutankhamun and the Golden Age of the Pharaohs."

One of the world's largest nonprofit scientific
and educational organizations, the National
Geographic Society was founded in 1888 "for
the increase and diffusion of geographic
knowledge." Fulfilling this mission, the
Society educates and inspires millions every
day through its magazines, books, television
programs, videos, maps and atlases, research
grants, the National Geographic Bee, teacher
workshops, and innovative classroom
materials. The Society is supported through
membership dues, charitable gifts, and income
from the sale of its educational products. This
support is vital to National Geographic's
mission to increase global understanding and
promote conservation of our planet through
exploration, research, and education.

For more information, please call
1-800-NGS LINE (647-5463) or
write to the following address:
National Geographic Society
1145 17th Street N.W.
Washington, D.C. 20036-4688 U.S.A.

Visit the Society's Web site at
www.nationalgeographic.com.

Published by the National Geographic
Society, 1 145 17th Street N.W.
Washington, D.C. 20036

Library of Congress Cataloging-in-Publication
Data available upon request.

ISBN 0-7922-3873-7

Printed in the United States